Passion and Craft

Passion and Craft

Conversations with Notable Writers

Edited by
Bonnie Lyons and Bill Oliver

University of Illinois Press

Urbana and Chicago

© 1998 by the Board of Trustees of the University of Illinois
Manufactured in the United States of America
1 2 3 4 5 C P 5 4 3 2 1

This book is printed on acid-free paper.

Library of Congress Cataloging-in-Publication Data
Passion and craft : conversations with notable writers / edited
by Bonnie Lyons and Bill Oliver.
p. cm.
Includes index.
ISBN 0-252-02387-0 (alk. paper). —
ISBN 0-252-06687-1 (pbk. : alk. paper)
1. American fiction—20th century—History and criticism—
Theory, etc. 2. Authors, American—20th century—Interviews.
3. Authorship. 4. Short story. 5. Creation (Literary, artistic, etc.)
6. Storytelling—United States. I. Lyons, Bonnie. II. Oliver, Bill
1949–   .
PS379.P35   1998
813'.5409—dc21   97-33749
CIP

For Grant and Eve   B.L.

For my mother   B.O.

Contents

Introduction   ix

Acknowledgments   xiii

Richard Ford   Important Acts   1

Bobbie Ann Mason   Quiet Rebellions   23

T. Coraghessan Boyle   Entertainments and Provocations   42

Gina Berriault   "Don't I Know You?"   60

Rick Bass   Out of Boundaries   72

Leonard Michaels   The Lyric Impulse   85

Christopher Tilghman   Grappling with the Holy Mysteries   99

Thom Jones   A Way of Feeling Better   112

Julia Alvarez   "A Clean Windshield"   128

Andre Dubus   "Passion Is Better"   145

Jayne Anne Phillips   The Mystery of Language   159

Tobias Wolff   Citizens and Outlaws   171

Index   191

Introduction

Books of literary interviews tend to fall into predictable categories based on theme, geography, age, reputation, race, ethnicity, gender, or style. Sometimes the categories are combined to produce hybrid collections—interviews with young Southern writers, for example, or African American women writers, or second-generation postmodernists. It's as if the editors were checking credentials, screening for membership in a club. For us, one of the most exciting aspects of American fiction continues to be its variety. Thus we have avoided limiting our selection of authors to those who belong to a particular school of thought or share a common background or aesthetic approach; no club members here. Fundamental and fascinating differences exist among the authors represented in this collection—differences in experience, temperament, voice, formal strategies, as well as in their most basic sense of the world.

Some of the authors in this book began working at their craft independently early on; some attended writing programs; most came to their profession by indirect routes. Andre Dubus and Tobias Wolff were soldiers; Christopher Tilghman a carpenter and technical writer; Jayne Anne Phillips a waitress and drifter; Thom Jones a boxer, an advertising executive, a janitor. Not surprisingly, these writers practice a variety of storytelling styles, from the discursive realism of Dubus to the often Kafkaesque strategies of Leonard Michaels. Richard Ford speaks of being guided by an abiding interest in the "sonority and rhythm" of language, while T. Coraghessan Boyle describes himself as an ironist and says ideas are the starting points for his stories and novels. Jayne Anne Phillips believes the story she means to write "is already there, whole" and her task is "to feel it out, to find out what it is and move into it and inhabit it." Rick Bass, like Phillips, senses something preordained about his stories but tries to resist that inevitability. "If a story's going well . . . then it's almost like water rushing down a canyon, or a culvert," says Bass, a professionally trained geologist. "That's when I start looking for side cracks or seams, fissures, where I can get some of the story to go, to keep it from all rushing down that culvert to the bottom."

We wanted to speak to writers from different parts of the country, and whenever possible, in places that mean something to them, hoping, in this way, to deepen our appreciation of place and geography in their lives and work. We met Bobbie Ann Mason in Mayfield, Kentucky, near the farm where she grew up; Andre Dubus in Haverhill, Massachusetts, where he has written and taught for more than thirty years; Christopher Tilghman in the converted Shaker meeting house outside Boston where he lives with his wife and sons; Rick Bass in a part of Montana that has more deer than people; Thom Jones in Iowa City, where he once served his literary apprenticeship and where he had recently returned to teach and to write a novel.

We chose to speak with both younger and older writers, and writers at various stages in their careers. We selected relative newcomers, like Julia Alvarez and Thom Jones, as well as Gina Berriault and Andre Dubus, who can look back over several decades of writing. Our hope is that the twelve distinctive voices in this collection will provide readers with something like a cross-section—or a "core sample," to borrow one of Rick Bass's geological metaphors—of the best American writers working today.

We live in an age of fiction rather than poetry or drama, and we began these interviews excited by the wealth of interesting and diverse fiction being produced in this country, especially by short-story writers. Our interest in the short story *is* one unifying element of this collection: the twelve writers we talked to are all masters of this uniquely modern form in which Americans, from Hawthorne to Flannery O'Connor, from James to Cheever, have distinguished themselves for more than a century and a half. The writers represented here are well versed in this tradition, and consciously indebted to it, even as they continue to push its boundaries. Considering their other diverse interests, however, we have not limited ourselves to a consideration of our subjects' short fiction but have attempted to address the broad range of their work.

We have tried to go beyond the usual chatting about career and craft, beyond the autobiographical as well. Such topics have their interest, and they are included in our book; we believe, however, that we have succeeded in doing more, in getting at what matters most to these writers as writers, and, in the process, shedding light on some of the motives behind literary creativity. The impulses that drive the authors we talked to vary. For Bobbie Ann Mason and Jayne Anne Phillips, there is the powerful urge to preserve and celebrate the rural people and places they believe are too often ignored in our increasingly urbanized landscape; for Andre Dubus and Christopher Tilghman, writing is a means of exploring the unseen, the spiritual dimension; for

Leonard Michaels, it is a manner of "singing"; for T. Coraghessan Boyle, storytelling is a way to entertain, to shock and astound his readers, all the better to reform them; for Gina Berriault, writing is a bridge to the world, a hedge against loneliness.

One thing that emerges as common to these writers, in spite of their differences, is a passionate dedication to the art of storytelling. The sense of vocation they bring to their work—which does not, by the way, preclude a certain playfulness—recalls the attitude of the modernists in its almost religious intensity, though our contemporary subjects do not appear to share some of their twentieth-century predecessors' superior and even disdainful attitudes toward the reading public. T. Coraghessan Boyle states that one of his aims is "to recapture some of the audience for literature," citing Dickens as an example of a writer who met the demands of both quality and popularity. Rejecting the notion of storytelling as primarily "self-expression," Richard Ford says, the excitement of writing, for him, lies in "the chance to make something new, which might be good and beautiful, and which somebody else can use." In a similar vein, Andre Dubus talks about how he "uses the senses in an imaginative way to connect with other people." Perhaps as literature becomes increasingly marginalized—Boyle notes, for example, that "literature" is merely another genre or category now—writers feel a special urgency about finding common ground with their readers. "Picture a reader stuck with a magazine in the dentist's office," says Thom Jones. "Why shouldn't the short story be the first thing [he] want[s] to read? Why do stories have to be boring?" Jones goes on to say that he thinks the reader should be "fully entertained" as well as "illuminated."

In a modest way, we hope the same is true of these interviews. We sought out the twelve writers in this book because we were genuinely excited by their work—found it entertaining and illuminating. We came to the interviews with considerable knowledge of and appreciation for the writers' achievements. That knowledge and appreciation, we believe, encouraged them to take the interview process seriously and to engage deeply the subjects we questioned them about.

Each of these interviews is an attempt to provide our readers with a lively sense of the mind and imagination that created the fiction, the distinctive flavor of each author's literary intelligence. We questioned the writers about their work habits, their sources of inspiration, their craft. We inquired about individual pieces of work and also asked them to consider individual pieces in relation to their writing as a whole. We encouraged them to comment on their work as it relates to the larger literary and social worlds. Not surprisingly, in this age marked by cultural wars, these interviews furnish some opinionated—and contradictory—responses to such current issues as censorship, multiculturalism, and political correctness. But ideally, the interviews that follow are more than a series of timely snapshots; rather, each is an enduring portrait of the author.

Acknowledgments

Earlier versions of some of the interviews in this book appeared or are forthcoming in the following publications:

Richard Ford: *Paris Review,* Fall 1996; reprinted by permission of the *Paris Review*

Bobbie Ann Mason: *Contemporary Literature,* Spring 1990; reprinted by permission of International Creative Management, Inc.

Gina Berriault: *The Literary Review,* Summer 1994

Rick Bass: *New Letters,* Spring 1993

Leonard Michaels: *New England Review,* Fall 1993

Christopher Tilghman: *The Literary Review,* Winter 1995

Andre Dubus: *Crazyhorse,* Spring 1993

Jayne Anne Phillips: *New Letters,* Summer 1994

Tobias Wolff: *Contemporary Literature,* Spring 1990; reprinted by permission of the University of Wisconsin Press

Bonnie Lyons's work on this book was facilitated by Faculty Research Grants from the University of Texas at San Antonio. Bill Oliver received financial support from the University of Texas at San Antonio and from Washington and Lee University.

Passion and Craft

Richard Ford

Important Acts

When Richard Ford's first novel, *A Piece of My Heart,* was published in 1976, he appeared to be a gifted Southern novelist much indebted to Faulkner. Since then his novels, *The Ultimate Good Luck* (1981), *The Sportswriter* (1986), *Wildlife* (1990), and *Independence Day* (1995), as well as his acclaimed collections of stories, *Rock Springs* (1987) and *Women with Men* (1997), have proved him a much less predictable writer and one harder to categorize.

Independence Day, which brought back Frank Bascombe from *The Sportswriter,* now as a harassed real-estate agent, was awarded both the Pulitzer and PEN/Faulkner prizes for fiction in 1995, the only book ever to be so recognized. In Frank Bascombe, Ford has created one of the most complex and memorable characters of our time, and the novel itself is a nuanced, often hilarious, portrait of contemporary American life. *Independence Day* has been called "the definitive novel of the post-war generation" and Ford himself "one of the finest curators of the great American living museum." In settings, types of characters, plots, point of view, and most importantly, in ever-broadening sympathy, he has, as he remarks in this interview, consciously kept moving on.

Our interview took place on a breezy July day at a large seaside house Ford sometimes rents outside Jamestown, Rhode Island. Dressed in khakis and a loose blue shirt, Ford seemed relaxed as he enjoyed the beautiful weather on the large veranda surrounding the house. Although originally reluctant to be interviewed, he was genuinely cordial and unhurried, referring to the afternoon as a "literary conversation" rather than an interview. He took obvious pleasure in his rented house, which has a view across high grass to the ocean (though he warned of deer ticks and the danger of Lyme disease). He said he was thinking of offering to buy the property and noted that one of his greatest regrets was selling his house in Mississippi. Frank Bascombe the real-estate agent did not seem far away.

John Foley

Is there any one aspect of fiction that is particularly central to you?

These days, when I'm writing every morning and afternoon, the distinctions among such fictive concerns as language, narrative strategy, story, character, and point of view don't seem very significant. I'm always interested in *words,* and no matter what I'm doing—describing a character or a landscape or writing a line of dialogue, I'm moved, though not utterly commanded by an interest in the sonority and rhythm of the words. Most writers are probably like that, don't you think? Sometimes I'll write a sentence that sets up an opportunity for a direct object or predicate adjective and I won't have a clue what the word is except that I usually know what I don't want—the conventional word: "The night grew dark." I don't want "dark." I might, though, want a word that has four syllables and a long "a" sound in it. Maybe it'll mean "dark" or maybe it'll take a new direction. I'll have some kind of inchoate metrical model in my mind. One of the ways sentences can surprise their maker, please their reader, and uncover something new is that they get to the sense they make by other than ordinary logical means.

You're unusually sound-oriented for a fiction writer.

I don't exactly know why that is, but probably it was just the way I *could* do it. And even though I may be "sound-oriented," I'm not sure that shows up in the sentences I write, at least not in ways the reader would necessarily notice.

Does your concern for language and especially for sound lead you to poetry?

I'd love to be able to write poetry, but I think if I ever brought my attention down to that meticulous level of utterance, I'd never be able to ratchet it back up to the wider level of reference that, for me, fiction requires. Quite a few of my teacher and writer friends have been poets over the years: Donald Hall, James McMichael, Michael Ryan, Larry Raab, Dan Halpern, C. K. Williams.

Putting aside the sound of language, how important is the development of character to you?

Well, we wouldn't have moral dilemmas and conflicts without characters. But when I started trying to write, inventing characters was hard for me. I thought about characters first from having read the practical criticism of E. M. Forster and Henry James and Percy Lubbock, who all talked about characters that were, in the first place, already written—and mostly written under the influence of nineteenth-century ideas of what human character is. Character seemed to me, therefore, a rather fixed quotient. Forster did say in *Aspects of the Novel* that characters ought to have the "incalculability of life." But I didn't find his own characters to be that way. Maybe I was naive. Let's say I *was* naive. But his characters seemed, say in *A Passage to India,* pretty hard-sided, pretty strictly representative of their class or gender or religion. I, on the other hand, already had a personal experience of character—mine and others'—which definitely stressed the incalculable, the obscure, the unpredictable. I'm not sure the word "character" ever came up in my childhood family life—except that so-and-so was "a character." Plus, my family was given to explaining almost nothing about people. People were just the mysterious sum of their actions. So, from a shortage of information, I was already making people up—actual people—long before I became a writer. I was doing it just to make them seem more knowable.

Today I think of characters—actual *and* literary characters—as being rather *un*fixed. I think of them as changeable, provisional, unpredictable, decidedly un-whole. Partly this owes to the act of *writing* characters, and of succeeding somewhat in making them seem believable and morally provoking. As I write them they *are* provisional, changeable, and so forth, right on through and beyond the process of being made. I can change them at will, and do. For instance, I can come upon an adjective which seems to have nothing to do with the person I thought I was inventing—an important adjective—"good" or "bad," for instance, and I can use it and see where it takes me. I can also erase it. Maybe I've convinced myself that we make ourselves up pretty much the way I make characters up in books. But this is the development of character, in my view; not the setting out of something fixed, which is how I thought of them when I was beginning. Maybe this view deviates from the conventional view of character. Maybe I'm guilty of writing deviant characters. But I don't think so. Of course not, right?

Well, don't you think people have characters?

I certainly think we have *histories.* And based on them we can purport to have characters—invent or allege character, in a sense. And sometimes histories predict what people will do. Though often not. But character is just one of those human pseudo-essences that is often used detrimentally. Certainly a lot of modern fiction derives its drama from the conflict between assumed character and some specific action that deviates from it.

But let me give you another kind of example of what I'm talking about. I was working on a scene in which a man goes over to a woman's house—a woman he's sort of in love with. All along I'd been thinking that one of the things that would happen in this scene was that she'd cut him loose, because earlier she'd seemed uncertain about him. In my plan, she was going to say to him that their relationship was heading nowhere and she wanted something better, and she wasn't married to him so why should she go on with somebody who didn't satisfy her. But I got to the part of the scene where she's getting ready to tell him they're not going to be lovers anymore, and she says, "You know, I was driving back from New York today and I was just thinking about you. I knew you were going to be here, and I knew we would have dinner." And I'm writing along and it suddenly seems right for her to say, "And I thought what a sweet man you are"—which is what I write. He's listening, and he says, "I try to be a sweet man. But what?" And she says (I have her say), "But nothing." What happened at that moment was that it occurred to me she needn't fall into this track that I'd predicted for her—into the form of her character that I'd devised. Based on how the scene felt, I completely switched the dynamics. What

happened next was that he—not she—tried his best to get out of their relationship as quickly and smoothly as possible. Which, for a time, he succeeds
in doing. But have you ever had to call somebody on the phone, somebody you
wanted to get rid of, only you end up doing nothing but getting yourself in more
deeply? Now *that's* something about life that interests me. That's incalculability, if on a small scale: how we cope with contingency in ourselves but try still
to accept responsibility for our acts.

When you begin a novel do you have the end in mind?

I certainly think about it a lot before I start, and I like to have some clear
idea of my destination. But I eventually get to the point in my planning when
I begin to feel I'm sacrificing useful time that I could be using to write by
holding off until I can figure out the ending. Then I think to myself, Well,
start. Start. Start. As I write, I, of course, think about these things more. Don
DeLillo said, "Writing is a concentrated form of thinking"—thinking, I assume, about the things that you sense are important and that could or will
find their way into your book, including where it'll end.

Did you have the title for Independence Day *when you started writing it?*

That was nearly the first thing I *did* have. The word "independence" had
some important-seeming appeal for me, an attractive density, and I wanted
to know what the constituents of that appeal were, what I could invent based
on that sensation. In this case I ended up trying to figure out a lot about
human independence, and so the Fourth of July seemed a good time to set
it. I like setting stories on holidays. The reader will be more likely to have a
set of personal, vivid memories I can engage—that is, if I'm any good.

During the course of your career has the way you work changed?

My first book was about the South and was captivated by certain traditional Southern themes—search for place, freedom of choice, s-e-x—all inherited literary concerns. And it was also probably directly influenced by
Faulkner and Eudora Welty and Flannery O'Connor and God knows who
else Southern. But during that time—the seventies—I was also reading a great
deal of what are now rather drearily called postmodernist stories and essays.
Their formal concern with language—words and phrases and sentences simply as sources of sound or as spatial objects or sometimes as nonsense—made
me recognize that my own attraction to and reasonably sensitive ear for language was an even larger virtue than I already thought. As I said, ideas are
things I'm interested in, whether I'm any good at negotiating them or not.
But the most palpable urge on the level of moment-to-moment writing is
following intuition as expressed in language—words. Of course, unlike some
of the so-called postmodernists, for me language is finally put to the service

of what I judge to be something larger—human concerns, such as affection or family ties or independence. William Gass's rather French idea of interest being in the pane of glass as much as in what you see through the glass is very powerful to me. But I'm also mightily interested in what you see when you look outside.

Besides length, is there any difference between writing a novel and writing a short story?

Novels are a lot harder to write. Long ones, anyway.

Why?

Because they hold so much more *stuff,* and the stuff all has to be related and make a whole—at least the way I do it. And from my experience of writing both, I do think writing a long novel is a larger human effort than writing a book of short stories—assuming that both are good. I used to say that a novel was a more *important,* a grander literary gesture than a story. And when Ray Carver would hear me say that he'd vigorously disagree, and then I'd always cave in. But he's gone now, and the fun's gone out of that argument. I don't care, to tell you the truth. Is a week in bounteous Paris more important than twenty-four hours in somewhat less majestic Chinook, Montana, if in Chinook your life changes forever? If it is for you, it is; if it isn't, well? Forms of literature don't compete. They don't *have* to compete. We can have it all.

When something comes to you, do you know whether it's going to be a short story or a novel?

That's a decision I make before I start to write. Somewhere in the mulch of my thinking, the material I'm attracted to and the selection of a form come together almost preconsciously; so that by the time I'm thinking to myself, Write this and then this and then this, I'm already supposing I want to write a novel or a novella or a story.

You said that when you began writing stories you weren't good at it. How did your stories go from bad to good? Practice? Breakthroughs?

Not practice. I actually gave up writing stories for a time because I couldn't do it and couldn't get better and didn't see any use in just beating my head against it. So I started writing a novel. I had been trying to write under the influence of Donald Barthelme, Robert Coover, William Gass—all writers whose work I still greatly admire. But my instincts, I guess, weren't particularly well served by those narrative practices and conceits. So when I quit trying to write that way I reverted to the more traditional, realistic fiction that suited what I could do. I, of course, had grown up thinking that what Faulkner and Eudora Welty wrote was what literature was. I remember very well that when we got married in 1968, Kristina gave me *The Collected Stories of Peter Taylor*. It was the first book she'd ever given me. Then when I got to Irvine as a graduate student, my teachers—Oakley Hall and E. L. Doctorow—were moving me back in the direction of more realistic stories. I read all of Cheever and Richard Yates and Bellow and Roth. Plus Babel. Plus Chekhov. Later on, when I started reading my contemporaries—Ray Carver, Joy Williams, Mary Robison, Ann Beattie, and others—I thought, Here are story forms that provide the opportunity for me to write the kinds of things that I know and am ready to put in stories. I was very encouraged by the good work of my contemporaries, which is what good work should do. It shouldn't make you feel intimidated. By the time my first decent stories started to get published in *Esquire,* I had already written two novels. I wrote the first story in *Rock Springs* in the spring of 1980 in New York. Another thing that encouraged me to write stories was that people were asking me to give readings, and I wanted to read new work. I wrote my little story "Sweethearts" because Dan Halpern asked me to read for the benefit of *Columbia* magazine, and I didn't have a new story, so I wrote that in one sitting—as usual—at a table in a rented house. Basically I just wrote one short story a year so that I had something new to read.

   What about editing?

   I've always had a lot of editing done on every book except the second one, *The Ultimate Good Luck,* which I completely rewrote. Donald Hall read the original version when it was in the first person. We met in New York in that little Irish bar next to the Algonquin, and he told me there that it wasn't any good. That was a horrible moment. We'd come into this little dark gloomy bar, and Donald put his hands on the table, looked at me and said, "I don't like your book." Whooh! You just have to take a deep breath and suck it up. I said, "Okay, okay, tell me what you can tell me." He told me all the things he didn't like about it and moreover told me he didn't know what the hell I was going to do with it, because it just wasn't any good the way it was.

   And what was the fate of that book?

   I took it back, and I changed the point of view from first to third, and it got published, though not many people read it. It's in paperback now, and somebody's making a movie out of it—so it's gone on to have a life and a readership.

   Did Donald Hall ever get back to you and say, "Well, I was wrong"?

   He wasn't wrong. It wasn't a good book as I'd written it. But I changed the point of view, and in doing so, let the book admit a wealth of material which the first person hadn't permitted. I didn't know what woes a change like that was going to impose on me. It took me a year to re-imagine the book in the third person.

Generally speaking, do you find the first-person point of view is easier?

I don't think it's easier, at least not in a generic sense. Each way of narrating has its beauties and its difficulties.

Some critics have said they consider you a particularly male writer. Do you see yourself that way?

That's a lot of crap. My narrators have so far been male, but they aren't always the principal characters. I give female characters equally good lines as male characters and, more importantly, equal opportunities within the stories to control their fates, which is what it means, in lived life, to be powerful.

Do you think you could have a female protagonist or narrator?

I think I could, but who knows? My basic feeling is women and men are more alike than unlike, and the ways they're different are both obvious and comprehensible and not as interesting as they're made out to be. The things that make a male character interesting are the same things that make a female character interesting: access to a variety of humors; a capacity to face moral uncertainty; the ability to surprise, to show compassion. I would never, for instance, say to myself, "What would a woman say?" Rather, I'd think, Given the circumstances of this person's life, what would this person say? Or do? Jim Harrison wrote a very good novella, *A Woman Lit By Fireflies,* in which the point-of-view character is a woman. And what he brought to that story, among other talents, was a great sympathetic sensibility. I think that sympathy for the people who are your creations is what's necessary—not a gender sensitivity.

Do you think of your audience as male?

My audience is women *and* men. I've had enough experiences in my life to know that my readers are a variety of people. Once Tobias Wolff and I gave a reading out in North Dakota, and a man came up to tell us he read our books during his lunch breaks, sitting on a tractor out in the wheat fields. He was followed by two women who said they were lesbians and wanted us to know they didn't think we were sexists, or whatever it was we'd been accused of that week. Maybe this isn't enough evidence. I could cite more if you'd like.

Are any of your protagonists like you?

They may be something like me insofar as they're people I have a sympathy for. I think I wrote about sixteen-year-old boys, in part, because I had sympathy from my own past. But I'm not interested in revealing myself directly in those stories. That would risk solipsism and, truthfully, I'm not that interesting. Plus, I get enough reward from my work not to have to make it be about me. Readers may conclude otherwise, but I feel stories are sold short by insisting on how much they supposedly do or don't rely on or reveal the writer's life. That insistence sells short the beauty and pleasing freedom of invention. My novella *Jealous* and many of the stories in *Rock Springs* are written in the first person, but I didn't grow up in Montana and none of the things that happened to those characters ever happened to me. When *Rock Springs* came out, occasionally someone would ask, "Were you born in Montana?" and I would say, "No, Mississippi." They wouldn't quite know what to say then. Asking the question may have helped them understand something about fiction, though: it's made up.

How about Sam Newel's memories in A Piece of My Heart? *Were they autobiographical?*

That book has a few oblique references to my life—altered and put to the service of some bit of invention. I didn't say I didn't *use* my own life as raw material. For instance the vignette about meeting a dwarf in the lobby of a hotel and going upstairs with him—something like that happened to me. Then there's an instance in which two women are lying in bed together drunk in the hotel room, and Sam Newel sees them naked. I saw such things. I saw a lot of fairly lurid things when I was a little boy. I don't mean I was taken care of poorly, but I saw a lot because my family ran a big hotel in Little Rock. Also my father was a traveling salesman and he'd take me with him on trips. Sometimes he'd be gone for hours at a time, so I'd get left alone in hotels. Not left alone in perilous ways, but when I was ten, eleven, twelve, I saw a lot of stuff. I seem to have some magnetism for lurid things. There must be some vibration that comes off writers, not just me. People tell me the most amazing and sometimes alarming things. They often ask me, "If I tell you something, will you not use it?" I say I probably *will* use it. Then they say, "What the hell, I'll never see you again" (which isn't always true) and tell me anyway. I'll write down what they tell me in my notebook, but nothing ever comes back up out of it exactly as it went in. Usually it comes back better.

You've written about your deep affection for your mother and your friendship with her. Is she a source for any of your characters?

I don't think I ever knowingly wrote about my mother, except in the memoir I wrote directly about her. But I know there are qualities I attribute to my mother which are qualities some of my characters have. There is the toughing-it-out quality of the mother in *Wildlife*. My mother was like that, particularly after my father died; so that if she made a mistake, or was less than extremely cautious in my welfare, which occasionally happened, she would look at me and say, "Well, I love you, and I tried my best and that's that." That's a quality I don't find in many people. My wife has that quality in even more admirable ways. Also my mother was humorous, without being exactly mirthful; and she was ironic in a quite obvious and superficial way that concealed (and not very well either) a vast storage of empathy. She was nicely inconsistent in most of her views except her view of whom she loved.

What I've always enjoyed about your writing is the humor, which is missing in much of contemporary literature, it seems to me.

In me, that comes partly from being a Southerner. When I was growing up, absurd humor was big in my and my friends' lives. We also mimicked each other and everybody else; we did voices; we were all blessed with a kind of aspiring-to-be-affluent fecklessness. Plus, we lived in an absurd racist society in which we—arrogant, ignorant, suburban kids—were the privileged ones. What could be more ridiculous! I guess I just didn't lose that sense of ridiculousness—mine and others'—when I came north.

Also the writers I always like are writers who *can be* humorous, whether they always are or not—a lot of Jewish writers: Stanley Elkin, Bruce Jay Friedman, Philip Roth. Plus Joan Didion, Walker Percy, Barry Hannah. Those are the writers I cut my teeth on.

Mark Twain must have been a big influence.

No. The Twain I read when growing up—*Huckleberry Finn* and *Tom Sawyer*—curiously enough evoked little river towns I myself knew, up and down the Mississippi, and just at the time when I wanted to get as far away from that kind of folksy, homespun, cracker-barrel sophistication as I could. I wanted to read about England; I wanted to read about New England; I wanted to read about France; I did *not* want to read about life on the Mississippi, because I knew what life on the Mississippi was like. I've gone back and tried to read *Life on the Mississippi* as recently as twenty years ago but couldn't crack it. I know that's a heresy. Sorry.

When you lived across the street from Eudora Welty in Jackson, did you ever go and see her?

She'd moved by the time I might have done that, and I didn't meet Miss Welty until 1981, when she came to give a reading at Princeton, where I happened to be teaching. I had only published one book. I had a feeling she probably knew about it; knew it was full of dirty words and sex and violence. But when I met her it didn't seem to have registered that I was from Jackson and had written a novel. I remember saying to her, "Miss Welty, I'm Richard Ford, and I'm from Jackson, Mississippi." She has a wonderful way about her; she said, "Oh, you are?"—but nothing else. I thought, Gee, what that means is, she hates my book. I felt horrible. I then published another book full of sex and violence, and I thought, Well, I'm just out of the Eudora Welty sweep-stakes here. We're never going to be friends. Then I wrote *The Sportswriter* and did a book-signing at Lemuria Books in Jackson. I was sitting there at my little table signing books, and I looked up and there was Miss Welty. She said, "Well, I had to come pay my respects." I felt beatified. I thought, Finally I've written a book you aren't too embarrassed by to come and meet me. I've gone on to be wonderful friends with her. I see her often. In addition to be-ing a great writer, she's also one of the wittiest people I've ever been around. She does voices, she mimics, she has a sensitivity to the absurdities of lan-guage. She also has a vivid memory for song lyrics. She's a performer who simply didn't choose to perform upon a conventional stage. Her work often doesn't seem funny but then is funny under the surface—sometimes even quite grave stories. I remember one time I was walking with her into a book-store. They had prepared a big celebration for her birthday. Someone was standing beside a helium cylinder and was filling balloon after balloon. Each time, the little machine would give off a kind of *ssshoou* sound, and Eudora said, "Oh, I thought it was someone sighing at my arrival."

You've talked about escaping Mississippi, the racism . . .

My family life was wonderful. I was raised by people I loved and I have great friends there, but the race part was bad. The cynicism of the whites, me included.

You didn't like yourself.

I didn't like what I was headed toward becoming. If I'd gone on, stuck in my niche, I would never have been a conservative, but I wouldn't have been proud of myself either. Another conflicted Southern boy. I simply didn't understand some very fundamental things in Mississippi in the fifties and early sixties: why it was we went to separate schools, why all the violence. Oh, I could understand it as long as it was sort of boilerplate, which is to say, "That's how things are down South." But if I had to say, as I began to do when I was a teenager, "Well, let's just piece this out a bit," I couldn't piece it out, couldn't make racism make sense. We didn't talk about that stuff much in my family. My father was dead by the time I was sixteen; my mother was not an analytical person. But neither of them was a racist.

How old were you when James Meredith was enrolled at the University of Mississippi?

I was eighteen. By that time I was at Michigan State. I was not brave enough or committed enough or selfless enough to stay in Mississippi during the civil-rights movement. I wanted to get out of it. I wanted to go as far away from Mississippi as I could. And it wasn't just about race. It was about wanting to get out of the South because I wanted to see the rest of the country. Television had alerted me to New York, Chicago, Los Angeles. I certainly don't want to paint myself back then as enlightened. I wasn't enlightened. I was nothing. But I knew I was nothing, which helped. I knew there were terrible things coming in Mississippi. I just thought, Uh oh, bad times are coming. I've got to get out of here to save myself. To reinvent myself.

How much of that anguish has worked its way into your fiction?

It's worked into my writing in one good way, which is that I want to write about dramatic, important things that engage my sympathies. That's been the most certifying thing in my life—that I've gone toward where my sympathies led me rather than where social pressures or convention might've led. That's good luck for a novelist.

Did you have black friends when you were growing up?

No, not in Mississippi. They lived on the other side of town. But in Arkansas I did.

What are the sympathies that have taken you back to Mississippi?

I'm proud of it because of the huge changes it's undergone and survived. And it's where I was born. I like it there.

Did you write when you were at law school?

Not much. But going to law school was probably very important to me because, when I started to try to write stories, I realized how much writing stories was like writing briefs. It's writing to persuade someone. I don't want to drag this similarity much further, but what I understand about the law (case law, anyway) is that it is something made up by lawyers to convince juries and judges, which then goes on to affect lived life in important ways. The novel is sentences made up by writers to persuade readers, et cetera, et cetera. They have very much the same rhetorical address.

I wonder if you feel you have to be more intelligent than your characters in order to understand or control them.

Is the potter superior to his exquisite vase? When I'm writing about characters, the discrepancy is as narrow as I can make it because I'm trying to make my intelligence act in the service of these creations who become characters. I only know what they don't know for reasons that are both obvious and unimportant. If I were less sensitive to this I think I'd have a condescending attitude toward my characters, which I don't want. Some critics have suggested I endow characters with certain thought processes or language or emotional experiences which they would not have, or to put it more grue-

somely, which those "kinds" of characters wouldn't likely have. But my attitude is that there are no such things as "kinds" or types of characters in fiction
or in life. Eloquence or penetrating understanding can visit anybody. In fact,
it's fiction's business to try to enlarge our understanding of and sympathy
for people. If, to do that, I have to strain your conventional understanding
about humans—well, that's also art's proper business, and my hope is that
I'll repay your indulgence.

Do you make all the decisions for your characters?

All of them. Unless I make a typo and I like the mistake better than the
word I wanted—which I did once. Somewhere, I think it was probably in *The
Sportswriter,* I meant to write that somebody was "cold-eyed," only I typed
"old-eyed," and Kristina told me how good she thought that was. So naturally I kept it.

*Elsewhere you've said you like story endings that "close like supernovas and
leave you gasping." Do you have the same desire for the endings of your novels?*

At the end of my novels, I certainly want the reader to say, "Boy, oh, boy!"
(that is, in an admiring way). However, I try to be cautious about creating
pyrotechnics at the end of a story or novel, effects that might cause the end
to have a luminous quality the story or novel itself hasn't quite underwrit-
ten. Many wonderful stories don't give the opportunity to end in a luminous
way. I admit that when I write a story that does provide that opportunity I
feel fortunate. It certainly intensifies a reader's experience at a moment when
he's notably available to the story. Endings are important for the life of the
story and, if I can demark that ending by making it significant to a reader,
then I have done the reader a service. I have a long and good relationship with
a certain magazine editor who has particularly liked the endings of some of
my stories. This is Rust Hills, at *Esquire,* who has been a wonderful editor for
me. Sometimes when he's encouraging me to write a story so he can publish it, he'll say, "And make it have one of those Richard Ford endings." But
that isn't always possible.

In your introduction to The Best American Short Stories, 1990, *you said, "I
only know one or maybe one-and-a-half ways to express verisimilitude." What
do you mean by that?*

I was probably exaggerating by admitting to an extra half. But I was referring, tongue-in-cheek, to Frank O'Connor's tongue-in-cheek remark in
The Lonely Voice, where he said there are dozens of ways to express verisimilitude—that quality in a piece of fiction, or the strategy in a story which makes
the story seem like real life, true to life on the page—a slippery matter in a
slippery world. My comment on the subject was just a way of saying that I

do things my way, though you can do things your way as you please. Fiction always uses language to refer the reader to lived life—life outside the story. This is true irrespective of how hermetic, how self-referring, how abstract, how language-preoccupied, how circular the individual story happens to be. The reader will always take what he finds in the story back to life, somehow, even if that's not the story's primary appeal, as in many of Borges's stories or in Barthelme's "The Indian Uprising." Even if it's just that you think about the story later, in another context or in another room, you've taken it to your own real life and you've somehow used it. This inevitability is built into the necessity that there be a reader for a story to be fully consummated.

In this way, fiction's a bit like a notative system in ballet, where there are instructions to tell a dancer where to step, et cetera. You can't take the analogy terribly far, unfortunately, because in the analogy the dancer has to be reader and author at once. But words are the notations in stories, and the reader covers them by reading. It's after that, I suppose, that all those diverse ways of bonding to the *real* commence: based on the words, the reader then entertains the multitudinous truth of life in a multitude of ways.

When I've written about Montana, some people have said to me, "God, you really got it right." And my answer always is, "Well, thanks, but I never tried to get it right, if by 'right' you mean I got it the way Montana is on earth." I mostly wanted to make it interesting on the page and to ignite the reader's imagination. What I'm sure happens in sealing the bond of persuasiveness or believability, or even verisimilitude, is that when people read sentences (particularly if they like them) they then go on and fill in from their own lives what that piece of fiction seems to refer to (I hope not too divergently from my own set of notations, of course, because then the story's a failure, or a kind of literary idiot savant). The completion of the illusion happens in the reader's mind—the way Sartre and Duchamp and hundreds of people who aren't French have said. I suppose another form of verisimilitude would be for me to call a landscape Montana but then have the details be from Mississippi. I haven't tried that yet.

You once talked about "committing a story" instead of writing a story. What do you mean by committing a story?

It's just a pretentious way of saying that for me, personally and emotionally, to write a story is to give myself up totally to this otherwise flimsy piece of business. I commit myself. It wasn't meant as an attempt to ennoble me or the product, but to describe the kind of emotional event in my life that I will eventually ask the reader to share in whatever way he can—to participate in the story as fully as possible. Though I suppose, too, it's another way of saying that I try to make the whole experience—the act of writing it and reading it—as important as I can.

Could you talk about the fact that The Sportswriter *takes place over Easter weekend?*

Easter was when I started to write the book in 1982. It's as simple as that. By the time I finished it though, I was aware of the way in which it was about various sorts of redemption—this despite the fact I didn't have an elaborate religious background or underground or any religious beliefs at all. But I didn't want to be one of those writers who doesn't understand his own books, so I tried to be aware of my book's unexpected implications. A writer for *Time* magazine pointed out that there were fourteen chapters, matching the fourteen stations of the cross. That was the first time I'd heard that. But when you start manipulating mythical narratives, whether you blunder into them or you do it by calculation, you'd better—to be in control of your book—reckon with their true potency and wide reference. They haven't persisted all these years because they represent trivial human matters. You heard it here first.

I want to ask you about names. At one time you said you "contemplate them very hard," and yet you've also said the fact that "Brinson" is the last name of the main character of "Optimists" and of Wildlife *"was quite an accident." Do you believe in accidents like that?*

There are always certain things I just don't notice, as much as I try to notice everything. I had the same problem with names in *Independence Day*. I repeat names thinking they're brand new. I do care a lot about names and once I find one I like and that seems serviceable, it keeps coming back in my head over and over. Good names seem so rare. Plus, my wife can testify to my general belief that if one of something is good, ten times is ten times better.

Have you had any other accidents with names?

I don't know, but I'm sure there will be in the fullness of time. It's one of those things about me that's unchangeable. I search and search for the right name to hook up with—some inchoate feeling that could develop into a character. I want to have a strong, good feeling about any name I use. When I wrote *The Sportswriter,* I was writing with a loose understructure which only I knew about and that probably isn't detectable by the reader. It was Joshua Slocum's famous book, *Sailing Alone Around the World.* To my brain, there are, in my book, certain focal points that are closely similar to events in his. Indeed, the whole time I was writing the book, I called Frank, Frank Slocum and not Frank Bascombe. I fully intended that he be Frank Slocum when the book was finished. But when Donald Hall read the manuscript, he pointed out that Slocum was the name of Joseph Heller's protagonist-narrator in

Something Happened, and because that's a book I think also had a distant influence on *The Sportswriter,* I felt I had to change it. But I was thrown for a loop. Of course, I realized that unless I wrote a garishly inappropriate name it probably wouldn't matter to the reader. But to me it mattered hugely, to my feelings of familiarity with my character (a character being, at least early on in fiction, his name). Frank's last name, though, had to be two syllables and had to start with a consonant. It also had to end with an "m" sound. Fortunately I had months to make a list.

In talking about The Sportswriter, *you once referred to Detroit and three towns in New Jersey and Florida as "the pylons of the novel." What does that mean? Is it related to the Joshua Slocum book?*

All I meant was that if you put a string around those places—Detroit and the little towns in New Jersey and Florida—the resulting rhomboid would basically form the geographical points of reference for the story's action. This geographic figure is one (rather obscure, possibly meaningless) abstraction that the book describes, and for some reason that's always important to me, to notice things like that—but probably *only* important to me. Such are the loony compulsions of novelists, spawned, I suppose, by sitting years alone in tiny rooms.

Is that the only book you see in geometric terms? Does every novel have a figure in that way?

In one way or another. It's like the line a ballerina strikes with her body. That line is dramatic in relation to something—empty space, another dancer, scenery. The context. (I don't know why I'm so attached to dancing today. Probably it's a means to escape my own dull vocabulary.) But so far, the human actions in all the stories I've written, by which I mean to include novels as well as short stories, have struck some kind of—for me—dramatic relation with a fictive place. There may be an actual place, too, a place on earth with the same name and similar geographical coordinates. But my places are all made up and used for my convenience, and sometimes my convenience requires alterations in the actual—say, if I like some word better than the word that actually describes the real place. Usually places are background for me, contexts made of interesting language and maybe even evoking striking mental pictures, in front of which the characters perform the important actions of the story. But in each case, there is some kind of dramatic abstract— call it a figure, shape, line—that the up-front goings-on make in relation to the setting. I feel it as a necessary tensiveness, and it's no less so as stories move from place to place. The reader, of course, may be altogether unaware of it, which is okay.

That's interesting because, when I think of The Sportswriter, *it seems a very mental book.*

But if it didn't have that movement among those places, didn't have that tensiveness in it, then it would be a static book, too. Some kind of movement or physical motion is important to me. Aristotle thought that action is physical action and that mental action is important as it prefigures physical action. You can say thinking is an action, but I've always believed that physical action is of higher importance than meditation and cogitation. No matter if that action is outweighed by mental activity in terms of how much time is dedicated to it. For example, I never believed we really sin in thought, only in our deeds. So I want people to move, to act, to have a dramatic relation with space. When I had Vicki smack Frank in the chops and knock him down in *The Sportswriter,* that's the purest example of what I find interesting in a book: not simply that she loves him or he loves her, but that it eventuates in her acting.

Another question about names: one critic pointed out that in the middle of Robard Hewes and Sam Newel is the word "ewe." Any relevance?

Accident. I'll tell you why I think so, though the Doctor Freuds of the world will snicker. Robard *Hughes* was the name of a boy from my childhood. I wanted to use that name because I liked it, but I wanted to change it so that it wouldn't be confused with my chum. Newel is actually the name of several boys from my childhood. Some other astute critic pointed out that the "ewe" sound must be related to the Lambs, other characters in the novel. But Mr. Lamb is in the story because of a Mr. Ham from my childhood. I changed Ham to Lamb because it sounded the same. In all cases it was a matter of sounds. I hate to be such a disappointing patient.

You've said, "I want everybody to look at [what I write] exactly as I do." Does that desire lead you to want to respond to critics?

Not unless the interpretation is totally off. When a critic says *Wildlife* is about incest between the mother and son, what I *want* to say is "No, it's not. You're wrong." Though in that particular case I didn't say anything to the critic—poor man. I didn't write a letter. Actually, I've only written one letter and never made a phone call or confronted someone to defend a book of mine against an unfriendly criticism. It doesn't seem appropriate or fruitful, though I've thought about doing it. But, in my books, I try to authorize everything. I do everything I can to narrow the range of divergence between what I understand and what the reader understands, though complete harmony is, of course, improbable. But I think books are successful in terms of how successful I am, at least as a first principle, in narrowing that range of response. You can get all kinds of critics to line up and say that my book states exactly the opposite of what I think it states, but that's rubbish. Unless I'm just nuts, and as yet I'm not.

Have any critical judgments or interpretations of your work been useful to you?

One that I remember. Walter Clemons wrote in *Newsweek* that he didn't think *The Ultimate Good Luck* took sufficient advantage of my sympathies and humor. It was one of the most significant things I'd ever read about something I'd written. I realized I shouldn't be writing books that short-circuit what I know or what I'm capable of, that I should be writing books which try to exploit what is valuable in me as a human being, without having to be about me.

Any unexpected responses?

Some that were hurtful. *Wildlife* got the most effusive praise of any book I'd written before *Independence Day,* but it also got the widest variety of responses—some very negative, which I found perplexing. I didn't consider it an unduly complicated book. But I concluded that it was about such a sensitive subject that some readers simply couldn't deal with it—and therefore rejected it—though it's possible I just didn't write convincingly enough to persuade everybody, which *is* what I always want to do. My favorite scene in *Wildlife* is the one in which young Joe's mother confronts him in the hall late at night, when both of them are only partly dressed—Joe because he's been innocently in bed, his mother because she's been with a man. But that scene really made some people unhappy. I've tried to figure out if it is because Joe has his underwear on or because his mother is partly unclothed. One young male interviewer asked me, "Why do you always write about women who are sluts?" I said, "Well, I wasn't aware that I do. But tell me what you mean by that." He said, "Here's the kid's mother and she's having an affair with another man." I said, "Is that what makes you think she's a slut?" He said, "Well, yeah." I said, "By that do you mean you think she's a bad person?" He said, "She *is* a bad person." I went on to have a long talk with him about it, trying to tell him the book was attempting to confront him on a serious subject, not advocate some kind of conduct—though I had sympathy for the mother and didn't think she was a slut, if there are such things as sluts. But he just wouldn't have it. He wrote something nasty about me, and disparaging about the book. I wrote him a letter—the only such letter I've written—and said, "Shame on you. Of all the people in the world the one who would be the most disappointed in you is not me, it's your mother." I thought maybe that would find a soft place in him. But in another way, if I wanted the book to confront him on that subject, and he rejected it, then the book failed. Pure and simple.

Some questions in a totally different line: Do you think you're unusual as a writer in the way you move from place to place?

I think I'm much more typical of Americans than atypical. Americans move around a lot for reasons not precisely like my own but not completely dissimilar either. They seek new experiences; they get bored; they see an opportunity.

Wouldn't most Americans say they move because they have to—for job reasons?

I think I move for my writing—at least, when I move, I also write.

Some writers say moving takes energy and time away from their work.

Maybe so. But they probably use their not-writing time in some other way. You can't write *all* the time. What a drag. Other people I know—Bob Stone, Tom McGuane, Jim Harrison, Joy Williams, Ann Beattie—they all move around, or they have. Of course, you have to be *able* to do it, you can't be strapped down to a job. You have to have a certain amount of financial and emotional independence. My life sort of conforms to my bank account. I go where I can go. Maybe another reason that I've moved around a lot is that I grew up in a sequestered part of the world—right in the middle of Mississippi. I grew up curious about the rest of the country. Later on, when it came time for me to try to be a writer, I pretty quickly realized that I wasn't going to be able to write very much about the South because it had already been written about so well by all the greats and was still being written about wonderfully by Barry Hannah, Josephine Humphreys, Ellen Douglas, and others; and that I was going to have to learn something else. And when I started learning those things, I found I *could* learn, and that I could function elsewhere rather than being consigned physically, or as a writer, to one part of the world where I wasn't comfortable. For a writing life to flourish, your mind has to go outwards.

Do you have particular requirements for your work place?

I've written everywhere. I wrote a novella, *The Womanizer,* on a plane coming back from Paris. I've written in hotel rooms in Milan and Great Falls. I wrote a screenplay in the Chateau Marmont. I've worked in fifty rented houses, in friends' apartments. It's a challenge to go into a place that's not yours and let the fact that you're doing important work there be the accommodating force. I don't think I could stay in one house continuously. I'm not contemplative enough, not interior enough, and that's another way of saying I'm probably not smart enough. I need a lot of external stimulation bulleting into my life. I'm not talking about exhilaration or thrills, I just want new sounds coming into my ears.

Is there any place you think of as home?

Mississippi. Unqualifiedly. My mother, who died in 1981, was my last close blood relative, and she'd moved from Mississippi back to Arkansas, her home, a few years before she died. So after she died I felt that I no longer had a home that she determined and that I had questions to ask myself: Where are you from? Where do you live? Where are you going to claim to be your home? Arkansas was a possibility because I had spent years there and liked it. But Mississippi was the obvious place because that's where I was born and had gone to school. I love the landscape. I can deal with the people. Of course, when I got back there and bought a house, I liked it so much it scared me to death. So I sold the house and left after four years. It is one of the silliest mistakes of my life. Though, if we'd stayed I probably wouldn't have written *Wildlife,* and probably not *Independence Day,* which I'd personally regret, though of course I wouldn't know it.

Have you got a house now?

I have a rented house in Greenwood, Mississippi, which I like a lot. Not as much as I liked the house I had before. But you know, I've been reading a lot of Auden recently. I'm not even a great fan of Auden poems, but he's always trying to find good uses for his neuroses. He said neurosis represents not necessarily a debility but an opportunity; that neurosis is a gift, something whose effects we can make use of in some inventive way. So when I think about not keeping that house, and God knows I've tried on occasion to buy it back, I begin to think that, well, maybe I get more use out of *not* owning that house than I ever would have gotten from owning and living in it today. Maybe that longing for and avoidance of a place of my own has made me write stories. Who knows? That's also the Presbyterian in me—to look at things that happen as part of your fate. Kristina and I often go window-shopping. She'll see something she wants, and I say, "Well, why do you want to buy it? There it is, you can see it. Take pleasure from *not* buying it."

How does she like that?

She doesn't always see it my way.

I wouldn't think she would.

But I can take a certain amount of consolation in not having something, or in some forms of low-grade duress. I've had migraines for years, and long ago it began to be quite clear to me that having migraines was actually a benevolent affliction, in one sense, anyway. Migraines are the ultimate neurotic Protestant's malady, because you get migraines often just at the point when terrible pressures are relieved and you have every right to feel wonderful. It's as though some stern angel was hovering around you. And eventually if you don't kill yourself or go nuts, you begin to develop a rapport with your tormenter and begin to consider what it's saving you from. Undue optimism, possibly.

In the past you said about teaching, "I was giving all my time away to somebody that I would never see again." What do you get from the process of teaching itself?

I have to say that I got a lot from teaching when I was younger. I learned a huge amount about making stories—not so much from the students' work, but from using conversations about their work to articulate principles for myself that I could then "teach" to them. Teaching was very useful to me when I was in my middle thirties. But then I quit so I could write more.

Still, you teach periodically. Do you get anything from your students now?

I can't think of one thing a student ever said to me except "Can I get a grade change?" or "Can I put off having my story discussed Wednesday because I have to go to my father's marriage in Venezuela?" All I remember are the things I don't want to remember. But has a student ever come up to me and said something so blazingly true I thought to myself, "God, I wish I'd thought of that," like Wittgenstein used to do with his teachers? No. Not yet.

What is your advice to aspiring writers?

My first advice to an aspiring writer is to talk yourself out of it, if you possibly can.

Why?

Because you'll probably fail and make yourself miserable doing it. I feel about myself that I'm anomalous—a rare combination of fear, affection for language, reverence for literature, doggedness, and good luck. Plus, I married the right girl. Shit, who's going to fall heir or victim to all those things?

Was there ever a moment when you felt it wasn't going to work?

All the time. Book to book or project to project, it's always scary. I remember the first time in my life when I ever said I was a writer. Toby Wolff and I were going to London—me, for the first time, at age forty-two—and I had to make out one of those debarkation cards that asks your profession. Over the years, I'd always put "None" on any questionnaire. Because I didn't have one. I don't think of writing as a profession. I think of it as a vocation. But I finally said, "Oh, what the hell, you might as well put 'writer,' because you aren't anything else. That's all you've done with your life and you're forty-two years old, and there isn't time to do anything else." And yet, even if I finally thought I was a writer, here I was heading into London, and though I had published two books and had a third finished, none were in print—I had nothing to show for being a writer when I was forty-two. So what was that about things not working? Things can always not work.

What is the exhilaration of writing, if any?

Primarily, the chance to make something new, which might be good and beautiful, and which somebody else can use. For me, that's come to be the most important thing. Put more succinctly, to write for readers. I've never thought of writing as principally a way of learning about myself, or even as self-expression. Anybody who writes books learns a lot about himself just by seeing what his preoccupations are, what generosities he has or lacks, what his abilities are to invent something out of nothing. I never think about writing in terms of self-psychologizing. That just doesn't interest me.

So you think of the reader when you're writing?

I wouldn't be a writer just for myself. If I were going to do something for myself, I'd do something else, something more practical and pleasurable, and probably easier. I want to write, partly at least, for the kind of reader I was when I was nineteen years old. I want to address that person because he or she is young enough that life is just beginning to seem a mystery which literature can address in surprising and pleasurable ways. When I was nineteen, I began to read *Absalom, Absalom!* slowly, slowly, page by patient page, since I was slightly dyslexic. I was working on the railroad, the Missouri-Pacific in Little Rock. I hadn't been doing well in school, but I started reading. I don't mean to say that reading altogether changed my life, but it certainly brought something into my life—possibility—that had not been there before.

What was it about Absalom, Absalom!*?*

The language—a huge suffusing sea of wonderful words, made into beautiful, long paragraphs and put to the service of some great human conundrum the author meant to console me about, if not completely resolve. When I was old enough to think of myself as trying to be a writer, I always thought I would like to write a book and have it do that for someone else.

An Absalom, Absalom! *for some nineteen year old in Georgia.*

Or Ohio. Or France. I heard someone say the other day, "You have to write for yourself." What shit, I thought. Write for yourself—why? (Though I guess if that produces wonderful work, who am I to argue over conceits?) But I once told an audience in France that I write primarily for readers, and several people got up and left the room. They said, "Hummmph. You're letting down your vocation if you're willing to admit that you write for other people." But I just don't agree with that. To me, it's the thought that you can make something out of words, which organizes experience in the way Faulkner is talking about when he says, "Literature stops life for the purpose of examining it." To be able to do that for another person is a good use of your life.

Bobbie Ann Mason
Quiet Rebellions

We met Bobbie Ann Mason in her hometown of Mayfield, Kentucky (population 12,000), where many of her stories are set. Before the interview, she drove us around the town, showing us the cemetery with its silver-painted iron gate donated by the Daughters of the Confederacy, the grain company whose elevator is said to be the tallest structure in western Kentucky, the town square with its Victorian courthouse and new jail annex, and the ramshackle white house used as Emmett's and Sam's home in the film version of Mason's first novel, *In Country*.

Mason talked about the film as she drove, said she liked it very much and also liked the people she met who worked on it. She didn't get to see the actual filming, because there was a rule barring the author's presence—a standard Hollywood practice, since writers sometimes prove meddlesome. ("They needn't have worried about me," Mason said.)

Her younger sister, LaNelle, who did the illustrations for Mason's second novel, *Spence + Lila*, had her life altered by the filming. A former art student with a degree from the University of Kentucky, she had been working at the local Photomat when she landed a job with the production company of *In Country* and began dating one of the set designers. Later they married and she moved to California, then Australia, where her husband worked on theme parks for Warner Brothers. Mason recounts this story of sudden and dramatic change—the kind that seldom occurs in her own writing—with obvious relish and faint disbelief.

We go by the family farm, where Mason's mother still lives. (Her father is dead.) The small, brown farmhouse sits close to the highway. Behind it, the fields—"Spence's fields"—fall away to a tree-lined creek two-hundred yards distant. There's a white picnic table behind the house; a dog (Oscar) and a cat (Abraham), both of whom appear in *Spence + Lila*, are asleep on the table. The farm now lies within expanded city limits, but as a child Mason attended a country school, with few books or other resources. She longed then, she says, to go to school in Mayfield, to be a "city" child.

Marion Ettlinger

We have our interview in the restaurant of the Mayfield Holiday Inn, where Mason's nephew is the night clerk. She has little to say about her work in progress (*Feather Crowns,* subsequently published by HarperCollins in 1993), a historical novel set in western Kentucky at the turn of the century. "Actually, I'm really eager to get back to short stories." Not that the novel isn't going well: "It's just bad luck to talk about it, because then you might not do it." She has a good deal to say about her other work, however, including *Love Life* (1989), *Spence + Lila* (1988), *In Country* (1985), and *Shiloh and Other Stories* (1982).

In an earlier interview, when asked about your taking up fiction writing fairly late in life, you noted that your background set up a number of roadblocks to the imagination. At the same time, however, you wondered whether, in an environment that totally encouraged creativity, "there would be any incentive whatsoever to resist, to bust out, any build-up of energy." Do you think there is an ideal balance between repression and encouragement? Did you need to encounter a certain amount of resistance?

I've often wondered what I would have done with my life if I had gotten a lot of advantages from the very beginning. I did start writing when I was eleven, but along the way I was stymied quite a lot. I don't know if it's necessary for everybody to have something to resist against for creative energy to build up. It just seems to be the way it happens at times. I think about Nabokov, who, to hear him describe it, had an ideal childhood. He had every advantage. He was pampered and indulged. I wonder what it would have been like for him if he hadn't been exiled and if his father hadn't been assassinated. We know that those experiences are the formation of his fiction and that's what his sensibility acts upon. Had he stayed in that comfortable place where he was the most important person in the world, would he have had anything interesting to tell us?

I sense that you have a rebellious strain, that some part of you is impelled to act against whatever people say you ought to be doing or ought to be writing.

You've hit it, haven't you? Because I was going to be that way about half of your questions. Actually I was going to try not to be that way because the last interview I did turned out to be perverse and not as polite as it should have been. I don't know, it is a very quiet rebellion. I'm not outspoken or politically verbal. I don't get upset very easily. I'm a stoic person. I don't get angry. I sit quietly in the corner and say "no."

Isn't your writing a way of saying "no" in certain respects?

I'm glad you see that.

You write about people, places, and subjects that others might tend to dismiss as not very "literary." Do you see yourself as reclaiming materials that otherwise would be lost or ignored?

Yes, it's somewhat natural for me to feel that way. I have my material, what's been allotted to me. And along with that comes a Southern defensive posture and a desire to reclaim a measure of pride and identity for my people.

There's a passage in In Country *in which a dilapidated barn is described. It's said to be like an artifact from dinosaur times. Are you something of an archaeologist trying to recapture pieces of the past?*

There are ways of doing that. I don't like to think of myself as romanticizing the quaint old days. Characters like Spence and Lila know all about how hard the past could be. I just had a conversation with my mother this morning. I was asking her when she was growing up in the country in a large household if she had her own spending money. She said no, never, she never had any money. Once she went to the local fair at the school and didn't take anything with her to eat and nobody gave her a nickel to buy a Coke or anything and she said the smell of the hamburgers and hot dogs just about starved her to death that day. She married my father when she was seventeen and when they were courting he would take her out to buy hamburgers and Cokes. I remember in my own childhood what an incredible experience a hamburger and Coke was. I think, by the way, that's why McDonald's is so popular. People have that residual memory of those days in their families, in American history. All those fast foods are basically farm foods—grease and starch. The past is very appealing to a lot of Americans. They see it as something to hold on to, something more cohesive than this fragmented, chaotic life that we mostly live now. But I find the chaos very exciting. People are getting free of a lot of that baggage of the past and I think that's good. People aren't always capable of dealing with change, and yet the possibility of dealing with it is there. I think that's what I was trying to say in the end of "Memphis" [Love Life] when Beverly is looking to her future and sees she has choices her parents didn't have. That seems to me an important moment.

Your characters are often enamored of trends and fads. Do you share with them an enthusiasm for what's new?

I'm probably more critical of pop culture than most of them, although they're getting more sophisticated all the time and less interested in a lot of garbage. I have a sympathetic understanding of why they're watching soap operas or reading the tabloids or whatever they do.

You don't seem to share the impulse of some writers to attack television, to lament the fact that it has replaced reading. In your most recent novel, television brings a harmony into the home of Spence and Lila.

Television has brought a lot of outside information and pleasure into people's lives. And whether it's good or bad the fact is that some of my characters feel something for the television programs they watch, feel an affection for the characters in the shows, admire their talent. Now those are real emotions, and we all see things on TV that mean something to us. So I accept that. It used to be that people in a town didn't go out at night, they stayed at home and watched the prime-time line-up. They had their favorite shows. They watched "M*A*S*H" on Saturday nights. Maybe they looked forward to it all day. They had it sort of notched in their skulls that that's what they were going to do. "M*A*S*H" was a very popular program; the final episode was watched by more people than had ever watched any such program before. I think that was culturally significant. The big change now is cable television. There is so much to watch that it all seems empty. People have caught on to that. Now they watch movies on their VCR or they go out because there are a lot of things happening since the seventies brought us groups to join. People just seem to be going out more. They're doing more things. They're more athletic, for example.

Is it greater prosperity?

I think so.

In Country *obviously has a lot of references to "M*A*S*H." Many of your stories have references to pop culture. Do you ever wonder if twenty-five years from now people will need footnotes?*

No, I don't worry about it.

You have said, "I feel I'm luckier than some of my characters because I've escaped the circumstances that trapped them. It's an insecure feeling so in a way I feel close to them." Could you talk about the insecure feeling?

I feel less threatened now, but for a long time I was afraid I might have to get a job in a factory or as an all-night clerk in a motel.

When you left Kentucky, how much of your leaving did you feel was geographical and how much did you feel was cultural or class?

Class. Which is bound up with the South and the North, because the South felt so inferior to the North. Southerners react to that sense of inferiority in two ways. One is to stand up fiercely for the South and sing "Dixie" all the time. The other is to reject it and say that the North is the authority and try to learn their ways and get rid of our accents.

Have you made a conscious effort to change your accent?

When I went away to school and later to New York to work, I made a real conscious effort to lose it, and I virtually did for a long time. Then I realized that was ridiculous, and I tried to regain the natural way of talking.

Recently you've moved back to Kentucky from Pennsylvania. Has coming back had any effects on your writing? Is it any different to write from Kentucky, about Kentucky?

I don't know yet. Here's what I imagine is going to happen: living away for many years, living in the North, I always wrote about Kentucky; coming back, I think I'm probably going to write about leaving. I'm probably going to send my characters out exploring.

Do you think they'll go north to Pennsylvania?

They might. I never wrote about Pennsylvania. I just wasn't motivated. I think the distance gives you a kind of perspective.

So now you think there might be some Pennsylvania stories?

Well, only if that's one of the places my characters happen to go. You see, my characters roughly evolve from what's going on in my family. It's not that the fiction is autobiographical but the family's my source, my anchor, my way of finding out what's going on with people and connecting with the region. In the last few years my family has gotten incredibly scattered. For almost all the time that I was away I was the only one who *was* away, and therefore it was my responsibility to come back, to come home at Christmas, to come home for vacation. Now just in the last few years one sister has moved first to Virginia and then to Florida. Her children have grown up and moved to Virginia and Texas, and one of them has moved from Florida back here and works at the Holiday Inn. And another sister has gotten married and moved to California and is currently in Australia. So it's hard to keep up with them. I find it very disorienting.

Could we discuss a moment the kinds of characters you write about? You said in another context that you see a shift in American writing away from the alienated hero toward characters who are trying to make their way higher into society, into a better position, because they've been down near the bottom. Do you see your own writing in this light? Do you see yourself as departing from classical American fiction with its heroes who typically reject society?

I did deliberately want to depart from the classics of American fiction in the beginning. Back in graduate school I thought I would like to do that. I tried to do it. I wrote a novel (it was never published) about a twelve-year-old girl, a sort of female Huck Finn. When I was in graduate school I had a wonderful teacher who said all American literature was about the American dream and the American hero who was alienated from American society. He said—this was back in the sixties—in the future, you're going to see a shift, where the hero instead of trying to get *out* of society is trying to get *in*. And of course already that has happened. Much of our fiction now is about marginal people—black literature, Jewish literature, people living on the edge—rather than people who have been in the center and are trying to get out. I have always remembered that my professor said the hero was going to come back in. I didn't know what to make of that, but I thought about it when I started writing about characters who had never been in the center, who had never had that advantage of being able to criticize society enough to leave it, like the hippies were able to do in the sixties.

You once observed that the literary hero of the past typically possesses a "superior sensibility." He is, in effect, an artist, at least emotionally. Your characters may feel things deeply, but they hardly ever strike us as being artistic. They often have trouble expressing themselves. Is there a special challenge in writing about inarticulate people?

A character like Spence knows plenty of big words, but he doesn't want to use them.

Why doesn't he want to use them?

I don't agree that he can't express himself. I don't think my characters are inarticulate. They do have a vital language and when they do talk it is quite vigorous. But they are inhibited in their relationships and they don't want to call on verbal ways of communicating. They can talk as well as I can. Certainly as well as I can in an interview. Their reticence is deep-rooted and it goes back generations and grows out of their class and their culture. They don't often know what to say, but that doesn't mean they don't know words. They don't know how to approach the subject or to find the courage to say what they could say, or maybe they don't want to say it because they are stubborn. At the end of "State Champions" [*Love Life*] there is a passage about how country children aren't taught manners, and so they don't say "happy birthday" or "thank you" or things like that. Manners are embarrassing. Verbal communication is very sophisticated and often empty. Saying "thank you" is something you are taught to do to be civilized. For some of my characters, saying "I love you" is a very negative thing, because the meaning is unquestionable and to say it is to commit yourself to a great emotional thing. It is one of those things you don't say. My people don't want to be that revealing about themselves. I said their language is blunt and saying "I love you" would be a very blunt thing to say, but I'm not sure they want to say that. It would be too embarrassing.

It sounds like your characters have two motives for not speaking up. One is a fear of revealing themselves, and the other is pride, a feeling that to say the words is to cheapen the emotion.

Yes, and to a character like Spence, a man of country speech, many words might seem comically inappropriate. To use a multisyllabic word that is not usually part of his vocabulary, even though he knows it, would seem like a pretension, and he does not want to put on airs.

You've said, "I feel if I can make characters know far fewer words than I know then I won't be scared of them and I'll be in charge." You were joking, but is there perhaps some truth in the comment? You don't often write about characters who have anywhere near your education. Is it partly a control issue?

Oh, that's probably it. I don't have the confidence to write about a lot of things. I would find it hard to write about somebody who has a lot of knowledge about something I don't understand, hard to grasp that person's way of expressing himself.

Most of your audience is, like you, more educated than your characters. Do you picture a particular audience when you write?

No, and I find it odd that I'm writing for an audience that is particularly well educated. I'm sorry the general public can't read what I write. I think that they are capable of it, but they don't have access to it. People don't know that they can go to the library and read. They feel a class inhibition. There are plenty of things that people who haven't graduated from high school are capable of reading, but their jobs and their worlds prevent them from taking an interest in it. A factory worker is not going to go to the opera. It's just unthinkable. That's not his world, he wouldn't be comfortable. People are taught that things outside their class are inappropriate and that's unfortunate because there are a lot of things that could be of interest to them. I don't think I write fiction that's for a select group.

What sort of reactions have you gotten from people around here about the way you portray them?

I haven't heard reactions. I'm not sure a lot of people around here read my work. I should qualify that. A lot of people wouldn't *want* to read my work because they might find it too close to their lives. They're not interested in reading something that familiar, it would make them uncomfortable. More have probably read *In Country*, which sold very widely once it was learned the movie was being made. I think most people are much more interested in the movie.

What do you think it is in your work that would make people uncomfortable?

Well, it's not television. It's not fantasy. It's realistic. A lot of people just look for escape, Danielle Steele novels, for instance.

You've said, "Letting the imagination loose is a way of getting at stuff that's underneath." Could you give us an example of a particular work where you did that, a breakthrough, when you felt like you got at something underneath?

I think I meant that in a more general way. I feel that writer's block is a common state of mind and almost constant for many writers. The act of writing is a battle to get at what's underneath, to break down the barriers to expression. Writing is a matter of opening up channels to your experience. I feel like mine is pretty far down there, so the act of digging it out is hard.

Why do you think it's so far down there?

It's cultural repression and lack of encouragement. My experience of going North caused me to repress my own sense of identity and to lose what confidence I had in my own intelligence. I don't even know what I know.

Is there a particular story where you really feel like you got into a vein?

No, I was thinking in general about letting loose and getting into an inspired state where you can feel like you're getting something.

What is that inspired state like?

It's like you're not conscious of your body and you're flying along in a state of excitement with high energy and a good feeling. Working up to that stage is hard because I have all these physical sensations that prevent it. If I can't get started I realize I'm hungry so then I eat, and then I'm sleepy and I drink coffee, then I feel bad. It's a daily battle. If you can transcend all that, you feel good.

How long do these periods of inspiration last?

If I control the coffee and the food just right and get a high energy level, then it could go on for a few hours. And on the best days, really the best times I've ever had, I can write a whole draft of a twenty–page story. That's good.

That's very good. How often does that happen?

It used to happen more often. There's a kind of innocence that goes into it, letting a story fly around like that. Once you do it often enough you get more self-conscious about it and then your vision of what's possible gets more complicated and you place more expectations on yourself. Then it's harder to get that innocent flow, because you start criticizing everything. So I think the writing ability has improved, though the vision of what's possible has become more complicated and so the writing's harder.

How do you handle the bad days, when the writing's not going well?

I play at it, and then I give up.

It doesn't affect the rest of your life if you have a bad day writing?

I'm not very emotional about it. I don't think about writing when I'm not sitting at the typewriter.

You've been called a minimalist, a dirty realist, a K-Mart realist, and so forth. Obviously these labels are more interesting to critics than to writers. But do any of the labels seem more appropriate than the others? And would you yourself distinguish the brand of realism you write? You once called it "hard realism."

I guess I used that description not so much as a label as a way of saying my writing is plain or matter-of-fact. I don't know about labels. But I got a kick out of that dirty realist tag. John Barth had one, too, that amused me— a blue-collar hyper-realist super-minimalist, something like that.

Do you think that's accurate?

I don't think any label is ever totally accurate.

What about the description of your writing as minimalist?

I'm not sure what's meant by minimalism. I'm not sure if it means something that is just so spare that there is hardly anything there, or if it describes something that is deliberately pared down with great artistic effect or if it's just a misnomer for what happens in any good short story, which is economy.

Your comments in previous interviews have emphasized style as important to you. You said once, "My favorite writers are those that have a unique style." What do you think your style is like?

I try to approximate language that's very blunt and Anglo-Saxon. Instead of saying "a decorative vase of assorted blooms from the garden," I might say "a jug of flowers." "A jug of big red flowers." A lot of it is not just the meaning but the sound of the words and the rhythm of the words and the way they come out of a way of talking. It's also a certain attitude toward the world. Imagine a person who would say "jug" instead of "vase." Style comes out of a way of hearing people talk.

Is your style an approximation of the sounds you have in your head from when you were a child and from the way people around here speak?

It's not literally the way they speak. It's something you fashion. It has to do with a projection from inside.

One of the complaints about minimalists is that they take too narrow and personal a view, they don't give us a broad context. In stories like "Detroit Skyline, 1949" and "The Ocean," however, you obviously do provide a historical context. Is this part of your purpose? Do you want us to view your characters as in some sense representative?

It just happens. It just turns out that way. I don't know that I typically set out to establish a larger social context for my work. But I did with *In Country*. My editor told me, when I started writing the novel, that the novel in general has a lot broader substance than a short story. Meaning a social context, I think. It has deeper issues. I bore that in mind when I was working on it.

You write almost exclusively in the present tense. Did that just happen or did you experiment with it?

Actually, I don't think I've written in the present tense in a few years. All the stories in *Shiloh* and most of the stories in *Love Life* are in the present tense. But the ones in the back of *Love Life* are more recent, and they're in past tense. This signaled a change for me. It wasn't a calculated effect. I wrote in the present tense because it seemed right at the time. It was a fashion; it was perfectly appropriate to the times and that's why a lot of people found themselves using it. It obviously came from television, you know. It's very expressive in a way. But I got bored with it. I started seeing it everywhere and it just made me feel like doing something different.

Did you discover the present tense on your own or did you read another writer using it and think you'd like to try that?

Everybody was writing in the present tense. I wouldn't say I copied it but I wouldn't say I originated it either. It was in the air.

Does writing in the present tense prevent your characters from having a sense of the past or an ability to step out of their immediate experience?

Mainly it has to do with the author's authority. If the author is writing in present tense then you get the impression he doesn't know any more than you do about what's happening. You're going along with the author. If the author starts in the past tense, if he says, "Once upon a time," then you assume he has sorted events out, he has a perspective on them, has judged them in some sense. I think the uncertainty of the present tense said a lot about what we were making of the late twentieth century or were unable to make of it.

But now your stories are primarily in the past tense?

One effect of using past tense is that you go along a lot faster. For example, here in the present tense, the phone is ringing. The waitress wants to answer the phone. She picks up the phone. Hello, she says. You could get bogged down for days . . . and you can't skip large chunks of time. You can't say she answers the phone today and then say it is three weeks later. How did that consciousness skip all that time? Who's doing the plotting? Who's behind the camera?

Ann Beattie once said that writing in present tense helped her to imagine everything happening.

Yes, that sense of immediacy is very valuable. And also, there's that habit people have, when they tell a story, "So I go . . . then, he goes . . ." The present tense is a natural storytelling mode. You turn it on and you go.

There are at least a couple stories in Love Life *where you do unusual things with point of view. Unusual for short stories, that is.*

You mean like two different points of view?

There's the shifting third-person point of view in the title story "Love Life." And the first- and third-person points of view in "Marita," which is even more unusual.

Also, in "Marita," I shift between present and past tense.

What was behind that, or do you remember?

No, I don't remember. I'm sure it just developed. I can't imagine that I sat down and said now I'm going to experiment with point of view and tense. It was a revelation for me to have hit upon the alternating points of view in "Love Life" because I'd never tried such a thing before. It seemed to make a breakthrough, force some shift. That story was written before *Spence + Lila,* in which I did the same thing.

What about the two different points of view and the shifts between past and present tense in "Marita"?

It felt very interesting writing it that way. I tend to write by piecing things together, and it may very well be that I looked at different fragments and then just somehow put them together.

That story is about an abortion, a critical decision. Are the different points of view and tenses perhaps supposed to emphasize the gap between the mother's feelings and the daughter's?

The daughter is the one experiencing it in the present and the one who's feeling it, so the first person/present tense seems to work more for that, but the mother has more critical distance, and third person/past tense seems to fit for her. That's the way I feel about it anyway.

You published a book on Nabokov [Nabokov's Garden: A Guide to "Ada," 1974] and have talked about having a strange affinity with Nabokov's sensibility. How would you describe his sensibility?

His extraordinary childhood allowed him to indulge a child's way of seeing that's up-close and particular. What I admire about Nabokov's work is his details, his seizing on the tiniest things. He thought these were the essence of reality, things you wouldn't notice necessarily. Nabokov said that the literal meaning is so much more important than what people find underlying it. He was much more interested in the pattern of the butterfly wing than in anything about symbolism or life on the wing or whatever butterflies are supposed to represent.

Do you think that's true of your work?

Obviously, my writing is nothing like his, but details and images can radiate and shimmer and evoke emotions. Whereas, if you talk about a story as showing a contrast between, say, the old and the new ways of life or as being about the New South, well, either that's very obvious or it is something I never even thought of. I have difficulty with abstractions, with questions about themes. I think that when you teach literature that's what you're dealing with a lot of times, because students want to know what it means. There was an article about "Shiloh," which reduced it all to these generalizations, and I felt like it was all very efficiently abstracted, so why did I go to all the trouble to write it as a story? Maybe most students are at an age where qualities and textures don't make much sense. When Nabokov taught modern European literature he typically gave his students exams with factual questions, like what was the color of Madame Bovary's dress, what color were Anna Karenina's eyes. He said he wanted them to read the work so thoroughly that they would remember even those details. I think that's a good approach. Writing is like making a quilt. You spend weeks and weeks doing all these intricate stitches and intricate patterns and colors. And then you finish it and somebody says, "Oh, this is about the Civil War." A total surprise! Abstractions have their place, of course, even for writers. I make up these terms that I use when I'm looking at my fiction critically to see if it's working. Things like balance and tone and emotional center and emotional direction, continuity, weight. Then somewhere along the way I'll discover what it's about or where the center is. But rarely am I able to reduce it to its meaning.

Something else you said about Nabokov was that you like the way he celebrates life.

He was the most positive writer, everything was just full of joy for him and he wanted to be intensely alive every second.

In Lolita *isn't the world ugly and unfinished and accidental? Doesn't it require the artist's vision to redeem it?*

Well, that may be true in the fiction. Some people think of Nabokov as a very aristocratic, snobbish sort of writer who looks down on anything crude and unformed and limited. I guess I'm influenced by what I read about him as a person and get that confused with his work. But I can see in his work the joy he took in the artistry and so I want to apply what I read about him as a person. By his own statements, the only things that he truly rejected and truly hated were deliberate cruelty and totalitarianism. I don't think he looked down on people. His whole background was very democratic and liberal, and I don't think he dismissed the human race. His critics also confuse the life with the work.

Do you think you also celebrate life in your fiction?

Oh, well, yeah, I'd like to think that. I can't believe anybody actually celebrates life every second. But I essentially have a positive view of things. Nabokov had a comic vision and I think that means celebratory.

Any theories about why Shiloh *was such a success?*

All I know is that people did tell me it struck a chord, and very often it was people who were transplanted from small towns and rural backgrounds. It seemed to ring a bell and remind people of something they've tried to get away from. As I have.

Is "Detroit Skyline, 1949" autobiographical?

It's not autobiographical; it's inspired by one little memory and two or three details, the memory being that I went on a trip to Michigan with my mother when I was nine and saw my first television set. I remember the buses were on strike and we couldn't go into downtown Detroit. And that's just about all I remember. I wanted to write about somebody encountering television for the first time. I was thinking about what that meant. Anyway, I got hold of the *Detroit Free Press* for that period and I found the bus strike and I also found the Red Scare which got me real interested. So I collected a lot of information from the newspapers.

*What differences do you see between the two collections of stories [*Shiloh *and* Love Life*]?*

The characters' world changed a good bit between the two. Life was changing so fast that they got more sophisticated, they've gotten more mobile, and I'd like to think that the stories have gotten more complex. My characters' lives were a lot simpler in the first collection.

Do you think the changes in tense and point of view in the second collection are related to the stories' greater complexity?

That could well be.

When you take individual stories and put them in a collection, do you just compile what you think are your best stories at the time or do you try to shape them into a unified whole?

I try not to put two stories that are very much alike right next to each other. In *Love Life*, I began with a story about an old person and ended it with old people, and I think I had the more recent stories in the past tense toward the end because I felt that moved things in a forward direction. "Bumblebees" was the central story that it all radiated from. I had a complicated scheme that I can't quite remember now! It was very organic. Maybe you can figure that out.

I really liked the story "Midnight Magic" in the second collection. One of the amazing things about it is that even though its protagonist is unintelligent and insensitive, we end up liking him, caring about him.

That story was inspired by a guy I saw sitting in a car eating chocolate-covered donuts and drinking chocolate milk. He looked like he had a hangover and felt horrible. He looked like a really mean person and I wondered about him, so I started writing a story. While I was writing it I couldn't make the person I had seen follow through in my imagination. The real person looked like he could be a rapist and really mean. But I couldn't write him that way. I made him a whole lot nicer than I thought he would be, and I kept thinking he was too nice. I had to explore and I don't know why he came out the way he did other than, as I said, I kept trying to tone him down. We've all seen thousands of people who don't have any sense of responsibility but they want to be liked, they want to do right. They want to be in love and they want to make people happy. They just can't bring themselves to put forth the effort. They're totally out of control.

In your stories religion is not very often a source of strength and solace for your characters, which seems a little surprising since they live in the Bible Belt. Can you comment on why that is?

It's a failing on my part. I haven't written much about religion, just like I haven't really written about any black characters. Religion is not a part of many of my characters' lives. I've tried to refer to it in passing, to make it a normal part of their lives in some cases. But I don't feel confident about approaching religion. It's a tricky subject. I do try to think about religion and I'm interested in the evangelists and what effects they've had on people. I even went to Heritage, U.S.A. to look around for inspiration for a story. I just haven't been able to write it.

Why is religion a tricky subject? Is it the difficulty of capturing the religious sensibility itself or is it the fear of seeming to belittle or make fun of people's beliefs?

It's hard to do seriously and delicately, and I don't know how to do it from the inside. One of these days I'll work on it.

Could you talk a little bit about how In Country *evolved, what your first thoughts were?*

I don't usually start out being inspired by a whole set of characters that just appear in my mind. Usually I discover the characters through writing and through exploring what they're doing. But in this case I had Sam and Lonnie and Emmett and Irene and the baby there all of a sudden. The story was inspired by some kids I saw on the street corner selling flowers. I thought how odd they would look doing that in Mayfield, Kentucky. They would be regarded as oddballs. So I started writing about a couple of kids selling flowers. That was a time when unemployment was high, and the kids I was writing about had just graduated from high school and so I had them try to be entrepreneurs. So I wrote a story about Sam and Lonnie and her crazy uncle, Emmett, and her mother being away. I couldn't make it work as a story but I liked the characters so much I thought I'd keep going and write a novella. I wrote about eighty pages and I had Emmett get cancer and die. I thought, this is crazy, I don't know what this is about. Then somewhere along the line I thought of Emmett being a Vietnam vet—I thought, *that's* why he's so weird. And so I went with that for a while, but it was such a stereotype I didn't know what to do with it. By that time I was talking with my editor and told him that I wanted to write a novel about these people and about this guy as a Vietnam vet, and he convinced me I should face the Vietnam issue squarely. Before that point, I realized that Sam's father was killed in Vietnam. That just came to me out of the blue. Then I realized that *that* would take a whole novel by itself. So I had discovered the focus for the novel. Sam's quest for a father was a classic theme and it was the first time that particular story could be written about Vietnam, because it was just about that year [1984] that kids of Vietnam soldiers would start coming of age. One thing led to another and I started on the novel and I stuck with it because I liked the characters.

Emmett is a great character. Where did he come from?

I originally wanted to write about his being out of work, dropping out, and I was interested in why a guy wouldn't work just because he made a moral choice not to work. I heard about somebody like that once. But he wasn't based on anybody in particular.

Why would you be interested in someone who refused to work?

I didn't want to work, not at any conventional job. That was my problem after college. It wasn't laziness. It's not laziness with Emmett. He just doesn't think there's anything worth doing in a conventional job. That was true for a lot of Vietnam veterans.

Recently you said that you had more sympathy for the men in the stories, that women seemed to be breaking through, finding new opportunities, and the men seemed to have lost their way.

That goes back to "Shiloh." I didn't have any worries about Norma Jean, but Leroy was quite bewildered by all the change.

Do you think there is a little of that same bewilderment in Emmett? He and the other men in the novel seem to have lost their way. They've lost the old definitions of manhood.

They went over there to do a man's job in the war and they felt ineffectual. A lot of them anyway. When they came home there was nothing they could do that could compare with fighting a war. I think it had an emasculating effect on a lot of men, making them feel ineffectual in anything they tried to do. Some of them decided then that nothing was worth doing.

When I teach "Shiloh" many of the women students assume it's Norma Jean's story and cheer her on for trying to take control and move out of her confining background. They overlook Leroy and don't recognize that it's his story, told from his point of view. Is that common?

Not uncommon. And you can imagine my surprise when I hear that some students think Norma Jean is going to jump because she's standing on the edge of a cliff at the end of the story. That's so weird. Maybe *Leroy* would jump but not Norma Jean. She's a survivor.

"Naming" and "writing" seem to be central motifs in In Country. *At the end of the novel when Sam finds her father's name and then her own on the Vietnam Memorial a whole symbolic pattern is completed. The narrator's words,*

"Writing. Something for future archaeologists to puzzle over, clues to a language," *fit both the Vietnam Memorial and the book itself. Any comments on this idea?*

I often have characters puzzling over words, because I do myself.

I thought Sam's journey through words, from books about Vietnam to her father's letters and journals, reached a climax at the Memorial. It brings together a whole pattern.

Cements it all together? Oh, that's nice. I don't know that I remember doing that consciously.

Doesn't the experience of naming for the characters parallel the novel's naming of experience for the reader?

Oh, that's nice. But as a writer I go at these things in such a different way. For example, you might think I called her Sam so she could find her name on the wall, but she was Sam long before I had the Vietnam focus. And I wrote most of the novel *before* I went to the Vietnam Memorial. When I went to the Memorial I found my own name where Sam turns out to find hers. Fiction is shaped very consciously, but what goes into it is so haphazard. Sometimes you see the patterns as you write and other times you're surprised. To tell the truth, I don't remember if I saw that writing pattern at the time.

Let me ask you about another pattern. Spence + Lila *celebrates Lila as a mother earth figure. At the end of the novel, when Spence goes up in the plane and sees the farm as shaped like a woman's body, doesn't that bring together the whole pattern of Lila and—*

The land? Yes, I considered that pattern consciously. And going back to that other pattern, while I was writing *In Country,* the words *sounded* right to me and went together coherently. And then you point out to me *why* and I realize that it's successful and that's because it *sounded* right.

You've talked about how you started writing In Country. *What got you started on* Spence + Lila?

At 11:00 o'clock one morning I was looking at this notebook I had been keeping when my mother was in the hospital having a mastectomy. I had taken a lot of notes. I started writing them out and after five minutes I realized, "I'm writing a novel." I had all this material and I could see the whole book.

How did you conceive of the story? What held it together?

It was Lila's attitude, her story.

Isn't there more physical affection, both maternal and sexual, in Spence + Lila *than in any of your other work?*

It was just the most natural thing to write. I knew their language, I knew how they spoke. It seemed to write itself. It wasn't like piecing together *In Country;* I had to *discover* that one.

It seems that heroic stature is being claimed for Spence and Lila, even though to the casual observer this farming couple would probably not seem very significant. On what basis are you willing to claim that importance for them?

They're very much based on my parents. But looking at the story, I would say they both face death with courage, they're both successful at having a good, long-standing relationship to their world and to each other, they're welded to each other, they have strong purpose, and they know what their work is. They're capable of great love and sacrifice. They know where they are and what needs to be done. Therefore they're strong models of moral integrity.

Why do you pronounce the title Spence *plus* Lila*?*

I saw it as a love story, with the title written in a notebook or carved in a school desk, with the words enclosed in a heart.

There's a moving passage in which Spence is looking over his fields and thinks, "This is it. This is all there is in the world—it contains everything there is to know or possess, yet everywhere people are knocking their brains out trying to find something different, something better. . . . Everyone always wants a way out of something like this, but what he has here is the main thing there is." Since this is what you keep returning to in your own writing—this place, these people— would it be accurate to say that Spence's view here is your own?

Yes, I think Spence is very wise and what he says is absolutely true. Somebody asked me recently to say what it was about Kentucky that inspired me and to name two places that always inspire me. Here's number one: walking through Spence's fields, the fields of my childhood. That always inspires me, always evokes memories. I see myself as a child picking blackberries or going to round up the cows with a collie dog. So I make the connection. And the second place that inspires me is the mall in Paducah, because there I can go and see all my characters. And I can imagine their journey from those fields to the mall.

What do you feel about that journey?

I understand it, I understand the emotional travel. I think of my own mother talking about starving for a hamburger at the fair when she was young. And the mall is just a big version of that fair. This mall attracts people from miles around. Some don't come to buy, just to look.

In that same passage, with Spence pondering his fields, we have this: ". . . the way things grow and die, the way the sun comes up and goes down every day. These are the facts of life. They are so simple they are almost impossible to grasp." Does this describe your own subject as a writer?

Yes, it might do. That's the way I feel about experience. Some of the most profound things are also the most obvious, and they're the hardest to write about. They're clichés.

Both novels, but especially Spence + Lila, *have celebratory endings. I wonder if that's your resistance to the part of our culture that suggests only the tragic or nihilistic is true or serious?*

I don't think it comes out of any sort of perversity or reaction. It's more natural than that. I did come from Spence's fields and I respect that. I think it's temperamental; I think people have different world views.

Just as you bring new kinds of characters to our attention aren't you also validating certain positive feelings that aren't very prominent in contemporary writing?

My stories tend to end at a moment of illumination, and that in itself is hopeful. For example, Leroy in "Shiloh" recognizes that his life has got to change. His situation is difficult, but he now knows he can't just deny it or ignore it, and I think that knowledge is hopeful. I see the excitement of possibility for a lot of my characters at the end of their stories. At the end of "Love Life" and "Wish" and "Memphis," for example, I'm really thrilled at what the characters can remember and can conceive in their imaginations.

T. Coraghessan Boyle

Entertainments and Provocations

Born in 1948 in Peekskill, New York, the grandson of Irish immigrants, T. Coraghessan Boyle has suggested that the "mad, language-obsessed part" of him derives from his Irish ancestry. His father, a school-bus driver, and his mother, a school administrator, both died of alcoholism before Boyle was thirty. Although his family did not have much money, he was pampered and encouraged by his parents to obtain a good education. By his own report, his youth was spent "hanging out and taking a lot of drugs." He first began writing in college with a one-act play about a young boy eaten by an alligator except for his foot. When the professor and class laughed and applauded, Boyle concluded writing was "a pretty good gig" and he's been at it ever since, transforming himself from a "degenerate youth" to a "megawatt generator of fiction."

The orange-and-black, zebra-striped jacket he often dons on public occasions (and which he obtained at a Liberace garage sale), his earcuff, his bad-boy persona, and his frequently outrageous comments have gained him recognition unusual for a hard-working literary craftsman. Boyle is well aware that flamboyance attracts audiences, and he is intent on being as fine a writer as he can be and also as popular as possible. He cites, as precedent for this two-fold ambition, the career of Charles Dickens, whose work Boyle studied while earning a Ph.D. at the University of Iowa.

Boyle's four collections of stories—*Descent of Man* (1980), *Greasy Lake* (1985), *If the River Was Whiskey* (1989), and *Without a Hero* (1995)—and seven novels—*Water Music* (1981), *Budding Prospects* (1984), *World's End* (1987), *East Is East* (1990), *The Road to Wellville* (1993), *The Tortilla Curtain* (1995), and *Riven Rock* (1998)—display black comedy, incongruous mixtures of the mundane and the surreal, wildly inventive plots, and ingenious word play.

In 1993 Boyle moved from Los Angeles, where he is a professor at the University of Southern California, to the Santa Barbara area. This interview took place in his recently acquired, still largely unfurnished Frank Lloyd Wright house. Boyle said he hates moving; in his words, "This is it. I've got my grave already picked out in the cemetery up the street. This is the last house."

©1995 Pablo Campos

Elsewhere you've said that you divide writing into comic and non-comic rather than comic and serious. Could you talk about that?

People devalue comic writing. But I don't think comic writing lacks seriousness. Good comic writing is deadly serious and from my point of view can be more effective than a non-comic approach. Take the end of *East Is East*. Because of Shakespeare and the Greeks, the reader thinks the ending has to be tragic or comic, one or the other. But when you mix the two modes you can take the audience way down, a lot lower than you might have otherwise. I learned this from Flannery O'Connor's "A Good Man Is Hard to Find," one of my favorite stories of all time. It mixes the modes and gets you off balance. I don't know if you recall the opening pages, but they are a hilarious satire of this Southern family, including the children who are incredible brats. Then, as soon as the Misfit appears, the story shifts into a much lower gear. It is a comic story but in a desperate, frightening way.

Was Flannery O'Connor's work a model for you?

No, although I've read most of her work, many times. That one story, though, is the one I like to talk about in terms of what I'm trying to do. The

use of the grotesque, sure we share that, but she had a very religious moral-
ity, which I don't share.

*Do you think comic writing leads to certain kinds of choices in characteriza-
tion? Do you find yourself relying on types?*

I don't think so. True, I dealt with types in *East Is East*, but that is what
the book was about. Other characters I've created, like Walter Van Brunt in
World's End or Ned Rise in *Water Music*, may be types in my own iconogra-
phy of characters, but in terms of recognizable types in literature I like to
think they are fairly unique. I certainly don't have types in mind when creating these characters. I create them as living, breathing people.

*Do you think there is a conflict between using a character for comic purposes
and exploring a character's psychology?*

There are a lot of levels of comedy and I think that I do tend to explore a
character's psychology, as I do with Ruth Dershowitz in *East Is East*. I create
characters who have recognizable problems and try to work them out. Of
course my universe is very deterministic and I don't give them the opportunity to work those things out. Sometimes I think the audience is a bit disappointed by that. They would like something more uplifting and gratifying.
That's just not the way I see things. I see us as victims of chance. It is a very
terrifying world. Earlier we were talking about the fire storms and about L.A.
seeming like Sodom and Gomorrah. Who's in control? Not us. We feel powerless. Often so do my characters.

Do you think that all your books are equally deterministic?

World's End is a kind of rhapsody on genetic determinism, the idea that
what we inherit from our parents may preclude free will. I wanted to work
that out, to deal with that. So obviously my hero couldn't survive to over-
come it. Hiro Tanaka [*East Is East*] is doomed from the beginning because
that makes a more effective statement about prejudice than if he lived happily ever after.

Doesn't determinism reduce all the characters to victims?

Walter Van Brunt certainly winds up being a victim of his biology.

*Aren't satire and determinism opposites? Underlying social satire isn't there
the wish for people to think and act differently? Doesn't a deterministic universe
imply that you could not possibly do anything but what you are doing now,
however terrible?*

That genetic determinism was a line of thought in the years I was involved
in writing *World's End*. Succeeding and preceding books go off in different
directions. The historical argument behind *World's End* isn't if you don't
know history, history will repeat itself; it is that history will repeat itself

whether you know it or not. We take our gifts for granted. They are given to us biologically, but what about our predilections for evil, for self-destruction?

Elsewhere you called yourself an ironist and said, "One doesn't expose one's true heart, that's what irony is all about. That's the way I view the world and view human conversation." Do you think that's true throughout your work?

Each is different. But in general I am an ironist. An artist reflects how he or she grew up. My friends always had a detached way of looking at things. The guy you saw in the backyard is one of my oldest friends from boyhood. He's out here fixing our house. We're a tight group; my old friends are the dedicatees of *Water Music*, in fact. As a result of our group style I've always approached things in ironic fashion. I like nothing better than to go on a talk show and deflate the pomposity of it. This is true of the way I work as well.

How about the issue of exposing your heart? Do you think you ever have in your work?

You will find several non-comical and, I hope, moving stories in each of the collections. There are very moving parts in the novels, too. That's fine; if I feel that way, that's the way I plan to write. I'm more comfortable, though, in my bizarre, wild mode. It's more playful and interesting in terms of language and idea. I think of stories like "The Miracle at Ballinspittle" or "Ike and Nina," which I don't believe anybody could have written but me. But the critics loved "If the River Was Whiskey" because "Boyle was finally getting a serious tone." I, too, loved that story. I titled my collection after it. But I think there are other writers who write well in that mode.

Going back to your interest in Flannery O'Connor, she said, "To the hard of hearing you shout, and for the almost-blind you draw large and startling figures." Do you think that fits your work?

That's terrific. Sure, I like that.

She was talking about feeling alien in contemporary culture because of her Catholicism, because her vision of reality and salvation was so different from most of her readers'.

I don't feel alienated from our culture, but I do feel estranged from the audience to the degree it is illiterate, TV-obsessed, and celebrity-obsessed. Part of my job is to show them that literature can be every bit as fun as TV or rock-and-roll. As far as my belief systems, I think I'm very much a part of my generation and American culture today. I re-examine it all the time and try to define it in my works, but I don't feel alienated in the way O'Connor did.

Do you feel there is a clear moral vision behind your work?

I think you know what I stand for if you read the books. Absolutely. I don't know if it could be codified, like O'Connor's vision, or even Cheever's. Recently I was reading his diaries and it was fascinating to me that he was a man from a previous generation tormented by things our generation doesn't give a shit about. He was tormented by what it means to be a good person sexually. Our generation says do what you want. In his generation, you couldn't be openly homosexual. He cried out to be a good person. But in whose estimation? In mine, he was fine. Fuck who you want, it's okay. It's amazing to see how his value system overwhelmed him in certain ways but also gave rise to wonderful work like *The World of Apples*. In my stories, I'm trying to find where the values are when there is no God and science is bankrupt and you've overturned the moral tables of the previous generation. What do you believe in, then? What are you going to put up to replace the walls you tore down?

Do you think ideas *tend to be the starting points for your stories and novels?*

Yes, the stories, in particular, are often the working out of ideas. In the novels, the ideas are more complex and need to be worked out over a longer period. I have an idea and then the work progresses organically. That's why I like to have a subject, a historical subject. That's why *World's End* was so difficult for me. I had to invent the subject. Doing historical research, like I did for the novel I'm working on now, *The Tortilla Curtain,* gives me a chance to formulate ideas. Then I work those ideas out. In the beginning, it's sort of a puzzle. Why are these my concerns? What are the ramifications of these concerns?

Do you always begin with an idea rather than a character, or is the process different from one book to another?

A line occurs to me. Voices begin to talk. I follow the voices. Each day I make discoveries. With the book I'm working on now, I have a pretty good idea of its general structure and length even though I'm only about sixty-five pages into it. This is a little different in that I've had a lot of time to think about it since it was interrupted by my being on the road promoting *Wellville*. A novel develops organically. The planning grows cumulatively, block by block. It would be an empty exercise to have a structure and then nail the shingles and the boards onto it, because you already know what you have to say. If that's true, then you should write an essay or be a historian. That wouldn't interest me very much. Each writer plays to his or her gifts and one of my strengths is that I am able, somehow, to lay out loose ends and make them connect finally. The plots of my books are well wrought. That's important for me. A lot of writers, particularly in the late sixties and early seventies, lost sight of the fact they were writing for an audience. Literature is an entertainment. It is fun. Everything else is secondary to that. You've got to move the story and I've always tried to be aware of that. Story is a spell you cast over someone. I love to read in public. It's a seduction. I love to suck them into my vision of things, to entertain them, to make them enjoy it—the story has to do that. Every beat, every scene, every movement has to go toward that end.

Is your use of the word "entertainment" a deliberate provocation?

Look at Graham Greene, he divided his books into the serious ones and the entertainments. I know that by using the word entertainment I risk idiot journalists saying, "Well, he's just an entertainer." But some very good writers, like Charles Dickens, appealed to a wide audience. Even people who had no sense of the deeper structures of his books could enjoy the story. That's the way it should be.

How about the argument that, for historical reasons, it's no longer possible to have a wide and sophisticated audience?

I think our biggest problem is with the media; people are losing their ability to concentrate. We have an increasingly large portion of society that has no experience with the kind of concentration required for reading. We're practicing a dying art.

Do you ever feel tempted to write for TV or movies?

I'm rather monomaniacal, to say the least. Writing fiction is a conscious choice and it accords with what I like to do. I try to recapture some of the audience for literature.

But what about the danger of all the attention being focused on you as a personality?

You've noticed all the stuff written about me is biographical. They're interested in my personality, and my bad-boy past, so on and so forth. If it helps sell books, hallelujah. The books are separate, they stand on their own. They're of the finest quality and they're the best I can do. If I were writing fly-by-night crap then I would feel a little ashamed to get on TV in an orange jacket and tell jokes. But I'm not. If some people think that I'm only interested in that sort of thing, well, fine. But, if they'll read the books they'll find that's not true. They'll find out that the books are very subtle and surprising.

Aren't you thumbing your nose at accepted ideas about what a serious writer should be like?

Of course, I enjoy that. Don't ever tell me what to do.

You did a three-month promotional tour. Does that mean you've left teaching?

No, I still teach at USC. I'm going back in January.

Why?

I like it. They hired me out of Iowa to start the program. Two hundred fifty of the five hundred students in the English department are in the creative writing program. I never take off more than one semester at a time because they are my farm team. I need them. They need me. It is something that I would have a lot of difficulty giving up.

What do you get out of it?

I get the association with people who are excited about literature. It fires me up. I love to see the passion for the subject.

Do you feel you have learned anything from teaching that is useful to you as a writer?

I don't think so, specifically; but in general, yes. You get out of the house. You get into the real world a little bit, as much as the university is the real world. You interact with other people. You get totally involved with someone else's literature and lose yourself in it. You get away from your own work for a while. It's necessary for me. I like being a professor. I like being a part of the university. I like using the library. I like the fact that I'm helping my students and that they like me and want to be there. All of that is very rewarding in a way that is different from the other things I do. It makes me feel useful.

Do you find that you are producing miniature versions of yourself?

I've always tried to avoid that. I think I'm a good teacher because I am able to avoid it. Sometimes the best writers make the worst teachers because they feel so strongly about their own aesthetic vision that they impose it on their students and make their students clones of themselves. That, of course, is anathema for the students. All I ever demand of them is excellence. I'm like a coach.

How do your students respond to your increasing success?

That's another service I perform for them. They see me and think, "Jesus, if that schmuck can do it, so can I." You know, no matter what your elder has done, he's nothing. I had the same attitude. You're nothing, nothing compared to me. Nothing compared to what I'm going to do. That's how students should feel.

How about you as a reader? Do you read your contemporaries? Do you read writers doing work similar to yours?

No, I read whatever appeals to me, anything good. Among my contemporaries I like Louise Erdrich, Denis Johnson, Don DeLillo. Ron Loewinsohn's *Magnetic Fields* is a great book. I've never taught a class without using one of Raymond Carver's books. Richard Ford. Ann Beattie. Ellen Gilchrist. Different sorts of writers, whatever is exciting and well done. The more you write though, the less you read, which is unfortunate. When I first began as a student I knew every contemporary writer. I read every word. Now,

I spend so much time in my own world working on my own projects I don't read as much. Most of my reading is associated with what I'm working on.

Can you talk more about what you're working on, or do you not like to discuss something unfinished?

I've blabbed it all over the world, so I may as well. I have always talked about books before they're finished, and I've always written them. The title *The Tortilla Curtain* is a reference to the border we share with Mexico. It's a contemporary story set in L.A. dealing with the problems of class division, particularly in the way that L.A. is the capital of the Third World, as David Rieff has suggested. Increasingly we have people living behind gates in private communities, while the hordes of immigrants from the Third World camp out in the ravines. I drive up Topanga Canyon all the time coming back from USC. Mid-summer I went down there because I have a scene set there in the book, and the first thing I saw as I went toward the bridge was a little encampment. Nobody was there, the guys were working. But people were living there in the canyon. There were bedrolls and utensils. I'm writing the novel in part from the point of view of Mexican characters, which of course I'll be crucified for, because how can I presume to write about Mexicans? But I feel that, as a creative writer and as an American, I'm free to do it.

You object to the idea that we should only write about people like ourselves?

I'm opposed to censorship of any kind. The politically correct attitude to which we all subscribe—that we should be fair to one another—has become a fascism in itself, and I refuse to be intimidated by it. I will do exactly as I please. And I'll suffer the consequences. Finally, the work speaks for itself. If you create a good work it should rise above political considerations. Look at Steinbeck's *Tortilla Flat* or *Cannery Row*. He was writing about Mexican characters, and doing it well. Why not?

Do you think there's more censorship now than in the past?

Definitely. I was banned in one town recently. The story "Greasy Lake" appears in an anthology and a teacher called me up to let me know the book had been outlawed because my story contains dirty words. My publisher sent a set of my books to the library so the kids can read them if they want to. In my letter to the superintendent, I suggested that before a story is banned the parents should be required to read it and it should be taught to them by the teacher as he would teach it to the students.

Then there's the PC censorship we were talking about a minute ago. Everyone is possessive of his own territory. How can you presume to write about a woman? How can you presume to write about a Mexican? How can you presume to write about a Japanese? You're not Japanese. You don't know our problems. I think that's horseshit. We're all equally human. That's how you write about and create Emma Bovary if you're a man. I hope I can be human enough to write convincingly about another sex or race. I would be a lesser writer and a charlatan if I tried to avoid it, particularly since that's where my interest lies. I want to be embraced and loved by the biggest audience possible, but in a way it's water off my back if I'm criticized from a particularly narrow viewpoint, whether it be feminist or Marxist or whatever. In every way, we seem to be getting narrower and narrower. Very few general interest magazines will even carry a piece of sophisticated fiction. Now there's *Runner's World* or *Self* or *Me* or *Sneaker Lovers*. There *is* no general interest or consensus. I was a fan of rock-and-roll. Now what are you? You're into heavy metal, or rap, or whatever.

Doesn't the attitude that questions your wanting to write from the point of view of a Mexican reflect a certain disbelief in the powers of the imagination?

Exactly. You should be able to enter anybody's head if you're a fiction writer. Look at Tolstoy. Would he say, "I can't write about serfs because I am a count"? It's ridiculous.

There seems to be a kind of possessiveness operating here as well. Various individuals and groups lay claim to a part of reality, and so if you write about their world, you've stolen something valuable.

Do you remember the book by Danny Santiago a few years ago, which was embraced by the Chicano community, acclaimed as the voice of the barrio? It turned out to have been written by some white guy in his fifties.

Wasn't the reaction to the discovery of the author's identity one of moral outrage? Didn't many people think he had committed some terrible sin?

In fact, *they* committed the terrible sin of idiocy. I have taken some of that kind of heat, but I don't care. I lived in L.A. for fifteen years and I want to address the questions: "How do I feel about it?" "What does it mean?" So, I'm opposing two groups of characters, as I often do. It makes for good comedy because it gives characters something to fight against. This book, *The Tortilla Curtain*, is comic, but by definition only. I don't think it would make you howl with laughter, like *East Is East* or *Wellville*. It's grimmer than that so far.

What do you mean "comic by definition"?

A comic, satiric vision underlies it but as we said earlier there are different levers to pull. It can be low gear, it can be high gear. It can be in-between. If you look at my work I have stories that are tall tales, purely absurd and surreal stories, slapstick stories, every kind of comedy, including intellectual comedy. Comic by definition? You probably won't laugh out loud, but you will know that it is not absolutely naturalistic, it's not played straight. There is something slightly askew there.

In a way comedy is more difficult. With something that's played straight, the cues are more apparent. Isn't some of your comedy uneasy-making because the reader doesn't know exactly what attitude to take?

I want the audience to be uneasy. What the audience expects and wants doesn't necessarily conform with what I see and what I want to say.

Have you ever been tempted to give an audience what they want?

I would love someday to have a purely happy ending. The closest I've ever come, I guess, was *Budding Prospects,* but that was following a true story.

So you were forced to do it. Is the happy ending why you called it a pastoral?

Right. I think, as an exercise, it would be fun to create a happy ending, but it would have to be in a short story rather than a novel. I don't think I could stand it otherwise.

Why the resistance to happy endings?

First of all, because they tend to be sentimental. But also because there *aren't* happy endings—we all die. Everything is going to fall to shit. You leave this house for three weeks and a pile of dust develops. That's the way of the world. There are never happy endings. They are too simple, too easy. It doesn't work that way.

Do you also resist tragedy?

Oh, I don't think so. The end of *World's End* should break your heart. So should *East Is East.* The ending of *Water Music,* too, is very moving. To me, anyway, but of course, I wrote it. I find it very moving and deeply affecting and true. It's genuinely emotional when Hiro kills himself and when Ailie gets no more letters.

Somewhere else you said writing novels taught you about inventing characters. Could you talk about the difference in inventing characters for stories and novels?

I don't think you can really talk about your career unless you've written ten books because until then you don't know what your themes and obsessions are. I'm on number ten now, that's why I said ten. The stories in *Descent of Man* were idea-based, conceptual stories. I was more interested in the design, what they would look like, how they would work themselves out. The characters were subsidiary to the ideas, the rush of comedy and language. To some extent my stories are still like that but they're a little fuller now because I've learned to invent characters and use characters. Probably the fiction is a little less wild than it was, but it is much more balanced now in terms of all the elements involved. You simply can't write a novel of five-hundred pages without getting into the characters and learning about them and learning to create them.

So you still see yourself continuing as both a short-story and a novel writer?

Oh, sure, I will always write stories. Recently, though, I've been doing a lot of reading for *The Tortilla Curtain*. Reading about Mexicans, in general, culture in Mexico, accounts of border crossings. I traveled in Mexico rather extensively in the past. I haven't been there in a while except for border towns. I did make a trip to Tijuana recently to look at the fence because I have a scene set there. It was just three or four months ago. Right on the beach in Tijuana, there is now this huge fence going out to the ocean.

In your fiction do you feel obliged to stick to historical fact?

To be successful in what I do or Thomas Pynchon does is to be rigorous and know what the history is. Of course history is just a version of events anyway. But I try not to violate the actual history as far as we know it. For example, we know when Mungo Park lived and how he died. We know that John Harvey Kellogg lived to be ninety-one. It would be difficult to have him run over by a train when he was twenty-three. But you could. Ted Mooney wrote a book recently that rewrites history and that's fun. It's like science fiction. But that's outside the parameters of what I usually do. I never say never, but I think part of the fun of the books for me, and for the reader, too, I hope, is in the subtle blending of the fictional characters and the real characters so that you really don't know. I know, but I don't think anyone except a scholar of the period would know what is actual and what is not. The movie people are real interested in knowing what is actual and what isn't because of lawsuits. They're never happier than to hear that events were invented. But as far as the character of Dr. Kellogg and his son, George, and his battles with his brother, Will, *Wellville* is very true to fact. And it is true to character as well.

Elsewhere you said you thought Wellville *was about letting your life be taken over by someone else. How important was it to you that it was about health fanatics? It seems to me particularly apt.*

Particularly apt for me, it's right up my alley. I think again we're talking about how you have to look back through your books to see what your obsessions are, what your themes are. You begin to make connections. Then you can see why you choose certain subjects over others and what fascinates you. In this case, obviously, since I've written so much about conspicuous consumption and food and body functions, people as animals, the impossibility of perfecting man as opposed to the progressive attitude, sure, it just seems natural. So, I love the subject. I wrote the book in eighteen months. The other two big books took three years each. Of course, *Wellville's* not as complex as *World's End*, but it wasn't meant to be.

Do you feel that of your novels World's End *stretched you the most?*

Yes, absolutely.

I think it is the most demanding on the reader, too.

I can't say. I think all my novels are a complete and utter joy and I can't understand why everyone in America isn't reading them instead of John Grisham. But *World's End* was difficult for me because it was dealing with my own history and it was the first novel I've written in which I did not have a ready-made story. For instance, we knew Mungo Park's life and I knew the history of *Budding Prospects*. But for *World's End* I wanted to go back to the area where I grew up, absorb some of the history, and see how I felt about it.

You've been criticized for the way you treat minorities and women in your work. Do you think there is any truth in the idea that your women and minorities are less individualized than the white males?

Obviously I'm a male and I do my writing primarily from a male perspective. In this new book I have two female characters and I'm writing from their perspectives. One is a Mexican immigrant and the other is a well-to-do white realtor. Those are two of the four main characters. In most of the other books the women have been secondary and I've been more concerned with the men.

Is it harder for you to write from a woman's point of view?

Yes, but it's necessary if you want to stretch. I can do the same thing endlessly and do it well, but you have to try new things. You want to be the complete writer. At least, I do. Again, Tolstoy really wouldn't have drawn back from writing from a female perspective. I think I did it with Ruth Dershowitz and I'm proud of the characterization regardless of what people may think of it. And I'll try in the future to do more of it.

When you look back at your earliest books, what do you see?

If I were to rewrite the earlier stories now, I would probably cut some of the language even though many would say that the language is pretty wild today as well. But I let them stand. I'm interested in what's coming next. I'm writing because it's what I do in life. It gives me meaning and focus. It allows me to live through each day. That's what I do. I work obsessively on one project and when it's done, it's done. I'm not going to go back ten years later and second-guess and rewrite it. I'm not going to worry, like Graham Greene, whether to call each work an entertainment or serious fiction. They're all my life's work, and I stand behind them.

You have a remarkable case of self-confidence. Do you have any idea where that comes from? You once said, "I knew I was a star before I ever wrote any-

thing." *When I read that I thought, "My, most people don't know they're a star until they get crowned."*

It's a kind of chip on the shoulder, a punk attitude. Everybody always said, "You can't do this or that." "You can't be a professor, there are no jobs." "You can't get a Ph.D., it's too much of a grind." "You can't be a writer, there's no living in it." I always thought, well, let's find out.

What you're describing now is different from saying you knew you were a star even before you wrote.

Okay, I cop to it, yes, I'm arrogant and conceited. So be it. It is all focused on one thing and that is to produce this work. That's why when you asked if I'd consider writing for TV, I thought, what a joke! I wouldn't consider working for anybody or writing for anybody. I don't want to write a script for movies. I don't want to be buddies with the movie stars who are calling me and asking me to do this or that. I just deal with exactly what I please. It is a kind of standing apart from everybody else and it is a chip on the shoulder. A lot of people are turned off by that. There are leaders and followers, you know. I'm not a follower. I've never joined anything and I'm not a part of anything. The bands I've been in I've been the leader. I'm interested in being the guy on my own. If you don't feel confident, you're out on the street with a six-pack. Maybe I'm afraid of that. So I keep going in this direction and try to control the habits for the sake of the work. Without confidence, how can you sit down and write a book?

Do you think your confidence helps make you prolific?

I know a lot of writers who are always second-guessing themselves and undermining their work. It's frightening. They are obsessing about what they should have done or they can't quite put the story before the public because they have to change a few commas. I'd hate to be like that.

I guess what I'm asking is, what is the source of your luck?

My luck is that I don't have to look backward. If you look backward you get depressed.

Sometimes you use miracles in your stories. Do you think a story like "The Miracle at Ballinspittle" is related to the work of the magical realists?

Definitely. García Marquez is one of those important writers in my background. When I began writing as a student in the early seventies, I was influenced by the magical realists and surrealist playwrights. However, García Marquez especially has staked out his own territory. Writers who try to write in that mode can never develop their own voices or their own territory. So if I do use the surreal or the magical I try to use it in a way that doesn't sound imitative. And don't forget that North American literature goes back to the bizarre and the surreal with Poe and Hawthorne and Washington Irving. Washington Irving, in fact, inspired *World's End* in large part. We have tall tales and folk tales. Paul Bunyan and John Henry. I try to keep that tradition in mind as well as the tradition of the South American writers like Borges and Cortazar, who were very important to me when I was beginning to write.

Do you think that your sensibility is scatological?

Wellville is an entire novel about shit. Years ago one of the reviewers of *Water Music* said this is a wonderful novel, a great big book about love and death and exploration, taking chances, and well, er, shit. So I thought, why not? If that was what the critics want, then I'll write an entire novel about shit. I think all higher aspirations finally come down to body functions.

Is the scatological a way of deflating?

Sure. If you say that what I want to do in person and in fiction is to make fun of things and ridicule things, deflate pomposity, as a satirist is supposed to do, then sure. It's wonderful fun to mix very erudite, sophisticated language and the most banal words that come right out of the id.

Have you ever felt the impulse to be a stand-up comedian?

I *am* a stand-up comedian, when I give readings. I almost always read comic stories. I have a good friend who is a comedian. We always discuss roles and audiences and the way it goes. Yes, I enjoy that aspect of performing very much. I have a good friend, a well-known writer, who reads very well and always likes to challenge the audience. In fact, if I'm present, he'll try to read something I haven't heard before, and I think that's wonderful. But I don't feel that way at all about readings. I think they're separate from the work itself, they're a performance. So I'll most often read the same stories over and over. I choose stories I feel will be effective in tandem. That's what a comedian does. A comedian's act is the same every night. If you see me on a book tour the first week or two you'll hear me being very spontaneous and getting the jokes and routines down. Two months later you'll find me doing the same routines and jokes. I don't get tired of that. I enjoy it.

In a performance you allow yourself to develop a routine but in your writing you fight against repetition.

A performance is an altogether different thing. The stories are set, they are what I wanted to write to be printed. For readings I select what might work well in public and then as I see that it does work well, I go with it. When I went to Japan I realized that I couldn't read funny stories because the Japanese are not very demonstrative, and it would be like telling a joke and having nobody laugh. So I chose the story "King Bee" to read to them. It was a new way of getting a hold on an audience.

Which stories do you usually read?

For several years now my favorite show has been "Modern Love," "Zapatos," and "Hard Sell." Now that I have a new book of stories coming out, I'll have to work up a new show from that book. The problem is that the stories from the new book are generally too long. I have to pick the stories that are accessible on a single hearing, and also pay attention to length and variety.

You've talked about how you don't read genre literature and mentioned your disdain for standard historical fiction. Yet you repeatedly talk about literature as entertainment. Do you think there's any contradiction in that?

Genre literature does only one thing, it tells a story. It has nothing else that we need or want. It doesn't have beauty of language, it doesn't have penetration, it doesn't have ideas or interesting characters or interesting situations. It simply tells a story. It is very unsophisticated in that respect. I can't read it. I'm perfectly happy to watch a moronic science fiction movie for two hours and numb out. That's two hours and that's another medium, but as far as investing time in a book, for me the most thrilling book does everything. It tells a great story; it does everything else as well. It's like a fully realized oil painting as opposed to stick figures.

Can somebody write in one of those sub-literary categories and transcend the category?

Kurt Vonnegut crossed those boundaries. So did Borges. We can't always put stories in categories, can we? What's a literary novel? People will say, "So you're a writer. What do you write?" I'll tell them literature and they'll ask, "Detective, science fiction, what?" Literature itself is a genre now, you know! I read what's good. Who defines that? I do. You do. People who have a wide appreciation and sophistication with regard to literature define that.

Is that bad?

No, it's great. Somebody has to make the taste and to lead people, show them the way, demonstrate what's good. Ordinary people could have a richer experience than reading a book from the supermarket if they only knew what to choose.

You clearly see TV as a threat and yet I see this big, very expensive TV across the room.

That's true. I'm often in the ridiculous position of being *on* TV and criticizing TV.

You've said you watched TV all the time as a kid. How did it not warp you? How did you keep your attention span?

I went to college and discovered literature. I'm worried about the average American family for whom TV is the main form of entertainment. They're mesmerized. If TV is your only source of stimulation, you're in deep trouble. After all it's a commercial medium and it exists to sell a product. It's not that we have great artists working to create these shows. And where's the artistic vision in a film where there are three different endings shot and the morons in the audience sign a card and choose the ending they want?

Tell me the difference between being mesmerized by TV and hypnotized by literature.

Reading is a very abstract process in which you recreate the book; you are in partnership with the author. You have much wider parameters. You have much more creativity when you read than when you watch TV or see a film. You bring your experiences into it in a way you are not allowed to in TV or film because the director has focused your attention there within the bounds of that screen. We can all agree on what Daniel Day Lewis looks like but we couldn't really agree on what Walter Van Brunt looks like. Books that are very well liked and widely read don't usually transfer to the screen successfully. The members of the audience don't appreciate the film as much as the book because they each have such an intense personal vision of the book that the one vision of the director collides with that and destroys it. So to be mesmerized by a book requires much more creativity on the part of the audience.

So when you're reading, some part of you is hypnotized but some part of your brain is necessarily active?

The same process goes into writing. You're working every day in order to bring up the unconscious and to be unaware of your surroundings, unaware that you have to take a piss or now it's two o'clock and you're hungry and the phone is going to ring or you have no inspiration. The same is true with reading. Sometimes you're just too concerned with other things and you can't focus enough to read. Once you do though, you're in your own world, and you aren't aware of time passing and you don't know where you are. You're focused on that imaginative journey. That's what's great about reading. The same state of mind is required to write the novel. We don't always get there. Each day's work is different. A lot of the beginning of the day is trying to get there. Sometimes you get there and sometimes you don't.

What do you do when you don't?

You rewrite. You work it up. You change the phrases. You get it closer and closer. I may work a day or two or three and be going very slowly, redoing what I've done and getting just to a certain point, not getting past it. Suddenly I leap ahead and write three, four, or five pages. Then the next few days I'm refining that and working to that point again. That's how the structure, the plot, and the characters develop.

Do you think your mind is working differently when you're engaged in work than when you're between books?

Sure. You feel great. You feel joy. Especially towards the end. Last year when I was finishing *Wellville* and I didn't know how it was going to come out, I was ecstatic. It's just the greatest feeling there is. When you work well there is nothing like it.

You use your hometown of Peekskill in several places in your fiction. Do you feel your future works will be more autobiographical?

I have written many semi-autobiographical stories. What I like is being able to write various things. If this week I feel like writing a story from my past, then I'll do it. An editor rejected one of my stories about racism saying, "The author is trying to atone for a shameful thing in his past." In fact, it was entirely fiction, entirely invented. It amuses me how sometimes the reader will read the author into the fiction. Another reviewer attacked *East Is East* because he felt I was so little a person as to savagely attack my fellow writers. I guess I did my job well because I've never been to a writer's colony and the writers in that novel are entirely inventions. I would never bad-mouth a fellow writer in any way, or a fellow human being for that matter, for any reason. That's beyond what I feel a person should do. But this reviewer felt strongly that I had written a *roman à clef,* that I was attacking my fellow writers because I was jealous of them. It amazed me. And it delighted me. I felt disappointed that thousands of people were reading the newspaper and thinking I was a jerk, but delighted that my depiction was so convincing the reviewer thought I am my character Ruth Dershowitz and these writers are specific people against whom I have a grudge. Anything with fictional potency is taken as literally true and autobiographical. We're talking third-person narration here, too. It's even more likely with the first-person narrator that they'll believe it is you. And they want to know. That's the thing. There is this whole cult of personality, and it is particularly true of me. The audience really wants to see behind the fiction. I'm guilty of this, too, as a fan. You are interested in the person who made a book you admire. You wonder, what human being made this? What are they like? Are they like me? I recently went to see Bob Stone read at my favorite book store in L.A. That night the first question was "So, what was it like to trip on acid and ride on the bus with Ken Kesey?" I would have completely deflected it and made all sorts of jokes and gone through my normal song-and-dance routine, probably got a top hat and skated across stage. Bob Stone very seriously addressed this stupid question which he has probably heard a thousand times, and I realized that *I* really wanted to hear the answer. It was a revelation for me.

Do you think when you've used your own experience the stories have a different tone, that they are more poignant?

Now that you mention it, my autobiographical stories do tend to be the non-comic ones. There are some, like "Greasy Lake," which are comic in a black way, but some of the others, like "Whiskey," tend to be non-comic and poignant, too.

A totally weird question: Elsewhere you've said your totem animal is the fish. What about "fish" is you?

I have always been fascinated with water, aquatic life, and fish. I don't know why, it's just some kind of rooted thing. If I weren't an artist, I could have been an ichthyologist. I'm just fascinated by fish. I like to catch them, view them, maintain them. I like to breed them, I like to eat them, I like to bread them and fry them. I just like them in every aspect and in every way. I like to think about them, dream about them. I have always wanted to go out when the grunion are running at high tide. They come up to the high point and mate in the sand. I've always wanted to go and mate with them.

You might get arrested. But think of the contribution to your career.

It could sell a lot of books.

Gina Berriault

"Don't I Know You?"

Gina Berriault has been writing stories, novels, and screenplays for more than four decades. Best known and most honored as a short-story writer, she has published three volumes of stories: *The Mistress and Other Stories* (1965), *The Infinite Passion of Expectation: Twenty-Five Stories* (1982), and *Women in Their Beds: New and Collected Stories* (1996). Her short fiction is marked by its subtle craft and the variety of its characters, settings, and subjects. But until *Women in Their Beds* received both the PEN/Faulkner and the National Book Critics Circle awards, Berriault's reputation was limited to a small but devoted readership comprised largely of other writers.

Her first novel, *The Descent* (1960), is about a Midwestern college professor appointed the first Secretary for Humanity, a Cabinet position designed to help prevent nuclear war. A plea for disarmament, *The Descent* depicts politicians militarizing the economy, harassing dissidents, and promoting theories of winnable nuclear wars. *Conference of Victims* (1962), her second novel, explores the effects of the suicide of Hal Costigan on his family and mistress. *The Son* (1966), Berriault's third novel, describes the devastating results of a woman's dependence on men for meaning in her life, a condition that eventually leads to her disastrous seduction of her teenage son. Her fourth novel, *The Lights of Earth* (1984; reissued by Counterpoint in 1997), focuses on Ilona Lewis, a writer whose confidence is undermined by the end of her relationship with a lover who has recently become a celebrity. Initially feeling unmoored, Ilona is finally drawn back into the world by the death of her brother, whom she has neglected.

In response to critics who have referred to her stories as "miniatures" or "watercolors," Berriault says, "Whenever I was referred to as a miniaturist or a watercolorist, I wondered if those labels were a way of diminishing a woman's writing. I believe that, now, because of the feminist movement, no reviewer would use those comparisons without hesitation." She adds, "I hope my stories reveal some depths and some strengths, but if those virtues are

not to be found in my work, then at least the intentions and the effort ought to call up a comparison with a 12' x 12' acrylic."

Berriault also rejects any category more limited than "writer," saying "I found my sustenance in the outward, the wealth of humankind everywhere, and do not wish to be thought of as a Jewish writer or a feminist writer or as a California writer or as a left-wing writer or anything else. I found it liberating to roam wherever my heart and my mind guided me, and that's what I've tried to do with each story I've ever written."

We talked with Berriault in the Sausalito apartment of her daughter, Julie Elena. Although she was initially reticent about discussing herself and her work, her comments have the same honesty, depth, and humanity as her fiction.

How do you think your childhood reading affected you as a writer?

That little girl who was me was a restless spirit, confined in a classroom and yearning to be out and roaming, either in the landscape or in her own imagination, and that restlessness was channeled into reading. I read more books than any other student in grammar school, roaming everywhere the persons in the stories roamed; I was those persons. Among the earliest books was *Water Babies*—that one belonged to the family across the alley and I remember climbing in through their kitchen window when they were away on vacation, reading it over and over, sitting on the floor in a corner. Also I remember loving George McDonald's great-hearted books, especially *At the Back of the Northwind,* about a poor family and their love for one another. That deepened me; I began to know who I was and began to realize that kids in poor families were worthy of having books written about them. I read A. A. Milne, who wakened in me a delight in dialogue, an intuitive ear for what goes on between us and our beloved small animals—conversations of pretend naiveté and subtle wit that can make a child feel she knows more than adults think she knows. And later, in the novels of I. Zangwill, who wrote about Jewish families in Europe, I found a secret kinship and I found that Jewish persons were worthy of being in novels. No one, all through my school years (except for a teacher who must have felt a kinship with Hitler), suspected that I was Jewish, and I must have been one-of-a-kind in that small California town. But those early writers were like my guardian angels. They helped me to see my own existence as valuable—why else would they write their stories for me?—and they seemed to be giving me their blessing to write my own stories.

Do you remember how you actually began writing?

My father was a free-lance writer for trade magazines and he had one of those old, stand-up-high typewriters. So I began to write my stories on it.

So you began writing when you were very young?

Yes, I began to write on that typewriter when I was in grammar school. I also wanted to be an artist and an actress. A drama teacher in high school offered to pay my tuition to an excellent drama school, but just at that time my father died and it was necessary for me to support my mother, brother, and sister. I never had any formal training as a writer.

Do you remember anything specific about how you taught yourself to write?

I simply wrote and wrote, and I was an avid reader. One thing I'd do was put a great writer's book beside the typewriter and then I'd type out a beautiful and moving paragraph or page and see those sentences rising up before my eyes from my own typewriter, and I would think, "Someday maybe I can write like that."

You mean you'd type the words of someone else's story?

Yes, to see the words coming up out of my typewriter. It was like a dream of possibilities for my own self. And maybe I began to know that there was no other way for that sentence and that paragraph to be and arouse the same feeling. The someone whose words were rising from that typewriter became like a mentor for me. And when I went on with my own work, I'd strive to attain the same qualities I loved in that other person's work. Reading and writing are collaborations. When you read someone you truly love, their writing reaches your innermost self. You're soul mates.

How old were you when you did that experiment with your father's typewriter?

In my teens. I did it a few times. You shouldn't do it more than a few times because you must get on with your own work.

Could you talk a bit more about how you began writing and publishing. That is, what happened after your experiment with your father's typewriter?

That was going on at the same time I was writing my own stories. Rejection cards and letters with hastily scribbled encouragement helped to convince me I existed. I remember a letter from an elegant, slick magazine, asking me to make a change or two and offer the story again. I did that, and when it was returned I cried for hours. By that time my parents had lost their house and the orange tree and the roses, and I wanted to earn enough with my writing to buy a farm for them. (I'd always wanted to live on a farm.) My father died before I could be of any help to him with my stories.

Elsewhere you mentioned that your mother began to go blind when you were fourteen. Could you talk about how that affected you as a person and as a writer?

My blind mother sat by her radio, listening to serial romances and waving her hand before her eyes, hoping to see the stories take shape out of the dark. That could be a metaphor for my attempt to write, hoping to bring forth some light from out of the dark. I haven't yet.

How much formal education did you have?

After high school I took over my father's job. Then after work I'd wander through the Los Angeles public library and pick out whatever names or titles intrigued me. Having no mentor to guide me through that library, I just found writers by myself.

Do you regret not having a mentor?

My father was a mentor for my spirit, and there were others from whom I learned about the world. I regret not having a formal, organized education.

I wish I'd studied world history, philosophy, comparative literature, and I wish I'd learned several languages. Really, there is no excuse for my lack of those attainments, of that intellectual exploring, except as it is with every unschooled person—the circumstances of each one's life.

You don't say you regret not having gone through a creative writing program. Suppose a young person wrote to you and said, "I admire your work and I want to write. Should I get a degree in creative writing?" What would you say?

I'd tell that person to learn more about everything, to rove, to be curious, and to read great writers from everywhere. If there's a true compulsion to write, a deep need, that person will write against all odds. And if that person enters a creative writing program, it would be for the purpose of learning how to shape what's already known and felt. Sometimes, when I taught workshops, I was glad I hadn't subjected myself to the unkind criticism of strangers. There's so much competitiveness, concealed and overt, among those who want to be writers and those who are writers. In Unamuno's *Tragic Sense of Life* he speaks about poets' desperate longing to be remembered, to be immortal. I think that concept of immortality is long past, long gone from our consciousness. There's such immense change going on in the world, so much that will be irretrievable. Now the vying with one another is only for present gain. When I asked the students if they'd read this-or-that great writer, most had read only contemporary writers, and if the ads and the reviews praised those writers, the students accepted that evaluation. Ivan Bunin, for example, has been almost forgotten, and what a writer he was!

Speaking of contemporary writers, whose work do you admire?

Nabokov, Primo Levi, Jean Rhys—aren't they contemporary still? I liked Raymond Carver's first collection. Those stories were like underground poetry. He must have felt that the reader possessed an intuitiveness like his own, and picked up on the meaning, just as with poetry.

Isn't that a way of taking your reader as equal?

And when you take the reader as your equal, your work isn't affected or false. You establish that collaboration, that shared intuitiveness.

In your career there's a big gap between The Son *and* The Infinite Passion of Expectation. *Why?*

That's a question that should never be asked. It opens a wound. What can a writer say about gaps and silences? The question can't be answered because the answer involves the circumstances of a lifetime and the condition of the psyche at one time and another. How can a writer possibly answer it without the shame of pleading for understanding of one's confusions and limitations and fears? You call it a gap, but that's the time between publications.

There is no measurable gap. I never ceased writing, but I destroy much of what I write or I can't work out what I want to say and I put the piece aside. The longing to write and the writing never cease. When I taught writing in order to make a living, evenings and years were given over to guiding students through their own imagination, to the neglect of my own. And there's the belief, so often at my elbow as I write, that I can't write at all.

Do you see yourself primarily as a short-story writer rather than a novelist?

Oh, yes. When my first stories were published, there was a lot of enticement from editors to write novels. But I wish I'd written twenty stories to one novel, instead. Short stories and some short novels are close to poetry; with the fewest words they capture the essence of a situation, of a human being. It's like trying to pin down the eternal moment.

Many critics have praised your work for the extraordinary variety of characters and settings, including characters of various races and classes. Do you think your life experience was important in developing that broad scope?

I never thought I had a broad scope. The way to escape from the person you figure you may be is to become many others in your imagination. And that way you can't be categorized as a regional writer or a Jewish writer or a feminist writer, and even though you may be confined by the circumstances of your life, you're roaming out in the world, your imagination as your guide. I haven't roamed far enough.

You've said, "Between the lines of every story, readers write their own lines, shaping up the story as a collaborative effort." As the writer, are you concerned about controlling or directing the reader's lines, leading him to a "correct" interpretation?

Of course the writer wishes to compel and persuade and entice and guide the reader to a comprehension of the story, but there's no such thing as a "correct" interpretation of a piece of fiction. That's demanding a scientific precision of the writer. Each reader's interpretation originates in his or her life's experiences, in feelings and emotions of intensely personal history. You get more from what you read as you grow older, and your choices change, and, since you're wiser, you bring more to that collaborative effort.

How do you feel about writing screenplays?

They're so mechanical to write, and you must leave out the depths you try to reach when you're writing your stories. A screenplay is a simplification and an exaggeration at the same time. By contrast, if you slip in a false note in a story, the whole thing falls. But a film can be packed with other persons' demands upon it, become a falsification of the writer's original idea, and then be hailed as one of the year's best. What makes a film work are the magnified, publicized, idolized actors moving around up there on the screen. And because the influence and the gain from movies are made to seem more real than from your obscure small stories, so many young writers think it's the highest achievement in life to write a movie script.

Were any of the interviews you wrote for Esquire *in the sixties memorable to you? To whom did you talk? In addition to your story "God and the Article Writer" did they have any lasting influence or effect?*

Whom did I interview? I interviewed the topless dancers, the first nightclub topless dancers; not first in the world, of course, but in San Francisco. I remember that an editor at *Esquire* asked me to write an article; they had published some stories of mine, and he said that fiction writers write better articles. So I offered the idea of the topless dancers, who had only recently stepped out onto the stages in North Beach. His "OK" sounded tentative to me, and so I was very surprised when he phoned a few weeks later wanting to know where the article was. I had only a week in which to research and write, and I got it to them in time. Synchronicity is at work when you're writing an article. Pertinent things—overheard conversations, random meetings—are attracted by your task as by a magnet, and the article shapes up in a surprising way. That's not always the case, but it happens. Then an editor at *Esquire* asked me to interview someone or two who were fallen from the heights and so I found a very elderly couple, man and wife, who had been Broadway entertainers in their youth, and, in their shabby apartment, I looked through their piles of old newspaper clippings and photos; I was moved. I interviewed the student at Stanford who was a leader of demonstrations opposed to the Vietnam War, and I interviewed the men who were the firing squad executioners in Utah, the last firing squad that wasn't, after all, the last. They all wanted anonymity—shame, I suppose—and the photographer took their picture together in silhouette, dark, against a yellow sunset, out in a field. Since I am an outsider, an observer at heart, not an interrogator, I'm not facile at asking people about themselves. And protective as I am of my own secret self, my own personal life, I am reluctant to inquire of others, even though I find that some others don't mind at all telling about themselves. Pride intervenes, too; you feel subservient, at times, to the person you're interviewing, and it was this attitude, this uneasiness, this feeling of being an intruder, that brought about the story "God and the Article Writer," wherein the lowly article writer transcends himself by becoming one with God. It's a bit of a satire and it amused me as I wrote it.

In the more than forty years you've been writing and teaching, what do you think has been the most significant change in fiction?

One thing that dismays me is the cruel pornography of recent novels and how they're considered an honest probe of these desecrating times. What's inspiring is the work of more African American writers and Hispanic writers, and the availability of the small presses and quarterlies. But most of the short stories in most of the large circulation magazines seem about the same as they always were—about the middle class, their mishaps and misapprehensions. An elitism in a vacuum. There's no sorrow and no pity. We're far from writers like Steinbeck and Dos Passos and Nelson Algren. I remember reading *In Dubious Battle* all through the night, I remember just where I was and what period of my life—like a vivid fragment. There's been an intimidation of writers in this country. We write to be acceptable. Some things I wanted to write about, I haven't because I was afraid I wouldn't be published, and writing has been and is my livelihood. I supported myself and my child with my writing. I like to believe that I never misled and that I wrote truthfully, but I've always felt the presence of anonymous and not-so-anonymous authority.

Do you think there is a connection between the superficiality you find in so much writing today and the fact that many writers are academically trained and remain in academia as teachers?

It may be that superficiality results from covert or implicit censorship of our work. The academy isn't to blame, I think. Some very fine writers, in both prose and poetry, are teaching in universities to keep a roof over their heads and to find pleasure in teaching. Superficial writers seem to make a good living and don't need to teach.

Right now, a first-person, present-tense style is very popular. How do you feel about it?

I imagine that the first person, present tense is the easiest way to write. But to me it seems to contain the most emptiness. It brings a sense of immediacy, and with immediacy you think you've got hold of the real, and so there's a touch of satisfaction about it, a conceit. Just recently I was looking at Sebastião Salgado's book of photos, *An Uncertain Grace,* and there was a short introduction by Eduardo Galeano, who wrote "Salgado shows us that concealed within the pain of living and the tragedy of dying there is a potent magic, a luminous mystery that redeems the human adventure in the world." When I read that I thought that's what great writers have always done. Salgado lived in Africa with those suffering people and he lived in Central America. He was right there, where the truth and the real and that luminous mystery are found. It can all be found in this country.

Do you see yourself as a woman writer or as a writer who happens to be a woman? And has your gender affected your career at all, caused you any difficulties?

I've known, and still know, a fear of men's judgments and ridicule and rejection. At the same time I've been acutely aware of the oppression and abuse and humiliation that men endure and struggle against, the same that women endure and now know they don't have to endure. In other words, I'm a humanist, I guess.

How do you think of your work in relation to the women's movement?

Most of my stories, early ones and later ones, are about women. My wonder and my concern over women are present always in the natural course of my writing.

When you look at your own work, do you think there are recurring themes?

I don't look over my past work, or I don't like to. I want to look over my future work. If there is a recurring theme, it's an attempt at compassionate understanding. Judgment is the prevalent theme in our society, but it's from fiction we learn compassion and comprehension. In Gogol's great story "The Overcoat" there's a description of the poor copying clerk's threadbare overcoat, how the cold wind got in across his back. I don't know why those lines move me so much, except when you visualize how the cloth has worn out without his knowing until suddenly one day he's surprised by that cold invasion—isn't that a description of an entire life? That copying clerk is always ridiculed and insulted by the younger clerks. I guess that in my work, in my way, I attempt to rouse compassion for those who are called demented or alien or absurd or ridiculous, for those who are beyond the pale.

I think you do that wonderfully well in your work, especially with the brother in The Lights of Earth.

That *was* my brother, and though I told only part of the story, it was the most grueling work I've ever attempted.

Because it is about a woman writer, set in California, and many of the details seem to parallel your life, The Lights of Earth *appears to be autobiographical. Is it?*

The Lights of Earth was an attempt to redeem and forgive myself, and maybe that's what autobiographical novels are all about. But it's impossible that characters and situations and scenes and plots be absolutely true to life. If you attempt that truth then you may be false to your creative spirit, which knows how to handle truths in its own way.

Toward the end of The Lights of Earth *when Ilona receives that healing letter from her daughter, Antonia, the narrator says, "For a moment now the earth was hers to know, even as it was known to everyone to whom the earth with all its wonders appeared to belong. A child out in the world can do that for you, can bring you to belong in the world yourself." That second sentence seems to leave Ilona and speak to the reader about life in general, in your own personal voice. Is that so?*

Yes, I suppose, and that's probably why, when you first came in and before the interview began, I spoke about my daughter. My child and my writing and others' writings and everyone I've loved, all have brought me to belong in the world.

It seems to me that although your writing is never propaganda, it is indirectly quite political and that you see social or political engagement as essential to serious literature. Do you agree?

Engagement is the only word you need, because it explains why some of us must write. And political engagement is essential to serious literature, but only as a part of that larger engagement, that dedication.

What do you make of the idea, popular in some circles today, that writers should only write about people like themselves, people of their own ethnicity, class, gender, and sexual preference?

How limiting that is. Your imagination is left to hang around the sidelines. Say that you're crammed in at a restaurant table with your friends of the same preferences as yourself, all speaking the same language, and you notice someone, a stranger, out on the street, who's glancing through the window, and your eyes meet his, and you want to get up and go out and say to that stranger, "Don't I know you?"

The Brecht epigraph to The Descent *reads in part, "Indeed I live in the Dark Ages." Does that seem applicable now?*

More so now than when I wrote the book. I construed Brecht's Dark Ages in his poem as our ignorance of others' suffering and degradation, our indifference. But recent events seem to add another dimension to those words. Wars and invasions everywhere, mass starvation, the torture and disappearance and assassinations of human rights activists everywhere, the ruination of the planet. We're still in the Dark Ages.

I'd like to ask you about another epigraph, the Auden epigraph in Conference of Victims. *It begins, "We are created from and with the world / To suffer with and from it day by day," and it ends, "We are required to love / All homeless objects that require a world."* Conference of Victims *explores the consequences of a suicide. Does your choice of epigraph indicate that suicide is forbidden? Is the novel suggesting that suicide is a refusal to suffer with and from the world?*

It might be so. But it's not an immoral act except for its effect upon the survivors. Sartre claimed we set an example with every act. Suicide can cause havoc and further tragedy.

Why are there only hints in Conference of Victims *about the causes of Hal's suicide?*

Maybe I thought hints were enough. I may be drawn to writing about suicide because of how I feel about life—that life is sacred. This belief in the sacredness of life is pervasive in my being. It may be a naive and unworldly belief, but there it is.

While you don't explore the causes of Hal's suicide in Conference of Victims, *the novel develops a wonderful pattern of imagery of coldness. Could you talk about what the cold means?*

Is there a pattern of coldness? When someone questions me about this or that character or motive or meaning, I'd rather not recall the intricacies of any past work that meant so much to me for so long. For me to inquire again into what I did and why, in all its particulars, only calls up for me the labor of the writing itself, the solving of problems. I'd rather leave it alone.

At the end of Conference of Victims, *Naomi seems to reach something like universal compassion, when she sympathizes with the solitary stranger struggling in the wind on the deck of the boat. Is that universal compassion the highest emotion in your work?*

I suppose it is. Maybe her seeing a stranger, as she does, from the back, repeatedly, as he goes round and round the deck of the ferry, allows us to see his human vulnerability for that brief time of watching.

As you can see, your choice of epigraphs intrigues me. I'd like to ask you about the epigraph to The Son. *That one is from an Aztec fragment which speaks of a midwife telling the newborn son "Your house is not here. Here do you bud and flower. Your true house is another." That seems to imply the existence of another realm, a religious dimension. When I thought of the epigraph in connection to the novel, I wondered if the root of Vivian's problem was her failure to recognize that sacred realm.*

Her problem was that many realms open to men were not open to her. She spent her life in the woman's role, seducing and bringing pleasure, being married, having a child. So the sacred realm was the farthest thing from her mind and, if she glimpsed it, it must have seemed for men only.

At the end of the novel the word "remote" is repeated again and again. Does that suggest all of us are ultimately alone or is Vivian's aloneness a result of who she is and how she has lived?

All the men she has known seem remote, every experience of her life seems remote, the world around her seems remote, because on that night she is lying alone, no man beside her, her son gone from her forever. A profoundly spiritual union with other human beings is a condition she never knew existed, but on this night she dimly perceives it, understanding at the same time how far beyond her grasp such a relationship is.

Rick Bass

Out of Boundaries

A committed environmental activist, essayist, and fiction writer, Rick Bass has two reading audiences. To those primarily concerned with the natural world and the preservation of natural resources, Bass is the prolific, persuasive author of seven highly regarded nonfiction books: *The Deer Pasture* (1985), *Wild to the Heart* (1987), *Oil Notes* (1989), *Winter: Notes from Montana* (1991), *The Ninemile Wolves* (1992), *The Lost Grizzlies: A Search for Survivors in the Wilderness of Colorado* (1995), and *The Book of Yaak* (1997). For readers of fiction, he is most importantly the author of *The Watch* (1989), *Platte River* (1994), *In the Loyal Mountains: Stories* (1995), and *The Sky, the Stars, and the Wilderness* (1997). His stories have been described as "true and desperate and full of longing," as "weirdly lyrical," and as "complex, compelling, and expressed in a unique and powerful voice."

A petroleum geologist by education and an environmental activist by bent, Bass nine years ago left the oil business and most of humanity behind by moving to an area in the northwest corner of Montana called the Yaak. This was much more than a geographical change; Bass has called Montana "the state of my rebirth." When we interviewed him, Bass was living in a cabin on a dirt road near the "village" of Yaak itself, which consists of a mercantile (general store) and a saloon, The Dirty Shame.

His house was difficult to find, but when we finally tracked him down, Bass proved to be a remarkably direct interview subject. In the following comments, he often uses geological metaphors in talking about his stories and essays and in describing his attitudes toward nature.

In Oil Notes *you say, "There's a deceit in writing, you're trying to pull all the clever elements together and toss out the dull and round-edged ones." Is there more deceit in fiction than in essays?*

When I write fiction I'm trying to see the characters so clearly there doesn't seem to be any question of it *being* fiction. I don't feel like there's any deceit in it. In nonfiction, I think I'm trying for more sleight of hand. It feels more

technical to do a good job in nonfiction. When I'm writing the first draft of a story it feels less technical, more emotional. I'm watching for seams and fissures.

Seams and fissures?

If a story's going well, if I've got the force of it moving all in the same direction, then it's almost like water rushing down a canyon, or a culvert. More like a culvert, because it's contained all around and there's only one direction for it to go, where gravity is taking it. The danger then is I have this mass of story, all going the same way, and it might become very predictable. So that's when I start looking for side cracks or seams, fissures, where I can get some of the story to go, to keep it from all rushing down that culvert to the bottom.

Are there times you can't find those fissures?

Sometimes I don't see any, or I don't make any. Those are real hard stories to work with. But with almost any story, even failed ones, I will later see where the fissures were and where I didn't have my head up enough to exploit them.

So you're resisting a kind of inevitability when you're writing? That is, you feel from the start where the story is going, but you don't want it to go there in a predictable way?

Yes, I can sense the shortest way for it to go, or I guess you could say the easiest way, and I have to fight that. I like that word "inevitability," it's a good way to put it. I'm looking for surprises as I tell a story. I've talked to other writers about this, and my favorite writers say that in their best stories they didn't have any idea they'd turn out the way they did. It's a good lesson, a hard lesson for me, not to plan a story ahead of time but just to gather what's important and start out on it.

Why is that a hard lesson for you?

My inclination is to try to control what I'm doing. Even to be talking about it like this is to assert a kind of self-conscious control over it. Later on I will really downplay everything I say here and the occupancy it took up in my mind.

Is that because you're afraid that talking about the writing process and its techniques will distract you from the storytelling itself?

Exactly. Shoot, the technical stuff is what editors are for. I like to get my first draft down, then deal with questions of plot and motivation. For me, there are two entirely different mindsets—creating the story and then fixing it. What we're talking about now feels like fixing the story.

As one who writes both essays and stories, how do you decide whether particular material will be treated in one form or the other?

The question of timeliness comes into it. If I feel it's not urgent for anybody to know it, if I'm writing primarily for myself and nobody else, I will think in terms of fiction. If, on the other hand, the subject bears a certain urgency, I tend to put it in nonfiction so people will be more inclined to act on it. I realize this way of thinking is flawed because great fiction can sometimes motivate people much more strongly than a piece of nonfiction. But I think it comes back to the question of urgency. If I'm going to issue a bulletin saying the woods are on fire, I'm not going to sit back and say, "In 1930 when he was seventeen years old Joe first began playing with matches."

Don't some ideas just naturally seem more appropriate to one form or the other—fiction or nonfiction? You don't always make a deliberate decision about it, do you?

I didn't used to, but recently I've been seeing things in double vision. I can see the same material handled either way. Since I'm more interested in writing fiction now, I'm trying to discipline myself to put the nonfiction away and save the best material for stories. I'm doing a lot of research on endangered species—wolves, grizzlies, caribou—and I'm seeing these things in terms of nonfiction, but I'm also trying to put some of the material away to write about later, more slowly and with less urgency, in fiction. I'm also doing research on J. Frank Dobie. My inclination is that it's a subject for nonfiction because he was a real person, but at the same time I can imagine a wonderful story about a character like him. I'm going to try as hard as I can to do the fiction first, even though I've got a lead for the Dobie piece in my mind and a theme and all sorts of facts for a nonfiction treatment. I'm trying to hold all that at bay.

How did you start writing professionally?

I wrote hunting and fishing articles just out of college, but I wasn't having much luck publishing them. I published several in a row and then the magazine stopped buying them because they were always the same: I went on a trip, I never killed a deer, I never caught a fish, I just looked around at mountains or felt the wind or something. They bought it a few times, then they said, "Look, you got to start killing stuff." I felt constricted by that formula, so I started looking to travel essays, then to fiction.

In Wild to the Heart, *you write, "If it's wild to your heart protect [it], focus on it." Is that how you feel about your writing? If so, what is the nature of its wildness?*

I certainly try to focus on it. By "it" I mean the stories and characters rather than my success or failure in the marketplace, the attention or lack of attention paid to my work, or the technique of it. When I write I want to preserve something that matters to me. That's how I feel about writing. It's something that can get away from you. A story is something that can be lost, just like natural resources. There's Hemingway's advice about storing up material or turning down the flame, letting it get crusty with the barnacles of time. That's a fine idea, but I feel many people just let stories get away. They'll hold onto a story for years, then another story comes up and the first one never gets written. I'll listen to people tell me great stories that they mean to write. After two or three years, if they haven't done it, I'll say, "Can I write that story? I really want it." They'll say, "No, I'm going to write it." But finally I just wear them down. They realize they're never going to write it, so then I'll write it. When I do, it feels just like it was my own.

You say you prefer to disregard the attention or lack of attention paid to your writing. The Watch *got a great deal of notice. Was that a mixed blessing?*

It made me self-conscious. For about a year after it came out, I was looking at all the reviews and I got real aware of people watching what I was doing. I started to have trouble with the fiction. But I got it figured out. The way I did it was with a kind of belligerence. I constructed an anger or defiance about people reading my work—I didn't give a damn what they thought, good or bad. I held that attitude as a sort of callus for a couple years and finally it fell away. In its place, now I truly don't care if some people dislike my work, because I know that as long as I like it some others will, too. That sounds simple, but starting out it was not that simple for me. Everybody had to love my work or I thought it wasn't good enough. I'm pleased I got out of that trap as soon as I did.

How did you happen to turn to fiction writing?

I read *Legends of the Fall* by Jim Harrison. It's a collection of three novellas, and when I read the third one, *Legends of the Fall,* I thought, boy, this is what I need to be trying to do. It was a quantum leap for my enjoyment of fiction—some of the devices used, the mixture of language, and the force of the story. It has a sort of breathlessness about it that carries you along. It's a great, great novella.

Has Harrison continued to be an important influence on you?

Yes. Lately he's been influencing me with his reading capacity; he reads everything and retains it. His striving not to repeat himself also impresses me, and I would like to follow his example in that. His determination to enjoy life, not just to be a writer but to enjoy life in great quantities, has been a real inspiration. So I've learned and continue to learn from him.

Your fiction has been compared to Richard Ford's and Raymond Carver's. Do you see any similarities?

I see no similarities with Carver's stories, to my great regret, but I do see similarities with Ford's. I used to model a lot of stories after his *Rock Springs* collection. It's a very powerful book. I remember the end of the title story, "Rock Springs," where the narrator asks the reader all these questions beginning, "Would you think . . ." I never heard of such a thing. We're always told it's bad to put rhetoric in a story. To put it at the *end* of a story, what kind of stunt is that? All of a sudden, five or six stories in a row, and he's ending them with questions. There was an opening of boundaries. Also, I like his roundabout way of telling a story, that air of relaxation mixed with immediacy. It's a fine tension, a fine ambivalence. That reflective tone can really get you in trouble, but you can also use it as a great tool with which to injure the reader, to get your point across.

"Injure" the reader?

Yeah, rough him up, bring him around to the truth. A lot of Ford's stories are bringing home unhappy truths which will make you more whole if you accept them. Sometimes the narrator grabs the reader by the collar at the end and says, "Did you ever think this, well, did you?"

In The Deer Pasture *you describe your father as a great storyteller. Does some of your interest in fiction come from him?*

Without a doubt. And my mother, too. She's a great observer. If somebody does something funny or there's some peculiar clash of personalities, she's going to notice that and she'll tell us about it when she gets home. My father will take something that's happened and he'll tell it in a way that's not quite the truth though you couldn't get him in a court of law. He takes something that needs telling and makes it larger and better. In different ways both my parents are a great help to my storytelling. When I go home there's always another story.

How is it, working on your nonfiction books with Elizabeth [his wife]? Did you meet her because she was your illustrator?

I knew her before I wrote the books. We've known each other for a long time. She's not only a good illustrator but a good editor. She's got excellent instincts. She either likes something or she doesn't, and if she doesn't, it's probably not good. She's a tough reader and that's the best editor to have. You know, it's great to have editors who can help structurally or with line editing, but the most important thing is to cut through all the nonsense and say this works or it doesn't.

So she's your first editor?

When I'm in trouble she is. If I know something is working, I'll just wait and surprise her with it when it comes out in a book or magazine. But if I'm in trouble, she's my first editor.

You say in Winter, *"The writing was more important than anything could ever be—which is sad, but the way it has to be." Why sad? Why the way it has to be?*

Writing is inevitable to me because that's what I do, it's what I am. It's in the definition, a writer writes. It's sad because there are so many other things I want to do. I wish I were compelled only to hike. I want to see every one of these peaks and side drainages and mountains and ridges. I want to know every tree in this valley and then the valley next to it and the one north of here, over in Canada where I don't have any maps. The days aren't long enough and I can't cover enough ground in the day, so that's sad. I'd like to read every book I own, it's very sad because I never will. A couple years ago I finally figured that out. Writing takes time from things I want to do. Every writer thinks, What if I didn't write? What if I didn't know there was such a thing as writing? Would I enjoy life more? Would I look at life differently? And of course you would, you would look at it with a cleaner, more innocent perspective. You wouldn't always be putting these double and triple spins on everything that comes to your eyes. You might be a little more rested. But this is a kind of self-pity. Whatever you do, if you do it fully, you're going to be running close to exhaustion all the time.

You say writing is inevitable because that's what you do. When you were working as a petroleum geologist, did that work also feel inevitable?

Not to the same degree. And it might have been something as simple as the fact that I did it in an office, more or less in daylight hours, and got regularly paid for it. When I was looking at the logs, moving my pencil across the maps, certainly I felt a kind of inevitability about catching the oil. It's the same as when we're talking about fiction being almost a kind of nonfiction—you believe in it, you see it so clearly. Mapping for oil had that same kind of inevitability. If I mapped it so that there was oil there on the map, then it was there. It was icing on the cake to drill and find out it actually was there. There were so many things I wanted to do, geology was probably borderline. If you're going to assign numbers to it, with writing being eight or nine, then everything else is fours and fives.

What might a ten be?

I don't know, I'd be dead.

But you leave open the possibility there's something you might be drawn to even more than writing?

I'm not looking for anything else. Maybe it's just something as simple as better writing. I think I have a fear of boundaries.

You come across in your essays as a happy person. Most of your fictional characters are much darker. Any ideas why?

I try to make the essays positive because I get tired of hearing the doom and gloom story of the environment and I know everybody else does, too. It's not going to change anything to say how bad things are; we know how bad they are. If you start droning on about increasing populations and present land-use practices, you turn into what Jim Harrison calls an "eco-bore." So the only other tack I can think of is to try to celebrate what's good, help readers to treasure certain things, so they will say, "Yeah, it would kill me if that was ever gone." In fiction there's not that same pressure to celebrate the good.

Would you talk a little about the organization of The Watch?

My editor for that book, Carol Smith, and I organized the stories for meaning and for development of attitudes, and also we paid attention to length, not wanting to put too much burden on the reader, because it's hard to read two or three long stories in a row. We didn't want successive stories with similar themes either. We wanted to have some diversity and also a cumulative effect that would lead toward the general theme of the book: time's passage and the acknowledgment of it, and the race to stay ahead of it or to hide out from it. The last story in the book, "Redfish," does, I think, have a closed, resolute ending, more so than the other stories. I think the resolution of that story could speak for any of the others. Arranging the collection was like putting a puzzle together. It was fun. A lot easier than writing the stories.

Why did you use the title of "The Watch" as the title of the entire collection? Do you think it's the strongest story?

I don't know that it's the strongest, but it seemed good. I was originally going to call that story "Field Events" because everything seemed to be taking place either at the edge of the woods or out in a field or meadow. I was living in Mississippi among some meadows, and a lot of that imagery crept into the story. Anyway, when we were putting the collection together, Carol suggested *The Watch* and it suited me fine.

At the end of that story, Jesse's got a stopwatch and is timing himself on the bicycle. What about other watches or kinds of watching in the story?

Jesse has his little pocket watch, and that was a big part of it. But also Hollingsworth was standing out on the porch through much of the story watching for Jesse to come riding by. So "watching" becomes a metaphor for loneliness. Jesse's also watching for Buzbee out there. The collection is going to be published in France and the title is driving the translator nutty, because there are all these different words in French that mean "pocket watch" or "to look out for" or "to look at." I think the one we're going to use is "to watch out for."

Doesn't "The Watch" suggest that freedom, as exemplified by Buzbee and as opposed by Hollingsworth, is the ultimate good?

Yes, and I'm most moved in that story by Buzbee's courage, his defiance. Would you rather be safe or happy? That's an old question. I'm doing this research on wolves. This federal biologist caught this old wolf who'd been suspected of killing some calves. The plan was to relocate the wolf where he wouldn't get into so much trouble, but he'd injured his foot in a trap and they didn't know if he could survive with the bad foot. If they kept him in a cage he'd get acclimated to humans and would be no good in the wild. So they let him go, and sure enough he starved to death. The biologist defended his decision rather eloquently, saying that, for the wolf, any period of survival in the wild is preferable to time spent in captivity. I think that's true.

Hollingsworth appears to represent all those debilitating forces that sap us of life, and not coincidentally, he's a big talker. Buzbee says about women, too, they "always wanted to talk," as if talk "could be used to keep something else away, something big and threatening." That echoes something you said in your essays, that actions are better than words. Isn't that a curious position for a writer to take? Logically extended, wouldn't it lead to silence?

For a couple hours a day you believe so strongly in your stories that they truly are actions, not words but actions. I'm not much on speaking, it's been abused so badly. It is so easy to lie when speaking aloud. It's much harder to lie when writing.

The opening sentences of the first two stories, "Mexico" and "Choteau," play off each other. In "Mexico": "Kirby's faithful. He's loyal: Kirby has fidelity. He has one wife, Tricia." And in "Choteau": "Galena Jim Ontz has two girlfriends and a key to Canada." Don't the opening sentences define Kirby and Jim as opposites, in a sense?

If you'd been editing these stories and mentioned that to me I would have gone nutty and never would have finished the collection. That's interesting what you say. But I really get paranoid about that sort of thing. I'll have to go back and look at that.

Why would that make you paranoid?

Well, I have the idea each story should be unique, a different mineral or gem, not different shapes of one mineral.

Of the stories in the collection, only "The Watch" and "Wild Horses" are not in the first person. Why did you use third person for those?

When I start a story in third person it's got something mythic or Biblical about it. With first person, it's like I'm down in the dirt just scratching the story out, trying to earn or create it. But the third-person stories simply are meant to be told. It's like that new age stuff, channeling.

At the end of "Redfish" the narrator imagines his friend Kirby and him riding horses into the surf and he talks about the horses' fear "of going down under too heavy a load, and of all the things unseen, all the things below." Is that a metaphor for what all the characters in the stories fear?

Yes. The stories tend to be about the characters' attempts to control whatever they're afraid of. Like Hollingsworth tried to control Jesse and Buzbee. But in "Redfish" Kirby and the narrator go get the horses and they start riding out into the water, further and further. It's dark and it's snowing but they keep going into the deeper water, into the Gulf, which opens up into infinity. Maybe that's why the story has more resolution, because the characters confront their fears instead of trying to put up a screen and block them out.

Three stories in the collection focus on Kirby and his friend, the unnamed first-person narrator. Are these stories autobiographical?

Yes, though I'm not the narrator. That's where the fiction comes in.

Since there are real-life sources for at least some of your characters, do you ever worry that the small number of people in this part of the country will prove a hindrance?

That's a good question, one that I asked myself when I first moved up here. But there are a lot of good characters in this vicinity. And here I'm speaking like a map guy. There's a greater density of good characters up here than anywhere else I've been. By "good characters" I mean people things happen to or who go out and make things happen, people who don't just accept life rushing at them. Interesting, lively people. I don't mean eccentric. They just feel *full.* They interest me.

You've called Montana "the state of my rebirth." Why?

It's like being a newborn when you come into a place about which you know nothing. It's an invigorating, almost giddy feeling.

Was it hard for you to make the decision to give up your career as a petroleum geologist and come out here?

No, it wasn't hard. It was hard work but it wasn't a hard decision. I mean, it was hard physical work and emotional work, saying, "Okay, I'm just going to write now. I'll do some geology but I probably won't make any money at it, being on my own." I had only published one story at the time. That part of it was hard, but the decision to try it was not hard. There was no decision at all. It just had to be done.

You suggest in your essays that happiness is within the individual's grasp. You write that "a state of mind, if you mold it right, is as real and durable as anything else capable of being retained in this world. Good things last longer than bad." That sounds a lot like Walden. *Is such an attitude on your part congenital or learned, or is it an expression of some kind of faith or philosophy?*

It feels to me like a learned attitude. In science there are theories about cell memory, and in weightlifting there's a theory: if your muscles have done a movement before, if they've lifted a certain weight or been a certain size, then they're going to "remember" that. If your muscles have reached certain boundaries, even if they get smaller or weaker later on, they'll be able to achieve that expansion again, and more easily than the first time. I think happiness is that same way. If you're unhappy and you work to be happy, then it doesn't matter if you become unhappy again because with effort you can be happy. If you've done it once, you can do it again. Maybe even a little easier. It just gets to be a habit. This is not to say happiness can ever be a constant state, but you can pursue it as a goal with more confidence, having achieved it before.

When you came to live here were you retreating from civilization, giving up on it?

Yes.

In Winter, *you say,* "Decay in our nation is frustrating. We truly are becoming senile. I feel as if we are very near the end." *Do you really feel that way?*

Well, at that point, I lost my resolve to celebrate. I mouthed off. But I do feel that way. Again, using the metaphor of boundaries and cell memory and muscle memory, I'd have to say we're losing our elasticity. We're becoming more crowded and therefore less tolerant of other people's space and other people's beliefs and values. It's ultimately a function of population—too many people in too small a space. I guess the definition of elasticity is movement, the ability to move in a certain space. We're getting old and brittle as a nation. We can't run as fast as we could and can't be as generous. I don't think people were meant to live as closely together as they do. We didn't evolve that way. You can plot population curves and in the mid-range, before the exponential climb that all populations take, things are normal. But when the curve starts to kick up, all the rules fall apart. They fall apart for bacteria and for rats, and I think they fall apart for people, too. We develop shorter tempers, shorter lives. If we are really doomed as a nation, and as a human race, I don't think that includes nature—only humans' place in the scheme of things. Nature will never end. If we fry from a nuclear war, some bacteria will survive and life will go on. But selfishly speaking, my primary concern is how people can survive in the world. And the way to do it is to keep things in the mid-range, keep the fluctuations from getting out of hand, from reaching highs and lows humans can't survive. Whether it's something as simple as air or water quality or something as complex as human sociology.

Do you love nature more than people?

These days that's probably closer to the truth than I would like to realize. I love my friends more than I love deer or elk, but I love the general condition of deer and elk more than I love the general condition of cities. So I guess my answer to your question depends on whether we're talking about the abstract or the specific.

Is your relationship to nature a spiritual one?

There's more country realism than Emersonian transcendentalism in it. But at the same time it *is* spiritual. I'm hesitant even to speak about it because I feel that only now am I being allowed to look at nature. I'm trying to learn more, if nature will have me. There's an incredible spirituality in these woods. When I go up into them the question is, will they have me or will they not have me? If I just relax, I see incredible things out here. Animals come up to me, bears wanting to play, deer and elk not the least bit afraid. Other times they'll run from me. I don't want to be like Emerson and say I know what's going on because I have a sense that would offend the spirituality I find here, that nature would turn its back on me. I'm cautious. I like to be in nature, and I figure when it's time to kick me out it will, and if it's time to take me apart it will.

Have you actually had wild animals wanting to play with you?

Yes, young bears. Coyotes and ravens, too. These are animals that folklore and history attribute spirits to—there's something to it. Those aren't just old wives' tales. Almost without fail science proves them. Sometimes I hike to some incredibly high spot that takes me all afternoon to get to and some storm will come blowing in and these ravens will be playing. They'll be diving and swooping at me and ripping right at the side of my head; they'll be spiraling around and showing off because nobody can see it; there's nobody around except me and the ravens. I was on a hunt one time and a coyote came right up to me and sat down and looked at me. I had a gun, so how did he know I wasn't going to shoot him? I made these dog noises to him, and he just sat there watching me, and every now and then he walked to the left or the right. Finally I started talking to him. I said, "Hey, puppy," like I would to one of my dogs, and he turned and ran and was gone. When I get into the woods, amazing things happen, if I just take off and start walking, not knowing where I'm going, not having a plan. I feel very much like a guest up here.

In one of your essays you talk about a snake acting embarrassed. Do you think animals can be understood in such human terms, or were you just being whimsical?

No, I believe that. We say animals feel cold or hot, pleasure or discomfort. It's not that much more of a step to say they can feel embarrassed or can feel pride.

In your writing there's a special value placed on youth and the intensity of feeling that often accompanies it. In Oil Notes *you say, "You have to fight to stay young. Everybody, no exceptions, has to do that." One of the most admirable things about Galena Jim ("Choteau") and Buzbee ("The Watch") is that they retain energy, youthfulness, intensity of feeling. Is there no value, or at least are there no consolations, in aging?*

The important thing is vitality. Youth most often possesses vitality but it's not always directly proportionate. Many of the stories I write are about characters losing vitality or fighting not to lose it.

You've been working on a novel. Would you care to talk about it?

It's a long novel. What I first thought was the end of it turned out to be only the end of the first section. I've got over two thousand pages now. It's about a wolf biologist and her father who is this old eccentric geologist oil millionaire. And it's about her boyfriend who is a student of the old man. The narrator is a young man from the Texas hill country who comes up to Montana and learns about wolves from the biologist and then goes down to Houston and learns about oil and gas from the biologist's boyfriend and the old man. Then he goes off on his own and becomes a geologist. It's fun. I really like the characters a lot.

What other writing are you doing?

I'm doing a long, book-length essay called "The Afterlife," about this valley. It's nonfiction, though it's starting to turn into fiction. It deals with seasons and age and youth, what happens when you go into the woods and what is man's place between animals and the afterlife. I'm also working on the text for a photo book about the wildlife in the northern Rockies. I'm finishing up a book about wolves. I'm also doing short stories, a couple collections of novellas that are either finished or in stages of being finished. I'm doing a series of essays about hunting. I'm doing a collection of oral histories of old people in this valley. There are fourteen or fifteen things I'm working on.

How many hours a day do you write?

I used to write just two hours a day, but I write four hours now.

With all these projects, how do you decide which one to work on?

I used to try to get it lined up before I went to bed so I could work on it subconsciously while I slept, and then I'd get up and go with it. But that was too constraining. So in the morning when I wake up, I decide while I'm eating breakfast. I put in my four hours, then it's over—and I go hiking.

Leonard Michaels
The Lyric Impulse

"A precisionist of painful emotions"—so one reviewer describes Leonard Michaels. "Reading [him]," says another, "feels like taking a number of hard blows to the head and groin." But while his often graphic writing style seems designed to elicit visceral reactions, Michaels claims this is not his intention: "I only describe the world and think only about the words I use, not about the effect my writing has on readers, or what readers might think about me personally. Personally, in my writing, I don't exist."

Despite the disclaimer, his writing appears to have modulated over the past three decades from Kafkaesque fantasy to autobiographical factuality. Not coincidentally, some critics have observed a new ease and expansiveness in his work, beginning with his novel *The Men's Club* in 1981 and continuing with his 1989 fictional autobiography, *Shuffle*. Michaels acknowledges a new voice may be emerging: "Maybe I've got apprehensions of life and death I didn't have earlier." At the same time, he insists that his focus in writing continues to be on the relation of one word to the next, and what he calls his "lyric impulse." Indeed, one critic, in describing Michaels's early work, points to his "unflagging metaphorical style," "the almost anti-narrative thrust of the narration," and "the shortness of all his stories" as evidence that "at least the roots of [his] talents lie in the nature of lyric poetry." As Michaels notes below, however, his actual attempts at writing poetry have proved disappointing, at least to him.

Michaels first attracted attention as the author of two highly praised short-story collections, *Going Places* (1969) and *I Would Have Saved Them If I Could* (1975). More recently, *Sylvia* (1992), which reads like a novella and was reviewed as such, explores his destructive relationship with his first wife, a subject originally broached in *Shuffle*.

Our interview took place at Michaels's small house in the Berkeley hills, surrounded by live oaks and bay trees, which obscure it from the street below but allow a view of San Francisco Bay and the Golden Gate Bridge through a wilderness of branches.

© 1990 Eric Slomanson

Why is most of your fiction written in the first person?

I suppose I'd rather write a poem or sing a song than tell a story in the conventional way. The lyric impulse finds natural expression in the first person.

Have you written poetry? Do you sing?

I can't carry a tune, but I sing. My kids grew up listening to me. Now, when I sing around my thirteen-year-old daughter, she says, "Shut up, Dad, okay?" I love music, especially popular Latin music, and I go dancing sometimes. I can more or less do the mambo. As for poetry, I've tried it, and the results are depressing. Once I thought I'd written a poem. I submitted it to *Threepenny Re-*

view. Thom Gunn, one of the editors, said the poem had engaged a problem and then not resolved it—only stated it. He was right. The poem probably resembled my mambo, which also looks as if I'm stating a problem. But there is a lot of contemporary poetry where no problem is stated, let alone solved. You get shreds of feeling, along with shreds of thinking. To write a poem you've got to have a very good brain. Mine is so-so.

A poet needs a better brain than a fiction writer?

I think so. Poets do much more with much less; certainly less words. And it's hard for them to lie about feelings and not be discovered and condemned, whereas some fiction writers have made a career of lies. Poetry is higher level stuff, closer to religious experience. But some of what poets and fiction writers do these days is merely the same. They are always thirty thousand feet in the air, flying to give a reading at some bookstore or college campus. Even as we talk, they fly.

When an idea for a story comes to you, does a kind of music or a particular rhythm accompany it?

I'll be driving along with my daughter in the car and she'll say, "What? What did you say?" And I'll realize that I'm mumbling to myself, trying to work out the first sentence of a story, looking for the beat, the sound, not the words exactly. Something like a meaning is at stake, but it comes to me as a picture or a mood. Not easily nameable. I might be working on a paragraph in a story and can't get it right, and I'm on the verge of throwing it all away. Then I notice a word that I can delete and improve a sentence. If one sentence improves, the next one does, too, and then the beat is suddenly clear and the whole paragraph might come to life. The point is, I deleted a word for reasons of sound. I wasn't using my brain particularly, but then a whole paragraph seemed to make a necessary sense. I wasn't concerned with sense, only sound, the rhythm of one sentence against another. Sound is just sound, completely meaningless, and yet it delivers sense, makes it exist.

When you're working on a story, do you read it aloud to yourself?

I hear it in my head. I used to read aloud to friends, but reading aloud, if you're a good reader, can disguise bad writing. Suppose your reading is terrific. The friends look happy. You're happy. Then the story is published. You read it, as if for the first time, in silence. To your horror, you realize the story stinks. You didn't know it before because the desire to believe you wrote something good overwhelms evidence to the contrary. Like falling in love with the wrong person.

Shuffle identifies itself as autobiography, but one of its effects, certainly, is to blur the distinction between fiction and nonfiction, and more specifically, to obscure the differences between journal entry, essay, and short story. Some of the journal entries in the first section, for instance, read like short stories, though you call them nonfiction. What, for you, distinguishes them from your short fiction?

Some of the entries *are* short stories and could stand alone. I call the book autobiographical fiction. Other journal entries are fragmentary, suggestive rather than complete—like entries you find in a writer's notebook. The journal section of *Shuffle* is supposed to seem continuous with my life, which is also incomplete. The fragments thus suggest a larger ongoing thing, a life from which they are drawn. They also suggest time passing and a subliminal plot. But plot, like a sentence, can't be understood until it ends. The journal section is largely metaphoric and much depends on the sound, which can be a big part of metaphor. The lyric impulse dominates the first section of *Shuffle.* Almost anything in that first section can be read aloud effectively. That's not true of the autobiographical essays in section two. Nor is it true of the long third section called "Sylvia." When I read those other sections aloud people seem to be interested, they have an impact, but they also carry the sound of my personal voice in a way the journal entries don't. Something stronger than the mere sound of my voice obtains in the journal, and it's a kind of music. I think, for the most part, when you begin to hear, in a piece of prose, only the writer's personal voice, his voice droning on, then the lyric impulse is gone and what remains is boring.

In one of the fragments from the journal section, you describe a woman recounting a dream she had. You say, "Her voice remains neutral, as if it mustn't interfere with what she sees. The secret of writing." Is that the sort of thing you're talking about?

Exactly.

How does the writer's voice remain neutral?

The writer vanishes personally. Only a voice remains. If the writer remains, the work might become oppressive, tediously sincere. It makes an irrelevant appeal to one's noble instincts, to human solidarity with some man or woman. You can always tell when this happens at a public reading. You listen to somebody read and as soon as you hear the author's peculiar, daily, non-imaginative voice beginning to interfere, you start to lose interest. You think, Oh, here's so-and-so trying to make me understand something or feel something. Here's so-and-so insisting, being rhetorical, not musical, and deaf to himself. That's when fiction turns into a kind of lying, or a tedious, expository form.

Isn't escaping the author's voice the same as escaping his personality, and isn't that opposed to the very idea of autobiography?

I'm playing with the idea of autobiography in *Shuffle*, nodding in the direction of hard fact. I'm acknowledging what I never have before, that I'm using data from my life. I'm showing a certain respect for actual experience, giving it moral weight. Still, the narrator in *Shuffle* isn't me, not really. It's not the me who would exist, say, in a report to the police, if I witnessed a crime, or participated in one, and told all. It's not that me; it's not scientific or confessional. Nevertheless, it comes very close, at certain moments, to being who I really am, because this time the material demands it. Anyhow, I'm not the kind of writer who tells all, and I almost never use the real matter of my life. Sometimes my work sounds terribly personal, but it's still not me talking. Never has been. I've considered those moments when I veer close to self-revelation as being failures, a betrayal of my instincts as a writer. I've paid a certain price for remaining true to what I think writing has to be.

What price is that?

I never got rich. Also, I'm not in anybody's gang, and I probably have more enemies than most writers.

Why is that?

Judging from some reviews of my work, some folks are made very angry by the things I write. I can't somehow project a benevolent authorial persona or tell readers what they need or like to hear. I wish I could because more than anything Americans like to like. It's a deplorable and boring sensation, but very commercial. We live so much in Disneyland I don't understand why anyone would pay to go there.

You tell the story, in Shuffle, *of your grandfather going to get emigration papers one day too late, on the very day of a pogrom. Do you regard this as the central story of your family history? In its terrible ironies and its timing, doesn't it have some of the same qualities as your fiction?*

That event had a tragic effect on my mother's life. It determined her view of the world, her idea of her fellow human beings. Also her relation to me. For a while, I was all she had left of her own blood. I never knew my grandfather, but his fate had a bearing on mine. I acquired my mother's fears.

What sort of fears?

Fear of the world, fear of becoming part of it, a piece of nature. Dehumanized. It's not an uncommon fear. It's everywhere in literature. Jonah, in the Bible, gets swallowed by a big fish. What do you think that means? A great story; maybe the only story. It happens to everyone.

In Shuffle, *you describe an incident from childhood in which you were forced to defend yourself in a fight. At that moment, you say, you became "a piece of nature" as opposed to "pogrom-obsessed Yiddishkeit."*

There are two worlds. One is very largely in your head and the other is the world outside. The world outside includes trees, birds, concrete, and the reality of people behaving in sometimes awful ways. It also includes sex. Inside your head you do not believe you can be a part of that world. It's dangerous, it's sickening, it's cruel, it's full of pleasure, usually bad pleasure. It's a world of force and action. It's not where you live, which is in this little intellectual cocoon. But all of a sudden I got into this fight on the playground, and I suddenly moved from one world to the other for the first time. That's what that incident is about: I made a fist, I hit back. It changed my life. I ceased to be entirely Jewish. Borges, talking about Israel, seems to believe, sadly, when Jews gave up victimhood, they became less interesting. All right, very sad. It happened to me in a small way. In a neighborhood on the Lower East Side of Manhattan, at the age of nine, terrified, I smashed another kid in the face and became less interesting.

In one part of Shuffle, *you describe brutish men eating—just eating. At another point, you describe an anxious mother, whose voice vibrates with awareness. Are these the two choices: to be unconscious and animalistic or to be hyperconscious and riddled with anxiety?*

That sounds correct. I also say Jews are obsessed with meaning, which is a way of escaping the allure of nature. Meaning limits pleasure, but this in itself is another pleasure.

In one of the journal entries, you say that "Every wildness plays with death. I wanted to do dull, ordinary chores all day and be like nice people only to forget death, only to feel how I'm alive." Isn't this the opposite of what Phillip Liebowitz [a recurring character in Michaels's fiction] says at the beginning of one of your best-known stories, "Murderers"? Phillip wants to escape the everyday. He's courting darkness, taking risks.

Phillip's a kid in that story. He doesn't know from nothing. He wants new experiences. The journal entry is written by someone much older than Phillip. He's had experience and encountered a real fear of death. He sees that experiments with life are flirtations with death. He thinks it would be nice to sink into dailiness, a round of dull chores, because that allows him to feel, safely, how he lives, how it is that he is basically and merely alive. The new voice says, I want to go to the grocery, clean the house, pay my bills, and sit up late organizing my tax records. I want to do these things because that's life. I want to creep in this petty pace from day to day.

Judging from the essay "My Father" [in Shuffle*], your father was a very dutiful, unassuming man, someone people liked and who had a lot of friends. Do you think your own life, in so far as it's mirrored in the persona of Phillip Liebowitz, is in part a rejection of patriarchal duty and self-effacement?*

Partly so. Phillip wants to be wild. He doesn't want to live with the feelings of others or the claims they might have on him. He doesn't want his existence limited in any way.

Phillip does a lot of running, literally and figuratively. Is he only running away from things or is he also running toward something?

In a sense, he runs from what he sees in other people, what they themselves can't see. Such seeing makes him feel nervous and guilty. He doesn't want to know anything about you that you don't know yourself. This moral uneasiness turns up elsewhere in my writing. It can also affect me as a reader. Sometimes I quit reading a novel or story because the author tells things about his characters that strike me as unfair, as if the characters were being reduced and betrayed, their freedom denied them. I despise certain kinds of gossipy knowingness. Many people hunger for it, can't get through the day without feeding on TV soap operas. The media loves the sex life of politicians and movie stars. There's a rage for the illicit, as if nothing else were real.

Are you talking about journalism or a certain kind of fiction or both?

Both. There's revelation and then there's revelation. Chekhov reveals his characters, certainly, but he's always magnanimous. His revelations enlarge the reader's intelligent sympathies instead of merely titillating. He never clutches your attention with brutal revelation. Never gossips. When a writer does that sort of thing, usually assuming an ironic superiority to his characters, it's murder. People like murder too much.

It's interesting you should use the word "murder." The Rabbi in "Murderers" screams that charge at Phillip and his friends, calls them "murderers" for spying on his wife and him.

Yes, they watch him and his wife having sex. They pry into his life. And that's exactly what I mean. There exists a terrifying lust for that sort of voyeurism. You see it every day.

In "City Boy," Phillip says, "My name was Phillip, my style New York City." Do you see Phillip as an embodiment of New York and especially of Jewish New York?

Yes, Phillip is a fast talker, sees himself as a kind of psychological and psychosexual adventurer. He comes on as if he knows this and that and can glibly summarize people and their lives. And yet at every moment he sees himself as walking the edge of absurdity. He can topple very easily into the condition of the perfect fool, as he does in "City Boy," finding himself literally naked in public. Even in the midst of such humiliation, he tries to save face, to project this New York character, which is savvy and aggressive. This story, in particular, plays with the experience of embarrassment that is New York. I was at a Knicks basketball game once. This was years ago. The Knicks were losing, but the people all around me were screaming with delight. I didn't know why. Then finally I realized they had bet the Knicks would lose by a certain number of points. To them, if the Knicks lost by less than five, say, it was better than winning by one or ten or fifteen. To lose was to win, if you lost the right way. I was embarrassed by my lack of sophistication. Anyway, that's the New York where I grew up. I still think of it as a more interesting, more exquisite time and place. Like a black-and-white movie rather than vulgar color.

In "Sticks and Stones," Phillip's friend Henry complains that "there were no frontiers left, nothing left for a man to do but explore his own mind and go to the movies." Doesn't Phillip see things similarly, and isn't this aimlessness, this lack of appropriate manly endeavor, part of his problem, the reason behind his compulsive womanizing?

In fact, he doesn't have many women in his life. Count them. Phillip is virtually a monk. But it's possible that he shares his friend's complaint. Henry is a kind of alter ego for him.

As Phillip is for you?

I can't compare myself to my characters. It's hard for people to believe you really aren't the people you invent, except in a limited way. I'm more normal than Phillip, I hope. Three kids, the same job for over twenty years, and never late with a mortgage payment. I think I'm a lot more various than Phillip, too, capable of all sorts of things he would never admit to. He would never tell you, for example, about the nice things he's done in his life. But if you ask me, I could go on and on.

At one point, Phillip describes himself as "the enemy of Freud."

Yeah, the jerk. He's such a jerk for saying that. There couldn't be a more appropriate patient. He wants to believe the answers to his problems are perfectly clear and available, but he's completely victimized by impulses he doesn't begin to comprehend. He doesn't want to see the depths of his own lust, his raging animality.

Were the Phillip stories that appeared in your first collection [Going Places] originally part of a novel?

Originally I did intend to write a picaresque novel about the adventures of Phillip Liebowitz, but it didn't hold together for me, so I let it break up and be the thing it wanted to be, a story collection.

Paul Zweig has said your typical protagonist "is the traditional schlemiel of Jewish fiction." But Liebowitz, he says, "is a schlemiel with teeth . . . he cancels the genre." Do you see Phillip as falling into the tradition of the schlemiel? And was canceling the genre your intention?

It wasn't my intention, but it sounds to me as if Zweig gets things essentially right. I like the idea of me canceling a genre.

Is it true that you burned your first novel? What was it about, and have you ever regretted destroying it?

No, I was never sorry I burned it. It was a modern version of *Huckleberry Finn,* in which a city kid gets into terrible trouble because of a car accident. He finds himself in a lot of danger and has to appeal to a black friend, this hard guy who comes to his aid. It was terrifically passionate and violent, and it was awful. In spite of that, it got me some attention from publishers. They took me out to lunch and kept saying the same thing: "This book ought to be published but not by me." Finally, I went home and burned it. I thought, if these encouraging, generous publishers don't want it, they must see what a failure it is and how painful it would be to me if it were published. The funny thing is, I wrote that book in a month and it gave me reason to believe that I could be prolific, turning out a novel a year without any trouble. But I never have. My lifetime production of fiction is equal to what some writers do in six months, or Joyce Carol Oates does in six minutes. Writing has never gotten easier for me. It's gotten in some ways more painful because of my genius for self-criticism. It hurts to look back at what I wrote years ago and see things wrong with it and how it should be changed. It's sometimes very hard for me to feel that I've actually managed to write something that I won't regret ten years from now. It's a constant worry. I don't want to feel ashamed.

In the last story in Going Places, *the character Beckman is left clinging to a pipe, way up in the air, holding on for his life, and the narrator says, "The tremor passed into muscle as rigid as the steel it squeezed." Is that meant to suggest that rigidity or hardness is necessary to survive?*

Well, it might. Beckman is frozen in his musculature and can't go forward or back, as if he were suspended without a past or a future.

So the idea that the suffering he's undergone can somehow be a way out, or a redemption of sorts, is wishful thinking on his part? He's wrong?

Yes. Life is infinitely resourceful and can always get worse.

Are life's surprises necessarily bad?

They're ordinarily bad, I would imagine. It's almost un-American to talk like this, isn't it? But I happen to believe the surprises life brings might get worse and worse.

Your work has sometimes been likened to Kafka's. Like him, you mix the re-alistic and the fantastic. Do you think you've been influenced by him?

I can't imagine any contemporary writer who hasn't been. I have actually been surprised to discover that I've said things in my work that I later dis-covered, in different form, in Kafka's diaries. I don't know what to make of that, except perhaps these coincidences arise from similarities in the culture we share. But probably Isaac Babel has been more an influence on me than Kafka. Kafka comes out of the same world as my paternal grandparents, that part of Eastern Europe, while Babel comes out of the same world as my mother's parents, who were from Odessa. Babel's world seems more artisti-cally congenial to me.

What is it about Babel's stories that appeals to you?

Again, it has to do with lyric impulse. I don't see too much of that in Kafka. He is less a singer than a religious visionary. In Babel's stories problems aren't resolved by a rational step from A to B but by beautiful flights from A to C. This is accomplished only in song. You don't usually find that in Kafka, though "The Country Doctor" is a magnificent exception. In Babel you find many flights of sound and dazzling imagery, which have the effect of plot resolutions or thrilling closures. In Kafka you find extraordinary motions of mind, vaguely like logic, or psycho-logic, or Talmudic commentary based on the text of life.

Whom do you read among contemporary writers?

I read Latin American writers. Machado de Assis, Luisa Bombal, Borges, Fuentes, Paz, Mutis, García Marquez—*Chronicle of a Death Foretold* is an as-tonishing masterpiece. Among American writers, many are friends. I can't talk about one or two without mentioning ten others. I've devoured the crime novels of Elmore Leonard, who I met only once, briefly. His work is tight, smart, scary, touching, funny. As for new, young writers, Cristina Garcia and Edward P. Jones seem to me outstanding. Mary Ward Brown's story collec-tion, *Tongues of Flame,* is first rate. All in all, I read too much to say what I read. It's like discussing my breathing habits.

You've often been compared to Philip Roth. Do you see any similarities?

I think we're pretty different. Roth builds a plot, I don't. His structures are brilliant, powerfully rational, mine are not. I suppose we have some of the same obsessions.

Sex forms a large part of your subject matter, and it's often described in very unappealing terms, as manipulative, violent, ugly.

I've described it in many different ways, but I guess in my early stories I was rigorously unsentimental, very much against romanticizing experience.

My subject was lust. The word sex has had a peculiar fate in America. When Lady Macbeth says, "Unsex me here," she uses it well.

Your novel, The Men's Club, *further explores sexuality, especially from a masculine perspective. Does the book now seem prescient to you? In the beginning, the white, middle-class male narrator says, "Anger, identity, politics, rights, wrongs, I envied them [meaning women]. It seemed attractive to be deprived in our society. Deprivation gives you something to fight for and makes you morally superior and it makes you serious." In claiming to be the victims of certain deprivations, aren't the men in the club forerunners of what we now call the men's movement? Have you read Robert Bly's* Iron John?

No. I haven't read any books about men, or books about women, or about men and women, or men and men, or women and women, and I haven't been explicitly concerned with deprivations suffered by men. I've been concerned only to describe certain men in my novel, in a certain place and time. In the quotation from *The Men's Club,* the narrator talks about the deprivations suffered by women. He talks from his point of view, and he wonders about the men in the club. The narrator is suggesting, ironically, that these men are envious of women because women have something to fight for. It gives them seriousness. So without admitting it, the men in the club are imitating women's groups. The narrator implies all this, distancing himself from the other men. By the end of the evening he becomes one of them. During the club meeting, the men talk as they might never have talked otherwise. They talk the way they imagine women talk to one another in their groups, and the men discover that they, too, have complaints. So the book is prescient, maybe, but it isn't a political tract. It's a novel with the flavor of an era.

The Men's Club *is written in first person/past tense, but the narrator never steps back and analyzes or comments. How do you conceive of the narrator?*

He's unlike any narrator I've used before. He is someone who vanishes before several other presences. This is supposed to happen in the novel as it might happen in real life. For example, when a friend tells you a story and says, "I was sitting on the bus and this guy behind me said . . ." your friend then allows the voice of "this guy" to take over. But your friend isn't a ventriloquist, like the first-person narrators of most novels. In real life, it remains obvious that your friend is talking, and the voice belongs simultaneously to him and to "this guy." I hoped my narrator would sound like that, inhabited by voices while remaining himself. I wrote in that inclusive spirit. One man and six other men and finally a woman talk, but it's always one man talking. At the end of the novel, when the narrator stumbles forward to tell a story in his own voice, he's been so used up by the other voices that his story is anticlimactic. No strictly personal energy remains in him, no voice strictly his own. His story fails. He's embarrassed. This had to be omitted in the movie version. It would be too hard, maybe impossible, to show, and it wouldn't be interesting visually. Not everything can be shown. Despite the fact they are called "movies," the form is essentially static, a million pictures flashing by, but never with the speed, flow, or indeterminacy of pychological life. The movie in your head is not for show. It will never appear on screen. The viewers are only you and God. A European director, who was approached to make a movie of *The Men's Club,* said, "It can't be done." I felt flattered and disappointed at once.

Why is it important to have in this novel the sort of narrator you describe?

I wanted to suggest how men lose themselves as they identify with one another. The men in the club dissolve into a male community, a situation not too familiar among men in our culture. The experience of the club becomes deep when the men begin to think about death. Death consciousness hovers over the meeting of the men's club. When Berliner hears that one of his friends has died, he is horribly shocked and this leads to a fight, after which the men start wailing together like a wolf pack, united by their maleness, their common relation to death. Then the host's wife comes home and they are reminded of something less sublime, which is domestic reality.

As you say, right before Kramer's wife returns, the men howl, or wail, and the narrator says he felt more and more separated from himself and closer to the others. He says they "sank toward primal dissolution, assenting to it with this music of common animality."

Yes. It is mainly represented in comic terms, but it's based on a tragic condition. Insofar as the narrator has maintained his separateness from the others, he's been fooling himself.

At the beginning of the novel, the narrator thinks the purpose of the men's club is "To make women cry." Later Solly tells the others that when his wife cried he got his erection back. At the end, Kramer's wife is left in tears. Is making women cry, in fact, the purpose of the club?

The narrator, at first, indulges an ironic distance from the club. That's why he says, sarcastically, its purpose is to make women cry. He sees these men as coming together to spite women. And in a sense he's right. Our society provides little in the way of worthwhile, dignified occasions for male intimacy—aside from war, if you think that's dignified and worthwhile. The club does have something of a semiconscious spiteful air about it. Part of its intent is to say, "We don't need women. Let them have their groups. We'll have our club." At the same time, the brutal treatment of women, or the idea of women crying, or women made wretched by men, isn't a central dramatic concern of my novel as it is, say, in Toni Morrison's *Jazz*. At least I didn't think it was.

You wrote the screenplay for the film version of the novel, didn't you?

Yes. I once felt it had ruined my life. The experience was especially painful because I liked all the people involved in it, but I didn't know what making a movie was like, didn't know how important the director was, didn't know actors would change their lines. It occurred to me that I didn't know what the hell I was doing in the entertainment business. Nobody cared about my opinions. I didn't belong there. I saw every scene in my imagination when I wrote the screenplay, and some people thought that it would work. Then I saw the rough cut and I felt ashamed. It wasn't at all what I'd imagined, but my name was attached to it. I won't complain anymore. I was paid. I took the money and had my house painted.

Stylistically, The Men's Club—*talking about the novel now—seems very different from your other work. One critic said it was more conventional. Do you see it as more traditional, formally speaking, than your short stories?*

Yes, I do. It's a book about human voices. It doesn't advertise any major commitment to literary art. It talks in another way. It concedes the possibility that there is some important human reality which doesn't give a damn about art, doesn't lend itself to art.

That reminds me of one of your stories, "I Would Have Saved Them If I Could," about the Holocaust. Isn't that story about the limits of art and about the suspicion of anything, including art, that might divert us from a difficult truth or reconcile us to it?

Yes. I try to suggest in that story that there's no way to deal with the experience of the Holocaust and that Jews are obliged to carry around with them a memory of horror to which they can never be reconciled. Things that may appeal to us in our distress, all that offers redemption from that experience, that horror, is specious, including traditional theological justifications for human suffering. The story is against any means of escaping the memory of horrors, even through art. Of course, there's a contradiction in this, since my story is itself, I hope, artful. It was written and rewritten. If you're going to write the language, you have to write it as well as you can.

So, in writing about the Holocaust, you feel the obligation to be artful even as you point out the limitations of art?

Yes, a dual obligation. There is, on the one hand, the obligation to speak the truth, which in this case amounts to a statement against making statements. There is, on the other hand, the obligation as a writer to make the statement the best way you can. I think of Primo Levi. One of the problems for me in reading him is that he handles, with superb elegance, experiences that are grotesquely inelegant; monstrous. There's an astonishing inconsistency in the writing, since the writing entertains. I have a relative who survived the concentration camps. He tells stories about his experiences, but if he tries to write them, he begins to have heart trouble. He survived the camps but wouldn't survive his typewriter. The subject of the Holocaust poisons the intention to make it into art. But Levi is a genius. One reads him with trust that he understands much more than oneself.

Are you willing to talk about what you're working on now? Is Phillip Liebowitz, for example, still a source of inspiration? Do you return to him sometimes?

He doesn't exist anymore. There's a new voice. It's Herman. I've been writing a series of stories and also the beginning of a novel about Herman, who's a waiter. The working title for the novel is *Herman, the Waiter.* He has idealized relationships with women. He goes through a series of enormously intense love affairs. As I say, I've already written a few stories about him. They're all about love, love, love, love, love.

So this marks a new direction for you?

Herman allows another view, makes possible a kind of talk that wasn't there for me before. His interests are different. They're more psychological, even spiritual. Less sexual as such. Maybe I've got apprehensions of life and death I didn't have earlier. My attitudes have changed. I'm still in the process of working it out. I'm not a very deliberate writer, I don't think things out in advance. I don't ever really know what I'm talking about until I've written it. I'll see an image, I'll hear a sound, and I'm usually surprised to see what it is I'm saying.

Christopher Tilghman

Grappling with the Holy Mysteries

Though he grew up in New England and lives in Harvard, Massachusetts, about thirty miles west of Boston, Christopher Tilghman thinks of his short stories as "Southern" in their focus on family and place. He writes dense, often traditionally plotted tales which, in the words of one critic, "do the work of novels." Noting his fondness for "the great nineteenth-century narratives," Tilghman says, "I want my short stories to be as big as they can be, overflowing with sensuous detail. I want them to bite off whole chunks of life. I want to write about something that is going to change somebody's life for good; otherwise, why write?"

Tilghman initially gained public attention when his first collection of stories, *In a Father's Place,* was featured on the cover of *The New York Times Book Review* in May 1990. The exposure followed a long period of frustration and literary obscurity. "My late appearance," he says, "is because it has taken me this long to write publishable stuff." In 1996, his first novel, *Mason's Retreat,* earned widespread praise; "a stately, absorbing tragedy," in the words of one critic, it tells the story of an expatriate's return home in 1936 to assume control of his inheritance, a once-grand estate on Maryland's Eastern Shore.

Tilghman thinks the difficulty in starting out for most young writers is not that they have too little experience to write about but that they haven't yet learned to have empathy for that experience. He has taught fiction writing at the University of Virginia and says, "What students need to hear is that writing is going to require them to be better persons. To write fiction, you need to learn some compassionate empathy. I think it's very difficult for young men, in particular, to come to that point."

Tilghman lives with his wife, Caroline Preston, and three sons in a converted Shaker meeting house built in 1791. We visited with him there on a snowbound March afternoon.

Elsewhere you've talked about the "fun of making people come to life." In writing a story, do you begin with character?

Almost always I start with a visual image. Sometimes it's a photograph, sometimes it's just something in my head. And that visual image has a great deal to do with the place and landscape. The process of discovering the story contained in that visual image is really what the first couple of drafts are all about. My stories are all rooted in place. I don't know why. I just have this undying interest in American landscapes. When I'm out traveling, if I come across something interesting along the road, I take rolls of film.

Are all your stories set in places where you've spent a considerable amount of time?

The stories in the book are. I grew up spending half my time in New England and half down on the Eastern Shore. During college I worked summers in Montana, in those parts of the state I portray in the book. So I know those places pretty well. I'm getting a little bit broader. You have to. The short story is so expensive of material. I'm learning to use more imagined landscapes. I don't know anything about cognitive science, but there does seem to be something special about what comes to a writer through memory, as filtered by the imagination. When I wrote "Hole in the Day" I hadn't been in that part of South Dakota since I was nineteen. So I wrote all those details of place, even though I couldn't really remember what the place looked like. When *The New Yorker* took it, I felt I had to go out there and check on the accuracy of what I'd written. So I flew out, then drove the character's route. It was lots of fun. Everything I'd imagined for the story was there to be seen. Somehow I'd held onto it. I had experienced it when I was in my teens, and I recall being absolutely intoxicated with it. So I guess it's no mystery why it stayed with me.

You said you like to photograph places. Do you look at the photographs when you sit down to write?

Sometimes. I have a couple of photographs of a school in South Dakota that I've been trying to write a story about for years. I'm not the kind of person who takes little notes, jots down story ideas. But I do flip through photos. I'm a great user of coffee table photographic books.

You said a minute ago that you sometimes start from an image but you don't always know how it's related to a story.

Yeah, I think it's even fair to say I don't always know what the image itself is. There is that moment when a mood and a sensibility and an emotional pitch are available; they seem to be revolving around some layout of people and landscapes. So the question is, What is giving me that visceral feeling? Something in there is doing it, but what it is I don't know. I have to go find it. Then when I find it I can begin to see where it takes place within a story.

Do you consciously pursue the story or just let it happen?

I let it happen by thinking about place. Often I meditate on the place. The opening story in the book, "On the Rivershore," begins on a beach I know very well. I had a very particular feeling for the time of day. I could see a fallen tree across the bank. I mulled these things over for about a week and had a great time. I didn't write a word. Then I started writing.

And in that week the story came?

No, the story didn't come at all at that point. The boy had come, but I didn't know what he was doing on that beach. Then I started to write, and everything that came to me was somehow tied up with my sense of that place.

Is that boy the age you associate yourself with at the beach?

No, because I think of myself at that beach from age zero to forty-six. It's my family's place.

That story does not seem autobiographical in terms of the boy's family.

No, his family works on the land, my family is from the big house.

So your family is more like the one in the title story, "In a Father's Place"?

Yes.

Speaking of the title story, more than one reviewer criticized your depiction of the son's girlfriend, Patty, saying that you were too hard on her, that you made her into a villain pure and simple. Do you agree with that?

Critics are always going to pick a fight with one or another of your stories. Every review I've read or written has the "but" paragraph. They can say what they want about "In a Father's Place," because I know it's the best writing I'll ever do. If they'd picked on one of my lesser stories, it might have hurt. But when they pick a fight with your champion, that's great. They can try to burn that story, it won't burn. It isn't written on paper. True, more than one critic thought it was loaded too much against the girl Patty Keith. I was telling my students the other day that any story has major and minor characters. And for me, whether they're major or minor has little to do with how much they're on stage. It has to do with whether they develop and change over the course of the story. So Patty Keith is the most minor character in the story. She's exactly the same from beginning to end; she's there as a dispatcher, a creator of tension. I had lots of fun heaping it on her and I suppose I could have been more ambiguous about what I thought, but I didn't want to be.

Is it merely coincidental that Patty's so interested in deconstruction?

Absolutely, yes. I wanted her to be reading something vaguely threatening to Dan, something he wouldn't know anything about. My younger brother had just been going to architecture school and Derrida was deep into architecture schools, God knows why. So I decided to have Patty read Derrida. Sometimes you're lucky and you get the right detail. As I went on, I began to appreciate the aptness of the detail. But I did not initially recognize the broader implication of her, as a deconstructionist, coming in and trying to destroy the house.

There's quite a range of humanity in your stories, characters from different backgrounds, social and otherwise. The dirt farmers in "Hole in the Day," for example, are absolutely real and convincing. How do you happen to know them so well?

I did a lot of rural work. I knew those people in Montana and I sure knew them in Maryland and New Hampshire. They were friends of mine. I also think that human behavior isn't rocket science. I have a strong feeling that if you take certain kinds of people in certain situations, socioeconomic, et cetera,and if you do nothing but live with them and imagine them for four or five months you are going to be right about them. Sooner or later you're going to know who they are and how they would behave. It just isn't that complicated. That isn't to say that people are simple. But what the fiction writer does is focus energy on seeing how people will behave, who they are. It's an endeavor that gets us well beyond our own experience very fast. I've been working on a novella for a couple years about the Shakers. I haven't researched the subject; I don't want to. I finally gave the novella to Caroline [his wife], who at one point had done a lot of research on the Shakers. She kept on saying, "How did you know that?" And I'd say, "I didn't know it, but there's just no other way for it to work out." And I don't think that's because I have some great intuitive power. I think it's because if you spend six months thinking about how a community—in this case, a celibate community of ninety percent women and ten percent men—would organize itself, how it would behave, what kind of people you'd find there, then more often than not you're right. My advice to anyone writing about something researchable is, write it first, then research it.

One critic mentioned that you always have your eye on history and nature and that this gives a timeless perspective to your stories. Do you try consciously to bring in history and nature or are these subjects simply bound up with your fictional material?

They're bound up in the places I write about. You can't think about a place and not think about its history. Each parcel of land contains everything that has ever happened there. If you talk about evoking place, it has got to be sensual, but also cultural, geological, historical. That's part of it. And then if you're talking about families, where do you stop? You play *Roots* one way or another. That's the way I perceive history. That's how I was raised.

None of your stories is set in the city. Is there a reason for that?

Yeah, I can't do it. I've tried and it just doesn't work. I think, "God, this bores me to death." I haven't lived in cities. I don't understand them, I don't understand the landscape. I don't like it. I've come to think my rural places are there for me to glorify and to understand, and that if we lose our rural places we're going to be in deep trouble.

You've been teaching at the University of Virginia this year. How has that gone?

One difficulty with teaching creative writing is that many young students have been rewarded all their lives for being bright and hard-working. The trouble is, neither one of these qualities matters at all in writing fiction.

Not even working hard?

I don't think so. At least, not working hard in the usual sense. There have been plenty of people, and we all know them, who have been bitten by the writing bug. These are people used to success and they work like hell and don't get anywhere. Why not? It's not simply a question of working hard or being smart. You don't get any points as a fiction writer for having a reader say, "That writer's smart. How did that writer know that?" In fact, that sort of response from the reader probably gets in the way of the story the writer means to tell because there's a sense the writer's saying "look at me" instead of "look at the story I'm telling." In writing fiction you grapple with the holy mysteries and if what comes out seems intellectual, fine; if it comes out "down home," fine. Whatever comes out does so by spiritual examination and by working more with the heart than the head. Being on display is the enemy of fiction. It gets in the way of that passage between the imagined world and the real world. That may sound anti-intellectual, but it doesn't mean in the end you don't use every faculty you've got. If you like to read critical theory, read it, maybe that will help. I'm not saying you have to be some troglodyte, but I do know that what students need to hear is that writing well is going to require them to be better persons. To write fiction, you need to learn some compassionate empathy. I think it's very difficult for young men, in particular, to come to that point. You get there by putting forth a more earnest and honest and dumber side. Just last week I wrote a comment on a very good graduate student's story, a comment that he found impossible to interpret: "Don't let your intelligence interfere with your ability to write good scenes."

Is compassionate empathy something you can teach?

It *is* something you can teach. I'm just beginning to learn how to do it and that's one reason I'm excited about this semester at Virginia. Like all of us teaching young people, I want them to go deeper. Now I'm trying to figure out what I mean by "deeper," and I've been hammering away at these points as we work on their stories. Why does this character seem thin to us? Well, because you've only imagined a thin band of the person; you have to widen this band before the character will come to life. I think by the time we finish being teenagers, we've all experienced pretty much what life has to offer us. Maybe not the absolute depths of tragedy, but most things. By the time I was twenty, I knew what hurt was. I'd been shit on by enough girls, my parents were divorced, and so on. The material about basic human behavior was there. I wrote badly in my twenties and thirties, but it wasn't because I hadn't experienced anything. I have students come to me saying, "Well, maybe I'm just too young to be in this program." I say, no, that's not true. The problem is not lack of experience; the problem is getting in touch with it, to use a slightly New Age term. Through compassion, to go back and feel a kind of empathy for those things you've experienced. I think people can be told to do that. I think they can be shown on the page where they need to do it. Here's a stick figure that you think is just words and here's what you haven't even asked yourself about this person . . . I think you show it to them on the page, on the level of craft.

Your idea of urging the student writer to become a better person is interesting. Yet isn't it true that everything we know about writers suggests, alas, there's no necessary correlation between the compassion and empathy writers show for their characters and the way they behave in real life? Dostoevsky and Tolstoy weren't always compassionate to their wives or friends. By saying a writer has to become a "better person," do you mean a better person toward his created world?

"Toward his created world" is a nice way to put it. The nature of the individual writer is off the issue. It's got to be. Writing is a relationship to characters. I think it makes sense that people can be nicer to characters than they are to people, since characters, in some final sense, can't talk back quite the way everyone else can. But I would also like to argue, although I know it isn't necessarily true, that this empathetic examination is a morally enlightening thing to do. To undergraduates, I say, "This is a classroom where you are going to be asked to change a little bit—at least during the hours that you have to fulfill the assignment of this class. After that you can go out and do whatever you want. But you have to be somebody different to write well."

You said earlier that writing involves grappling with "the holy mysteries." What mysteries do you mean?

It certainly seems to me that one reason I write fiction is, in some way, to prefigure what has not happened, to examine and try to understand what is to come. I don't think we need to understand what has happened to us. We understand that. We need to understand what might happen to us. That's where literature makes life easier to live. As a churchgoer of indeterminate faith, I would say the holy mysteries are the things that don't make sense but seem to be with us, death being the big one. It seems to me as I'm working on a story I eventually crash through all the things I already know. I keep writing until I've gotten to the unknown. That's where I'm trying to get the story to take me. Contrary to what some readers may believe, you're not manipulating little pieces of fact, withholding information, creating artificial suspense. The real suspense lies in coming face to face with mystery.

Was it this line of thinking that led you to explore the afterlife in "A Gracious Rain"?

Yes, it really was. And it hurt my feelings when so many critics picked on that story. That's a little favorite of mine, and I feel very strongly about it. I had to defend it to my editor all the way through. There's a lot of Episcopalianism in that story, particularly in its emphasis on the importance of doubt and mystery. In the Episcopal prayer book you give thanks that you are fed in the holy mysteries. That's similar to what Stanley is saying at the end of "A Gracious Rain." The ultimate mercy is that now he has died and everything is still as confused as when he was in the world. He realizes that he's still "alive" because he doubts and questions. To have all the questions answered is to be dead finally. And then what would be the point of writing fiction?

You call this an Episcopalian view. Maybe it is, I don't know. It's certainly a fiction writer's view, the idea that nothing is ever resolved, the conflicts and the questions continue. When you started that story, did you know it was going to be about the afterlife?

I did. It's very rare for me to start and know where I'm going, but in this instance I just knew I wanted to run the story through in its three parts. When I submitted it, one magazine wanted me to let them have it without the third section. I thought, there's no story without the third section, so I wouldn't let them have it. The editor said something like, "We love all this about his family's reaction to his death. We'd love to publish that. But we don't want this yucky spiritual stuff." It seems to me that the reason I write is to get to a place where Stanley is, to get Grant [in "A Hole in the Day"] to where he can listen to the grass and look at the mountains and sense some great being or maker, feel some semblance of transcendence. This is the only reason I write. I would find life unlivable if I didn't believe we were somewhere held in faith and love by a higher power.

One critic said, "What is distinctive about the transcendent impulse that surfaces in so many of Tilghman's stories is that it doesn't take the characters away from the world so much as it returns them to it." It struck me that's even true of Stanley, who dies. Could you comment?

Yes, Stanley's back where he started. That's the great mercy, he's back on his porch. There are different kinds of spirituality. There's the kind that leads to

David Koresh in Waco; people like that are looking to be lifted out of the world. I'm not looking for that, I'm looking to glorify my life and my children and the time I get to spend with them and everything I love. That line from Frost's "Birches"—"Earth's the right place for love: / I don't know where it's likely to go better"—that's true for me. In order to be successful, to be happy, to be who they are, characters need reference to all the things outside them, from the simple aspects of place and landscape, to history, to larger issues of spirituality and belief. I think these are the things I need as a person, too.

You said once that the writing of "Mary in the Mountains" was different from the writing of your other stories, that it was "written in hallucination." Could you talk about that experience? Is the fact there's a woman character at the center of the story important? Is her religious interest a factor?

Her religious interest is very important. The opening line of that story came to me in a kind of waking dream: "Send me a picture of the boy we never had, the one with blue eyes, big ears, and a smile that says, Nothing, so far, has hurt too bad."

Talking about Mary, one critic mentioned the "lethal coldness in the heart of a gentle woman." Do you see her that way? Do you think some readers mistake her detachment and religious serenity for coldness? It's a rare woman who could write to her remarried ex-husband saying send me a picture of the child we never had.

Her ability to do that is deeply spiritual in my view. It reflects a certain forgiveness and worldly detachment.

Considering In a Father's Place *as a collection, how important to you was the order of the stories?*

I worked hard at it but didn't really have any big plan in mind. My agent suggested we could use the ages of the protagonists as an organizing principle, beginning with the young boy in "On the Rivershore," and that made sense to me. Also, at some point, it became clear that the whole collection could be read as a cycle about fathers. My agent came up with "In a Father's Place" for the title story. (I'm no good at titles.) And when I looked back at the collection, I realized that six of the seven stories do end up in a father's place.

Could you talk about your own family? Are you the oldest?

No, I'm the third. My father is still alive, quite disabled from a series of strokes. He hasn't been able to talk for twenty years. He was a wonderful father of young kids, the nurturing kind. He grew less attentive in some ways as we got older, and naturally we had our fights. The humanity of Dan in "In a Father's Place" is basically my father's humanity. He was a wonderfully forgiving, empathetic person. I think the sense of who I am as a writer as well as the material I try to cover is because of him and who he is.

What do you mean your material is because of him?

The fact that I'm trying to find some kind of joy or kindness or redemption. That's his way of looking at life. I remember a stupid little incident, but it speaks volumes for me. My father and I were driving along, rounding a corner near our house in Maryland. I was maybe seventeen, rich kid. There was a car parked along the road and I saw some teenagers making out. I wanted to honk and flash the lights, and he said, "Stop it, they don't have any place to go and they're trying to be together. You've got a house and you can do anything you want."

That's an unusually sympathetic attitude for any grown-up to adopt toward teenagers having fun sexually.

That was my father.

Is there a bit of your mother in Mary of "Mary in the Mountains"?

There's a little bit of her there. I love her dearly, but she can be kind of tough. The problem is that every time I write a story that has a mother in it, my mother reads it and says, "I did not." She never calls and says, "Gee, Chris, what a good story." It is her strength and self-reliance and spiritual understanding that engaged me in "Mary." Those qualities in her taught me many lessons. Actually my parents have taught me the gender opposites: the empathy comes from my father and the strength from my mother. Her style was, "Shut up, Chris. Wipe the tears from your eyes and keep going."

Could you talk a bit about your first two unpublished books? Is In a Father's Place *a much better book than they were, or was it just bad luck those two earlier ones weren't accepted?*

They were just silly. The first one was about what fiction is. It had some clever things, ten years late, but clever still. The second one was about my hippie life in New Hampshire. The title of it was *A Finished Place*, which I took from Bernard DeVoto. It was actually a collection of interrelated short stories written in this wry, forgiving, almost Trollope-like voice. Then I began to think, this isn't the way the world is. The fact is, I feel more kinship to Dostoevsky than Trollope. I've often tried to mine these fifteen stories and I can't. The reason I can't is that the voice is wrong. That's the one fundamental thing. That's how we stand in the face of the existential condition, the voice. So Trollope's lovely, forgiving, sweet tone, which is fun to read, can't be turned into gritty reality. There's no way I can salvage any one of those earlier stories. I think my late appearance is because it has taken me this long to write publishable stuff. I had every advantage, got the attention of anyone I would ever have needed, had I the work to follow up on it.

What happened? Was there a breakthrough story? When and how did you learn to write better stories?

Well, it was "Mary in the Mountains." Now this sounds rather sentimental and mawkish, ridiculously Hollywood, but I was just weeping away as I wrote that story. I got in touch with something, I don't know what. If only I could get to that same place again and again.

How interesting that the breakthrough came with a story that has a woman as the protagonist.

I know. How interesting that there are so few women characters otherwise in my fiction. The other thing I've observed about my stories is that there are no friends. Not a single one. *In a Father's Place* is a kind of man-alone body of work.

Aren't your stories basically about family?

They are and that's sort of enough, whether good or bad. It seems to be enough for the drama of the thing. In short-story writing you have to keep widening your territory. For me that means the emotional territory. I have a story coming out in just a few weeks ["Things Left Undone"] that is about a couple losing a baby to cystic fibrosis. It came out of a nightmare and the worst forty-eight hours of our lives, with a misdiagnosis of our son Matthew as having this disease. As it turned out, the tests came back negative. Both of us burst into tears and I was sitting there thinking, "There is going to be a parent sitting in this chair in half an hour crying just like I am, for the other reason." In some sense I wrote that story out of sympathy for people who lose children. I also wrote it because it was my nightmare, the one I cannot face, which grows out of the feeling that I can't control the world anymore. I felt I had to write that story. It was there to write. I worked on it for a couple years and finished it while Caroline was pregnant with our second son. I couldn't get my career around that story. I couldn't pretend that it was not there to be written. I could do little well-made pieces here and there, but this great emotional logjam was going to have to be dealt with. Having written it, I do feel I have a greater understanding of certain kinds of relationships between a husband and wife, certain ways of thinking about sex, certain ways of thinking of love, that were unavailable to me before. The thing is, now I have in mind to do a story about something really ghastly, something monstrous and unimaginable. That story is going to start to assume the same urgency and I'm going to have to go there, too. I really don't want to go into the mind of a parent who is a child murderer, but somehow I feel I have to. I think that if you don't do it you die. That is my message to the students. If you don't write these damn things that come along which tend to broaden you, then you die.

Your stories typically have substantial plots, with traditional rising and falling action. Could you talk a bit about storytelling in general, your style of storytelling, and your reaction to the spare minimalist approach so popular in the 1980s?

When I write, I am absolutely conscious of writing the kind of story I want to read myself. I want to make my stories as big as they can be, overflowing with sensuous detail. I want them to bite off whole chunks of life. I want to write about something that is going to change somebody's life for good; otherwise, why write? As a reader, I like the great nineteenth-century narratives. That's the experience I want in short-story form, not something stripped down. As far as storytelling in general goes, I think it is not being taught in a lot of M.A. programs. Plot is somehow regarded as one of the baser elements in fiction writing. It has struck me lately that the simple notion of story and how it works is becoming very confusing and in some ways is lost to us even as we continue to need it. Here's one anecdote: I was sitting in the office of Bob Gottlieb, who was at the time the editor of *The New Yorker,* and I was there for him to tell me why he was not taking my latest story. He was very kind, let me down easily. At the end of it his frustration emerged and he said, "You know, we just can't get enough good stories." I thought, what a cruel irony, that this magazine so long derided for delivering plotless, dramaless, meandering pieces of fiction has an editor-in-chief saying there just aren't any good yarns out there. After that conversation, I really thought a lot more about my own work. Storytelling ought to be about event and consequence and people. That's where I seek my rewards. Every story I write that fails does so because I'm unsure about where to take it. Why can't I just write a story? How can I work for six months and not have told a story? There's a mystery to it, a mystery to story. I'm devoting a lot of time to it. One of the reasons I'm working on a novel right now is to think about storytelling in the longer form and to see how it works. I think the most common comment/complaint I get from friends who are maybe not big readers but are good, smart people is that contemporary writers seem to have trouble with endings. Readers want a story that has a dramatic arc and shape and lands someplace. Writers can keep spilling out a situation forever, but to get that sense of story is hard. Maybe because we don't sit around the campfire telling stories anymore, our age is unclear about plot. There are thousands of fine writers but there aren't that many good storytellers.

Do you want to talk about the novel you're writing? Does it use any of the characters you've written about before?

It's a Maryland story set in the thirties. It's a story I've been working on for a while and my original intention was to do something very "told," no dialogue, just a narrative, thirty pages, dense as hell. I got it as good as I could do it with that approach and it still wasn't very good. More importantly, for the first time in my life I wanted to write every one of the scenes implied in all those sentences. In the past with a short story I was delighted that I didn't have to go into that. But with this one I really wanted to do it. I had intended for my next book to be another collection of stories, which I'm nearly done with. For a couple reasons it just made sense to do what I've always been nervous about doing, which was to get an advance, take a couple years and write a novel. So I'm doing that.

Two years to write a novel, with no other obligations—that will be very different for you.

It could be too much freedom.

Caroline can lock you in the room upstairs. Wasn't it Conrad who made his wife lock him up and not let him out until noon each day?

Writing is all I've ever done. I've never really had a job. In fact this teaching position at Virginia is the first thing I've had that resembled a job, so discipline is not the problem. I was thinking of that line of Joyce Carol Oates. When she was asked how she accomplished so much, she said, "Well, my impression is that most writers are rather lazy." I think she's right. I know I have plenty of discipline, I'm out there working, but I could finish things quicker and let them go quicker. I could learn not to go on wild goose chases.

But you never know until you've gone whether it is a wild goose chase.

I know, but with that story about the dying child, I was a basket case. I was scheduled to teach in a summer workshop and I was getting ready to leave. I'd taken that story all over the block and had nothing to show for it. I was thinking, this is a sham. Here I'm supposed to teach these people how to write stories and I can't even pull one together myself. This is absurd. Then I happened to look at the manuscript from eight drafts ago and realized, "That's it!" I had it right way back then. Why hadn't I recognized it before? I think I'm beginning to get a little more intelligent about these matters. I hope so.

Thom Jones

A Way of Feeling Better

Though he attended the Iowa Writers Workshop in the early 1970s, Thom Jones worked only sporadically as a fiction writer for the next twenty years. Like Ad Magic, one of his recurring characters, he wrote advertising copy and traveled in Africa and India, designing campaigns for hunger relief. Later he was a journalist, reporting on the Washington state legislature. When budget cuts cost him that job, he wrote a novel (unpublished) and collected unemployment. Then he worked for eleven years as a janitor at the high school in Lacey, Washington, where his wife was the librarian.

Jones says now that being a janitor was a good job for him because it left his mind free, mostly for reading. But he also talks about the sense of desperation that sent him, finally, back to writing: "I thought the only way out [of this professional impasse] was to write. I told myself, you said you wanted to be a writer all your life, well, now's the time to do it, you're running out of time." Within a year his stories began to appear in *The New Yorker, Harper's, Esquire,* and *Playboy.* His first collection, *The Pugilist at Rest* (1993), was praised for showing "the gritty side of life as a man, not only in our time but throughout time." It was a finalist for the National Book Award. *Cold Snap* (1995), his second collection of stories, solidified his reputation as one of our most compelling and original new writers.

This interview took place in Iowa City, where Jones was recently an instructor at the Writers Workshop and where he is now working on a novel, as well as trying his hand at screenplays. His wife and daughter have returned to Washington state, so the family is temporarily separated. "I don't like living this way," he says, "but for now my work is here." "Here" is a small street-level apartment with blackened newsprint taped over the windows in lieu of curtains or shades. There are stacks of paperbacks and manuscripts scattered about—also magazines, including several issues of the boxing publication, *Ring.* Jones lives with the family pet, an exuberantly friendly boxer named Shelby. He has owned several boxers, he says; the first was given to him years ago as a prize for winning an AAU boxing meet.

His father was a professional fighter, and one of Jones's earliest and fondest memories, he says, is being introduced to Joe Louis by his father. Jones's own amateur career in the ring ended with a brain injury sustained while boxing for the Marine Corps; as a result, he suffers from epilepsy. Three years ago he was diagnosed with diabetes. As he discusses below, his health has become ever more precarious.

The Pugilist at Rest was enormously popular with critics and readers alike, but along with the praise came the almost universal description of your work as "pessimistic." Are you a pessimist?

The pessimism is tempered with humor and absurdity. But I make no apologies. It occurred to me early on that life is sad. We really are like actors; we come on stage for a little while and then we go off and it usually ends badly. I remember feeling this, in some sense, even as a small child, about the people who would pass in and out of my grandmother's store. It's one of my first memories, being there in the back of the store and thinking that life was very sad, something that would have been better never to have been. I felt like Hamlet. Baby Hamlet. And those were the happy days. I was much loved by my grandmother and she was a remarkable person. She quoted and paraphrased Schopenhauer from the German. I guess you could say I was temperamentally inclined toward pessimism and then instructed in the true science of misery. They call Schopenhauer a philosopher of pessimism but that's reductive. He addresses everything that accrues in the course of a lifetime—love, war, politics, everything. According to his philosophy, we're driven by blind will. I suppose that's a dark view; it certainly has the effect of stripping away your illusions. The older I get, the fewer illusions I seem to have, but there's an advantage to that—you can see into the nature of things more deeply.

What illusions have you lost?

I was just thinking of the difference between my last trip to Paris and my very first. On the first trip I was a young man drunk with Hemingway and Henry Miller, out prowling the streets until dawn. The last time Paris was nothing more than another hot and expensive big city. The second or third time around the show isn't as pretty.

Maybe travel loses some of its appeal as you get older.

I've had it with travel. One kind of trip I don't mind though—I like going around in the Third World, or I used to. Americans are such falsely optimistic people, but when you go to places like Africa and India, you see people starving, you see them sleeping in the streets. The world looks like the shit it is, and it confirms for me, like Schopenhauer's philosophy, that I'm not so far wrong in feeling bad sometimes. I thought it was just something the matter with me.

We masquerade in this country. We even hide from ourselves the fact that we're going to die. We're pretty good at it, too. Because life is comfortable here, in a materialistic way. But I think we pay the price intellectually and spiritually. It's easy to be a robot in America, but I always wanted to feel *real*. I didn't want to feel numbed to what life was about.

Despite the sometimes depressing subject matter, your stories are anything but numbing. Maybe that's because they contain such lively and colorful voices, especially your first-person narratives. Do the voices just come to you? Do you hear them? Or do you have to work them up?

Almost always my stories start with just one line, possibly something I've overheard in a recent conversation and didn't think much of at the time but which, in a stroke of grand inspiration, suddenly strikes me as apt. I got a call from a friend last night and he was telling me how he had been afflicted with insomnia, depression, and impotence. He complained he couldn't even conjure up a happy fantasy before he fell asleep and said that the impotence was a real drag. So he went to a porno shop and bought a sex tape called "Cherry Busters" and a device called Debby Diamond's Water Pussy. On the way out of the porn shop he found he had left his car lights on and had a dead battery. Because of his location and recent purchases, he was ashamed to call any of his friends for a jump start. He felt like the biggest loser in the world. I could pretty much write a story all about that right now. I get my first line and that line carries me to the next, and so on. I don't worry much about what my characters will do, but once the first draft is done, I can shape their actions, push them along so they will respond for me. Ultimately there is an artistic fullness to it all. This technique involves writing from the heart— you must learn to trust your subconscious to drive the story. I'm sensitive to certain cues and especially to the sounds of language and voice. I also tape pictures of interesting looking people near my desk. Their faces, clothing, and body posture reveal all I need to know about them as characters.

What about "Rocketfire Red"? Where did the voice of the Australian girl who narrates that story come from?

I spent a little time in Australia, and I was interested in the way people talked frankly about evacuatory processes and other earthy things. It was fun to listen to them, I'd never heard anything quite like it. Anyway, I was getting ready to come here to Iowa to teach. I was depressed and sick, suffering from diabetes, though I didn't know that yet. My weight had shrunk to 145 pounds. I went to get a haircut at this little beauty shop not far from my home in Washington state. I drew a beautician who was overweight, sullen, and depressed. She had a picture on the wall; it showed the trailer where I guess she lived and some dogs and some rotten, dirty kids digging in the dirt with a broken bottle, and I thought, Jesus, her life is probably not that great. So I said to her—I was struggling to find something to say to make her feel better—I said, "That's really beautiful hair you've got." She was a redhead. She said, "It's called 'Rocketfire Red.'" As soon as those words were out of her mouth, the whole story came together for me. I couldn't wait to get to Iowa and write it, and I thought, maybe God is paying me back. If you're nice, he gives you a little gift back. He gave me that story. I believe that. Many readers cite that story as their favorite one in *Cold Snap*, and others deplore it as not even a story, little more than a voice exercise.

What do you think?

It feels finished. Once a story's over, I know it's over. I can't make it any better. So I send it off, and then I go into an incubation period, wondering what I'll do next. Sometimes I get panicked and depressed, though I know on some level the source of stories is inexhaustible. Eventually I'll get a voice and I start writing and I'm all charged up. I feel good, very good—almost manic. Then by the time that story's over and I send it off, I'm so tired of it I usually end up hating it.

You say you know when a story's finished. How?

I like to break my stories down into little scenes. When I'm writing a draft, I'll read up to the point where I stopped the day before, read all the scenes. And maybe one of them will strike me as good. At some point I'll work on that scene, really get it up, then I'll see where the other ones aren't nearly as good and I'll try to bring them up to strength. Then sometimes they'll surpass the original strongest scene, so pretty soon I'm bringing them all up. It's like when your daughter is getting ready to go to the prom. She comes down the stairs and asks everybody, "How do I look?" You say, "You look all right, but I think you've got too much eye shadow on" or "Your hair—do this or do that" or "Adjust your bra." Up and down the stairs she goes, maybe five or six times, until everybody says, "It's done, you're perfect. Let's get out the camera and take a picture."

So you think of your stories in parts?

Yes, but I write the first draft whole, as fast as I can. I think I wrote "The Pugilist at Rest" in one sitting. And then I go back and start working on things.

Would you comment on your unusual manner of telling a story, perhaps best exemplified by "The Pugilist at Rest"? Incident is interspersed with philosophy and history in that story. One critic said, "It is these stunning leaps over time and history that move [Jones's fiction] past the mimetic concerns of rendering a moment and into the larger concerns of rendering a culture." You do the same thing in "Mosquitoes," where the structure of the story seems to be determined by a string of loose associations in the narrator's mind; he moves from his brother's marital troubles to his own reflections on gorillas to an account of Robinson Crusoe's life.

I was working as a janitor in the days when I wrote those stories, so I always had time to read. I'd read anything. For a while I was reading a lot about Robinson Crusoe. I'd try to tell the other janitors all about him. "I know you don't want to hear it," I'd say, "but I'm going to tell you anyhow." It got me thinking back to my English lit. days. Somebody said the purpose of literature is to enlighten and instruct. I think readers enjoy hearing information about how things happened in history or about how doctors do things. Or even some philosophy. You can feed things like that into a story, the way I injected Schopenhauer into "The Pugilist."

So your motive for including such things is to inform the reader. Is it also to provide a context for the story you're telling, to give it resonance?

Sure, something like that will work. You're reading "The Pugilist" and you're going, well, this is a story about war and boxing and some other things, and then all of a sudden you've got a couple beautiful quotes by Schopenhauer, and they punctuate the story. It occurs to the reader, oh, this is literature. The narrator has more credibility because he's quoting philosophers. It's a trick of craft; it adds another layer. The story has to be there, of course, but plot has never been my thing. Alice Turner, an editor at *Playboy,* told me, "Thom, you're going to have to turn out a plot, because otherwise you're just going to end up being another cult writer." I said, "What am I supposed to do about that, read Mickey Spillane?"

In Cold Snap *you acknowledge the editors who have helped you, especially with the structure of your stories. What is the nature of your working relationship with editors?*

It varies. Some editors will actually point out structural problems. Colin Harrison, at *Harper's,* is able to do that. He has diagnostic vision; he can see through to the skeletal structure of a story. He helped me with "I Want to Live!" He showed me how cutting a section here and there can make a story much cleaner. I tend to be a little repetitive. But I'm getting more experienced and don't need as much help as I did in the beginning.

For a while, editors were clamoring for my stuff; they were buying up my stories almost as soon as I wrote them. I look at those stories now and think how I would do them differently; there are problems in every one that I wish I could work over. You know, Stuart Dybek will even rewrite stories that have been anthologized. He never stops. I never stop either, until a story goes to press, and then I figure, it's too late now, it belongs to the reader.

Does the demand for your work date from 1991, when "The Pugilist at Rest" appeared in The New Yorker? *Were you writing before that? What happened to turn things around for you?*

I was a student at the Writers Workshop here from '70 to '72. After that I became an ad writer and never thought of writing again. With a job like advertising, you write yourself out at work. I did journalism for a while and it was the same thing—even worse. There was nothing left for fiction writing.

Why did you go into advertising after Iowa?

You have to make a living, and my early work was undeveloped. You read books and you love them and you hope that you might have the vision and talent to write your own one day. But I was young and didn't have a lot of experience, and I tried sending stories out and nothing much came of it. In those days, baby boomers weren't editors yet. I think my stuff was a little too different to find an audience.

I wrote only off-and-on for a number of years after that. There'd be great gaps of time when I wrote nothing—five, six, seven years. Then maybe I'd sit down and write a story on the typewriter, do only one or two drafts, because I didn't like to keep retyping. Finally I got a word processor, which made revision easier, and that was something of a breakthrough for me. The first story I wrote on the word processor was "Rocket Man," and I felt like I knew what I was doing at long last. But nobody picked it up. I said to a writer friend of mine, Jon Jackson, "Jon, I can't write any better than this story." He said, "You just have to write something that's so good they *can't* reject it." As soon as he said that, it was like, "Why didn't you tell me that a long time ago? I can do that." Suddenly I felt tremendously free, and the next story was "The Pugilist" and the one after that "I Want to Live!" I felt awakened and wondered why it had taken me so long. It's like Zen—you get it when you get it.

On the acknowledgments page of Cold Snap, *you thank North Thurston High School in Lacey, Washington, "for providing me with sanctuary some eleven years." Is that where you were a janitor? What was the nature of the sanctuary the school provided?*

I left advertising and journalism. I took a year off to write a novel, which was so bad I didn't bother to send it out. I didn't have it as a writer at that time. So I took this job as a night janitor at the high school. It gave me time to read and to think about what I read. Sometimes I'd read a book in a day, or two or three books, just scanning them. Sometimes I'd get hold of something meaty and pour over every word for a couple weeks. I read and re-read the classics. For several years, I read. As always, I was trying to figure out what life was about. I was getting older. I was a janitor. I went through an alcoholic period. At one point I tried to get back into the ad business. When they saw my portfolio, they wanted me in a big way, until I explained I was working as a janitor. It was like I'd just gotten out of prison, as far as they were concerned. Then I knew I was too old and had too much explaining to do. I thought the only way out was to write. I told myself, you said you wanted to be a writer all your life, well, now's the time to do it, you're running out of time. So I got that computer and decided I'd take one more crack at it. I think a lot of times a writer will be 99 percent there and not know how close he is. It's like being out in the desert and there's an oasis just over the next sand dune, but you can't see it. It would be a tragedy to perish within hailing distance of sweet water.

So you can look back at earlier stories and see they were very close to being accomplished pieces?

Oh, sure. Part of the problem was, they weren't ready for the general audience. They were a little too much "in your face." Even "I Want to Live!," which has been anthologized about seven times, was close to the edge. Some people who read it said a sixty-seven-year-old woman dying of cancer wouldn't think that way. As a writer, you try to be fresh and original, without pushing it too far.

Returning to the situation you were in before you made your breakthrough, it sounds like you had to be backed into a corner before you started writing again.

I guess that was it. Even though my job at the high school wasn't hard, it was still work, and now I had to come home every day and do something that was much harder than work. I had to get psyched up to write. But I found I could do it. I'd learned as an amateur boxer how to fight my way out of bad situations. I wasn't that gifted physically, so I would think about how to win, what you have to do. Every time you don't work out or run or whatever, you're going to regret it on fight night. I saw a lot of boxers who would be a few pounds overweight two days before a fight. I realized they just wanted to have an excuse if they lost. They didn't want to have to say, "I was in the best shape of my life and I lost, period." It's the same with a writer sometimes. He'll say, "I don't want to put my whole heart and soul into this, because what if it's rejected? Then I'm a failure."

One of the unusual things about "I Want to Live!" is the way its morbid subject—your mother-in-law's death from cancer—is handled in a breezy, slangy voice. Was that a calculated effect or simply a reflection of your mother-in-law's personality?

The story is from her point of view but filtered through me. When I showed the story to my wife and some of her friends, their reaction was, "Women don't think this way. They don't talk this way. You make her sound like an angry teenybopper." But at that point I had confidence in what I was doing. I thought, I'm right, I know I'm right on this. I sent it to *Harper's* and they loved it.

You make it clear the woman's life is taken away by the cancer long before her actual death. The knowledge that she's going to die colors every waking moment. But before the end, she recovers "the Will to Live," in part through her childhood memories of Mr. Barnes, the tough little rooster that embodies the life force.

Roosters are mean birds. They're totally into the Will to Live. They embrace it fully, so, yes, a rooster is a perfect symbol for this thing that drives life, which cares not for the individual, but only the species. If you ride the wave, this force will drive you to do what you're meant to do. I often wondered why I didn't go to Vietnam. I wanted to go, I was ready, but then I got injured in a boxing match and developed epilepsy, which at the time seemed like a real bummer. As it turned out, though, everybody in my unit was killed, including my best friend, and presumably I would have been killed, too. The universe sends a few prophets down to call it out, and Schopenhauer was one, and I'm just mirroring it, channeling a lot of it.

Back to the end of that story for a minute. . . . The dying woman has the memory of the rooster and she captures some of that spirit for herself, then the story ends this way: "There wasn't any tunnel or white light or any of that. She just . . . died." Why no tunnel or white light? Why the flat, anticlimactic "She just . . . died."?

If there were a tunnel or a light, that would have pushed me into the realm of sentimentality. It would have been like saying, "Oh, death isn't so bad after all." It *is* bad, goddamnit. It's like going to Africa and seeing people walking around starving. Why shouldn't we say so? Why do I have to pretend there's this wonderful tunnel and angels?

Is that why you send your characters to Africa so frequently? Is it a reality check?

Like my character Ad Magic ["A White Horse" and "Quicksand"], I traveled in the Third World when I was working on ad campaigns. Knowing the kinds of problems other people have to face provides a sort of ballast for us, yes. But it's funny what readers will focus on. The reaction I got most about "Quicksand" was that there was too much unrealistic sex between Ad Magic and the young woman doctor. The thing is, I wrote that story for *Playboy* and the editor, Alice Turner, said, "Can we have a little more sex?" I said, "Sure."

That reminds me, your male protagonists tend not to be, shall we say, "enlightened." They typically regard women with a cold, appraising eye. The sex scenes are raw and often predatory. Have you been criticized for these things?

Absolutely. But women are my biggest fans. I think they realize the heavy sex scenes are written with a certain amount of irony. The only readers who miss that are the ones who believe everything you write is directly from life and you really are a misogynist, like the people you write about. In fact, I'm not. I think women are superior creatures to men.

Why is that?

I just did an article for *Details* about male bonding. My editor there has a theory that men only approximate intimacy with one another and then only while playing sports or drinking. Women can be intimate with one another, it's not so difficult for them. They can be kinder, more empathetic. This was the idea of the piece. Not that women are perfect. Not that they can't be corrupted by power and competition. I wrote about my experiences in the Marine Corps where the testosterone levels soar and there are few women to mitigate this poisoning. Machismo and elitism are part of the program. Buy into it and you become accountable to the group, loyal to your comrades, and filled with hatred toward the targets of "evil." It wasn't just communists we were taught to hate. I remember hating everybody who wasn't in recon and even there I hated a good half of the people.

That's the mentality of the narrator in "The Pugilist at Rest." He cracks Hey Baby's skull with the butt of his rifle because Hey Baby's giving Jorgeson a hard time.

He was programmed. Jorgeson was the narrator's buddy, and in that context your buddy is everything; your very life depends on him. You never can get a tighter bond than that. That's why men have a hard time recovering from the war. It's hard to find that same intimacy and intensity in civilian life. Hey Baby was a real guy and he got on my nerves in a big way. I was laying to get him, waiting for the right moment, and when he pushed my buddy, I went for him in an extreme fashion. I did not worry about consequences.

And you acted this way because you'd bought into the program?

Jorgeson was my friend. A friend will stand up for you. Be there for you. I was devastated when he was killed in combat. He was cheated out of the rest of his life. It rattled around in my mind for years. Finally I wrote that story after I saw the First Marine Division, my outfit, on TV, preparing to charge the Republican Guard's first line of defense in Kuwait. Those guys were stoked. I don't think they realized what it really meant. I remember feeling exactly the same way, but it's a different picture when you're older. I could only think of my buddy, and there was nothing to do for him except to write a story, straight from my heart. When you write from your heart like that, it's hard not to move the reader. Some people write in a plotted, studied way. I like to go with characters, people who *do* something, break out in some way, because they've got problems and they can't contain their emotions.

The combat scene in which Jorgeson dies is almost surreal in its vividness. How did you write that?

I'd been in the Marines, I knew weapons, I knew how those patrols worked, I'd talked to other Marines who'd been in the war. Also, I always read everything I could get my hands on about Vietnam. I read Tim O'Brien, his story "The Things They Carried." It's such a perfect story I was in awe of it. I read it many times. But I felt competitive about it, too. I needed to find some chink in that story that would give me the confidence I could write a story as good as O'Brien's. What I latched onto was the boy/girl thing in the story. The lieutenant carried a picture of his girl friend and he daydreamed about her all the time, though he eventually realizes she doesn't love him. I thought that particular aspect of the story was like O'Brien dropping his left after a jab; it was an opening for me. Not that O'Brien made a mistake exactly, but it gave me some room and a competitive urge to tell my own war story, which I was determined would not have any such romantic heartbreak in it. Tim O'Brien set the standard and I went after him in my own way.

So you feel competitive toward other writers?

As a reader, I love them. But when I sit down to write, it's another matter. Why let somebody else best you? I'm fairly Darwinian. It comes from fear probably. When I was boxing, there were fighters I had to face that I was so afraid of I didn't know how I was going to do it. That's a problem every boxer has. There's always going to be somebody bigger and stronger than you, and it doesn't take long to find him either. Usually on the first day you find him. I would go out to my garage on Sunday afternoon—that was the day you weren't supposed to do any training—and I would turn on WLUA in Chicago and worry myself sick trying to think of every contingency: if I got knocked down, if I got a guy who was faster than I was, this, that, the other thing. I wouldn't work out, I'd just try some punches—and worry. I think it's at the point when you abandon any notion you're going to succeed that the universe comes in and answers your question, as a boxer, as a writer, anything. That's why I disagree with boxing abolitionists; they miss the whole point. I don't think Ali or Jerry Quarry ever regretted fighting. I don't regret it and I got epilepsy from it. Because I learned so much.

I want to ask you about the ending of another story, "I Need a Man to Love Me." Like "I Want to Live!" it concludes with the female protagonist's death. But it's a very different sort of death—an ecstatic one. She thinks "the only hell she would know was about to end. In fact, it was over. She felt warmth and love and she wondered if there was a heaven. It seemed very likely, contrary to what common sense had previously deemed." In the other story you insisted there was no

tunnel and no light—just death. Here you permit the dying woman to antici-
pate heaven. Why the difference?

She's relieved about making a choice to die after a life of misery. Also she's
racked out on some really good drugs. I didn't mean to suggest she's on her
way to heaven. Nobody has ever come back from the other side to tell us what
death is, so how could a writer presume to say?

You said once, in another interview, that you're interested in spiritual quests.
And yet your narrators, when they ponder such matters, tend to be skeptical,
like the boxer in "Pugilist," who wonders if his own visionary experiences aren't
simply chemical episodes. What are your thoughts on that?

It depends on what time of the day you ask me the question. Alone at night
faith comes a little more naturally. By day I'm the stalwart rationalist. My
characters often wrestle with questions of faith. I'm influenced in that respect
by Dostoevsky. He was the author who first made me want to write. Sometimes I see religion from the perspective of the Grand Inquisitor in *The Broth-*
ers Karamazov: there are a select few who run things, dispensing religion to
the masses while living themselves with the terrible knowledge the universe
is chaotic and random. Yet I want security like everybody else, and it scan-
dalized me when I learned what an unabashed atheist Schopenhauer was.

Temperament probably inclines us to believe or not to believe. I'm a mel-
ancholy and depressive type. Others seem to be congenital optimists, happy
and trusting; they're always going around trying to cheer you up: "Isn't life
great? I'm going biking at 6 A.M., do you want to come along? Blah, blah,
blah." I try to avoid people like that. They aren't looking at the evidence. At
the same time, I've seen people who shouldn't be happy—and are. In India,
in Africa, living in the worst conditions, they're certain about life, they know
their place in the world, where they belong.

It's like some of the epileptic experiences I've had, which seem to me, ultimately, the most knowing moments in my life. What you realize then is, you
have a role to play, you act out your part. You don't necessarily have to be a
chief or an Indian, you could be a piece of furniture or a molecule.

You sound like Rocketfire Red when she's describing "Australian Dream time."
What's she say? "In Australian Dream time everything makes perfect sense. There
is no judgment. Thems that massacred me ancestors will receive no eternal judg-
ment. Neither will your Mother Teresa win a Brownie medal; she's just playing
her part in the cosmic play. Doing her bleedin' job. Good and evil all happen
for a reason."

I saw the truth of that in one of my epileptic auras: go ahead and keep
drinking and kill yourself, I thought, you won't be judged; or get sober and

be a writer, it doesn't matter. You're not going to gain any blame or merit. You're just doing what you're doing; relax and do it. *Amor fati.* "Love your fate." It's happened to me like that three times, once in a very powerful way. But it's an elusive thing. When you try to remember it and explain it, you can't. There's a lot of noise in America; it's hard to think, and it's very hard to be spiritual. You have to quiet down. And here I am, a coffee-drinking freak who doesn't know what "calm" is. Don't want to, really. Don't care to know it, though I'm interested in those sorts of visionary experiences.

"Manic" is the word often used to describe you, your characters, your writing style. You used the word yourself earlier, when you were talking about the super-charged state you get into when you're working.

I recently read a critic who described my voice as "first-person psychotic." I considered it a high compliment. When I'm writing well I do feel manic. My brain is on fire. It smokes. I don't know how a normal human being can compete with that.

Life is what you seem to value most in your characters—energy, vitality. Rocketfire Red has it, even to the color of her hair. Mr. Barnes, the rooster, has it.

Picture a reader stuck with a magazine in the dentist's office. First he'll check out the cartoons. Second he'll look at the ads. Third he might read about the war in Bosnia. And finally, if he's really desperate, he'll look to see who wrote the short story. He won't read it, he'll just check to see who *wrote* it. Why shouldn't the short story be the first thing you want to read? Why do stories have to be boring? Why do we always have to read about some angst-laden, upper-level executive driving around Cape Cod in a Volvo? I think the reader should be fully entertained—and illuminated somewhat.

"Illuminated"?

I'm not sure how much illumination I have to bring. I've been told my voice is everything and without it the substance of my work is fairly second-rate. It's been said my thinking consists largely of second-hand Schopenhauer and baked-over Nietzsche.

Who told you the substance of your work was second-rate?

Some critics have. They say without the voice it wouldn't work.

You could say the same about any writer, couldn't you?

Oh, sure, you can look at any writer and find trouble. Negative criticism doesn't bother me too much, because I know I'm learning. And you have to expect some people to come after you. It irritates some critics when a guy like me comes out of nowhere. Suddenly I'm in all the magazines, and they're thinking, who's this guy? Also I was pretty isolated and maybe some of my stories sounded odd to them. I wasn't reading what other people were reading. I wasn't reading the *New York Times,* I wasn't reading *The New Yorker.* I wasn't fresh out of some writing program.

Don't you think that was to your advantage?

It was up to a point. There's a raw power in my work and now I'm trying to become more of a stylist. But really, I don't mind being the outsider. I like that edge I get from feeling I have something to prove.

I understand you're working on a novel.

My publisher has been after me to do it. The return in money and prestige is much bigger with a novel than with stories. I've done very well with the stories, and I'm not complaining, but I haven't made any big score. I think about my health and the fact I'm in my fifties, and it's not like I'm going to write thirty more books, so I have to choose my projects carefully. A novel might be a chance to write something really wonderful. Then, too, with short stories, you have to create a whole universe each time out. With a novel, you're putting that same investment in, but you get to stay with the people you create and get more out of them. You're not closing the door and starting over all the time.

I read that you were expanding the New Yorker *story about the doctor in Africa and his baboon pal, George Babbitt.*

"Way Down Deep in the Jungle," yes. I wrote another chapter. I've got the baboon in ICU, he just got into a fight with a leopard. He's in a strait jacket and they've got him on Haldol.

So is that the novel you're working on?

No, I got stuck. Part of the problem with that story, and others I've written that had the potential to be novels, is that once the thing is published as a story, I go, well, I can't do *that* anymore, because it's in print. To keep working on it seems ludicrous; it's finished. Whereas, if I didn't publish it but kept working on it in private, then maybe I'd have a novel at the end of a year instead of ten stories. It's a matter of patience with me. Writing stories has been very gratifying, and an instant fix. With a novel, you have to drop out of sight for a while.

Besides the fact it takes longer and requires more patience, how does writing a novel differ from writing a short story?

It's easier in a way, because the pace can be more relaxed. In a short story, everything has to be tight. You can't bore readers, even for a minute. You can't have a bad line, especially in the beginning, or they're going to bail out on you. In a novel, nobody requires that sort of intensity. When I read a novel and the chapter is going on a long time, I think, all right, I'll ride it out, see what happens next. The chapter ends and I'm looking to see what happens and then the next chapter may pick up in a different place with different characters, and pretty soon I'm interested in those people and what they're doing. Then I'm back with the other people for a while, and so on. That's the trick. And it's not hard. Only the hardest thing in the world. You're creating something out of nothing. It didn't exist until you made it. Who would want to be a doctor or a physicist or anything when you can actually be a creator?

You mentioned Dostoevsky as an influence on you. You've said elsewhere that Salinger, too, was an early favorite of yours.

I was a freshman in college, complaining about everything, and this friend of mine says, "You ought to read this book. This guy complains almost as much as you." So I read *The Catcher in the Rye,* and the fire was lit.

Your own work doesn't seem to have much in common with his, except maybe for "Cold Snap." The tender, mutually protective relationship between the brother and sister in that story, along with the easy, humorous way they have with each other, is reminiscent of Salinger.

That was a popular story and probably one of the easiest I've ever written. I heard recently it's gotten into the Norton anthology. The sister in that story was a girl friend of mine who tried to shoot herself in the head and ended up lobotomized, like the character in the story.

You mention in the acknowledgments at the back of Cold Snap *your indebtedness to certain drug companies for "manufacturing Effexor and Elavil; drugs so good they feel illegal." I think that's the first acknowledgment of pharmaceuticals I've ever read.*

I thought maybe I'd get some free drugs.

So you had an ulterior motive.

No, I meant what I said. Those drugs make it possible for me to function.

In her review of Cold Snap, *Joyce Carol Oates said, these stories force us "to realize how rarely the mysterious life of the body is evoked in literature." Do you think your reliance on medication and also your experience as a boxer have made you more attuned to what Oates calls "accidents of blood chemistry, caprices of metabolism, illnesses, organic breakdowns"?*

Our body colors our view of the world, especially if it's a sick body. I had a healthy body once, but I abused it. I'm obsessive. I never do anything in moderation. When I used to go running, I'd run too far and the next day I'd feel like I had the flu—sicker than a dog. It was the same with boxing. You feel great while you're doing it, but you're getting knocked around all the while and you come out of it all banged up. It didn't matter to me in those days. I'd recover, then I couldn't wait to go back and do it again. Maybe it was just a way of feeling good for a little while, the way some people reach for alcohol or drugs to feel better. They don't make a decision to be degenerate or evil, they're just trying to get by. They're in pain and they're trying to make it go away. Life is a tough place. Everybody is trying to feel good in spite of it. I haven't got many ways to feel good anymore except through my art. I've run through the things that don't work.

You taught the past two years here at Iowa. How was that?

I liked it a lot, because Iowa tends to get the best writing students. Some of them are 97 percent there already. Knowing the magazines as well as I do, I could look at a story and see how to fix it. My students were selling their stories, and I was getting more pleasure out of that than selling my own. I developed a reputation for being a good line editor and people were coming at me from every direction. I'm a hypochondriac, and I'd be at the doctor's office every other day with some complaint, and even the doctor was giving me manuscripts—things he'd written! It got so, if I was feeling sick, I'd ask myself, "Are you *really* sick?" And I'd think, "Maybe not."

So your doctor cured you! It gives new meaning to that epigraph in Cold Snap, *about the healing power of art.*

It sure does.

Why did you pick that epigraph? ["Now the spirit of the Lord departed from Saul, and an evil spirit from the Lord tormented him. And Saul's servants said to him, 'Behold now, an evil spirit from God is tormenting you. Let our Lord now command your servants, who are before you, to seek out a man who is skillful in playing the lyre: and when the evil spirit from God is upon you, he will play it, and you will be well,'"—1 Samuel 16:14–16]

It's a reference to how David would play the lyre for Saul and the evil spirits would go away. That's how it is when you're engaged with a good book or a good movie or whatever. You forget about yourself and your troubles. Remember the scene in *Cabaret* when the Joel Grey character comes out and says, "I'm going to make you forget about all your troubles and we're going to have a great time"? Well, I'm thinking, "Right! Nobody can make me forget about my troubles because mine are considerable." But all of a sudden I'm into this great movie, and then the Joel Grey character is back and says, "I told you I'd make you forget your troubles." And I go, "Oh, you did! Hey, I like this guy!" Schopenhauer said that's probably the best we can do in life: become engaged in art, and in so doing, become objective and dispassionate about our own worries. When I was young, I'd go to bed with a book at night and that would be the best thing of all because I knew Somerset Maugham was going to take me to the South Seas and I was going to forget all my troubles. It worked. And it still does.

Julia Alvarez

"A Clean Windshield"

The interview with Julia Alvarez took place in her home on the outskirts of Middlebury, Vermont, a college town with an inn and trendy shops and restaurants on the main street. Alvarez and her husband live on a quiet lane that becomes a dirt road before it reaches their house. The house, constructed with wood from trees that grew on an old Vermont farm owned by her husband's parents, abuts a pasture where sheep graze. There are beautiful views out the living room windows, but what dominates the room is a long table crowded with family photographs.

Brought up in the Dominican Republic, Alvarez came to the United States in 1960 with her family, in flight from Rafael Leonida Trujillo's dictatorship. She began her writing career as a poet (*Homecoming* [1984] and *The Other Side/El Otro Lado* [1995]), but is best known for her two novels, *How the García Girls Lost Their Accents* (1991), an episodic and loosely autobiographical account of a Dominican American family, and *In the Time of the Butterflies* (1994), a fictionalized telling of the 1960 murder of three Mirabal sisters who opposed Trujillo's dictatorship. Her third novel, *¡Yo!*, appeared in 1997.

Alvarez divides her time between writing, teaching, and political activism in the Dominican Republic. She has become increasingly involved in the affairs of her native country over the past several years.

She has received prizes for both her poetry and fiction, including awards from PEN and the American Library Association for *How the García Girls Lost Their Accents*.

Do you see yourself more as a poet or a fiction writer?

I began as a poet, and it's still my first love. Poetry is harder to write than fiction, metaphysically: it requires such nakedness and accuracy. As Emily Dickinson said, there are no approximate words in a poem. You can get away with a few approximate words in fiction. But the other side of it is, if you want to be a writer full-time, you can't overlook the fact poetry doesn't pay. Every once in a while I find myself having to go back and write a poem.

Maybe it's like doing finger exercises. The other night when I was coming back from a reading, I was driving the car down these country roads, and this poem started to come into my head. I had to pull off the road. I was right by a rumbly bridge, and I was afraid someone would come by and not see my car and run into me. And there by the overhead car light I started to write this poem. The next day I really worked it, but that night the lines were coming.

Typically, in the mornings I always read a little bit of prose and a little poetry before I get going on my own work, and it's always the poems first and then the prose. It's the fine tuning of poetry I turn to first. The word before it completely descends into flesh—that's poetry for me.

Right now I'm reading essays, because I'm working on essays. People ask me to do a piece on this or a piece on that. I have about twenty essays at this point. These days I'm very interested in how essays work. With an essay it's a matter of pursuing a question straightforwardly.

What effect do you think being a poet has on your fiction?

I'm picky about words. I'm writing this essay now, inspired in part by my students, because they go, "Ms. Alvarez, you're like so picky." They just sling out words, they're so inaccurate. I'll tell them, "Tears cannot 'pour' down her cheeks." And they say, "Oh, come on, Ms. Alvarez, everyone says tears pour." They write, "Her eyes were 'glued' to the television." And I say, "No way!" I think writing poetry gives me a kind of intense particularity about words. What I have had to learn writing prose is not to get so obsessive and to re-member that with a novel I'm not working on a 2" x 2" square. To get myself going, I've got to put that poetic sensibility aside and save the fine tuning for later drafts. It's something that I have to convince myself to do. But the sen-sibility of the writer, whether of fiction or poetry, comes from paying atten-tion. I tell my students that writing doesn't begin when you sit down to write. It's a way of being in the world, and the essence of it is paying attention.

Isn't the theme of naming and word choice important in both novels?

Yes, and that's in my poems, too. Sometimes just a list of words will catch my eye, the naming of things. I love that. Naming is a way to control or crys-tallize, or to make meaning of experience that otherwise runs through your fingers. Naming experience, verbally putting it together, somehow redeems it for me. My heroine of all times is Scheherazade, who by the telling of sto-ries gains her life, saves the other women in the kingdom, and transforms the sultan's hatred to love.

The last word of The García Girls *is "art," and the last word of* Butterflies *is "story." Isn't a primary theme of both that the art of storytelling is a means of survival, of recording and also transcending history?*

And for Dedé it's also a political gesture, being the one who remembers. One of the most moving things about the Holocaust Museum in Washington is the button you get at the door, which doesn't say "Holocaust Museum"; it says "Remember." To remember and keep alive the Mirabal story is how Dedé be-comes politicized. Her politicalization happens much later than her sisters'.

In Butterflies *you very adroitly link the political events in the Dominican Republic to the Holocaust, including the survivor's need and responsibility to remember and to help others remember.*

What is it Conrad says? That art is rendering the highest kind of justice to the visible universe. In a sense he is saying clarity of vision and precision of expression, looking at life through a clean windshield, is a moral act. It is also the artist's job. And for me it is also a political way of being in the world. Because if you are looking at the world clearly and with your heart, something about the unequal distribution of wealth, something about the way the environment is treated, something about the way Third World countries are used for their slave labor, will be apparent. I don't want my writing to be political in any dogmatic way, maybe because I hate being preached at. But being transformed—who doesn't want that?

Would you make a distinction between the political and the propagandistic novel?

My writing is not allied to a particular program that the reader should follow. It's more like what Rilke says in "The Archaic Torso of Apollo": "You must change your life." I'm not going to tell the reader how to change it. Dedé's telling the Mirabal story is her political act, equivalent to the sisters' starting their underground, protesting, and politicizing the people. In the same way, writing is my political act.

Is Dedé's politicalization anticipated in the scene in which she claims to be Minerva?

Yes, and for Dedé her personal tragedy was that she had to be the one left behind to tell the story. But her telling the story redeems the past and the present and allows her to go on. The same is true of *The García Girls.* In that book surviving by telling the story is central. You have to remember who you are, where you came from. You hear stories, and no matter where you go, those narratives come with you. That's how the family retains a sense of cohesion through all its falling apart.

One of my sisters works with so-called Third World populations in Boston; she's part of a group of mostly Latino therapists trying to work from a different model than the Eurocentric Freudian and Jungian one. Some of their clients come to therapy because they've seen their whole village wiped out. Their problem is not penis envy. My sister says she knows they're going to be all right when they can tell her the story of what has happened, when it's not just weeping and fragments and protective numbness. They are on their way when they can start telling the story, when they have a way of saying, "This, too, I can take in. This, too, becomes part of the story. And this, too, I won't forget."

How did you go from writing poetry to writing fiction?

I was writing poems that were telling stories, so I was already moving in that direction. All my training at Syracuse—where I went to graduate school—was in poetry. One summer, when I was four years out of grad school, I took a fiction workshop from David Huddle. Basically he is a very hands-off teacher, and I kept asking him, "How do you write a story?" It is wonderful to give yourself that experience, after you are out of school and you're not supposed to be needing this kind of instruction. The experience helped me focus on the craft of writing fiction in a group setting, rather than trying to do it all by myself. I wrote some stories in that workshop that were well received, so I began to think, "Well, maybe this is something I can do."

Did you start your first novel as a series of short stories?

Yes, what happened was, one of the stories won a prize, and I was taken to New York to read it. There was an agent there, Susan Bergholz; she is also the agent for Sandra Cisneros and Ana Castillo. She really has put Latino/ Latina writers on the map; we call her our angel, not just our agent. Susan liked the story and she had me send her some others, and she sent them around. She could have told me the number of rejections and it would have been depressing, but luckily she didn't. Then she sent them to Shannon Ravenel, at Algonquin, and she said, "I like what I see here, but this isn't a book. There's a larger story here, a story of a whole family." She got me thinking about the book, and I got to working with it like a quilt, seeing that this little piece could go here, and that little piece fit there, and here I had a gap. And was I going to tell the story of this family from this point of view or that, and how was I going to organize it? I decided I didn't want the traditional *Bildungsroman,* with time going forward and the character growing up. I wanted the reader to be thinking like an immigrant, forever going back.

So you always thought of writing the novel in reverse chronological order?

Oh, no. I tell my students that one of the most liberating parts of writing is that you don't have to know where you're going, that you figure it out as you go along. This is important, especially for women, because we don't think of plot the same way men do. We don't structure our lives the same way, don't think of them as having a certain trajectory, as moving toward a certain apex, or ourselves as on a solitary voyage, whether like Odysseus or Satan in *Paradise Lost.* For us there were always the babies and the grandmother to take care of, the house to be kept. We move through experience relationally, so multiple points of view have always been much more interesting to me than the single perspective, which tunnels through and gets what it wants and is the hero. I once heard a Native American critic address the issue of Louise Erdrich's use of multiple points of view; the critic said she thought it made sense, not only as a woman, but as a Native American. The truth, she said, is not this single thing that you head for and tell; it's the points around the thing that tell the whole story.

I see many parallels between your work and Erdrich's. Both of you started writing poetry, and she also began Love Medicine, *her first novel, as short stories.*

That's true. I also think that, in many ways, Native American culture is like a traditional Caribbean culture, with that same emphasis on *la familia,* the tribe.

Was it hard for you, in your first novel, to create all those different voices?

Wait until you see the new book—the story of Yolanda the writer.

How much of that is you?

Quite a bit of what I write comes out of my own experience, altered, played with, and embellished. Things I hear combine with things I make up, until I don't know where facts end and fiction begins. In the traditional story of the making of the writer, the emphasis is on the writer with his or her sensitivity, how this person develops through life and goes through all these experiences and crystallizes into a writer. I'm not interested in that in ¡*Yo!* This is about the revenge of the people in a writer's life who don't usually get to tell the story because the writer is always co-opting the experience. So there's a story from the sisters of Yo, and the mother tells a story of Yo, the father tells his story, the third husband tells a story about her, the step-daughter—everybody gets to tell a story. We get the story of how this woman got to be a writer, but not from the writer's point of view. She never gets to utter a word in the book. She's not any of the voices. There's a stalker, there's a Midwestern landlady, and I had to hear all these people's voices. I love that kind of listening and being taken over by other voices, because as a writer it's not just your story that you are telling. You are the storyteller of the tribe, and there are many stories to tell. So it's important to me to be able to imagine experience from different points of view. I'm much more interested in that than I am in one person's story.

Both books are about sisters. Do you come from a family of all sisters?

I do, I do! I was just talking to this woman who has five daughters who said, "I always send my daughters your books because I say, 'Here is a writer who understands sisters and the dynamic of an all-sisters family.'" I think it's a special dynamic, especially for me having grown up pre-women's rights movement. In our family there was no question that women were powerful, that they could run the world. It was sort of like the phenomenon people talk about when describing the benefits of going to an all-women's college. I knew about sisterhood from having grown up with sisters, and I felt that women were capable, and that helped when I had to go out into a world that did not believe the same thing.

In the second novel, isn't the theme of sisterhood extended to women in general?

What is important is not just biological sisterhood or the blood family, which is what I was taught in the Dominican Republic, but *mi familia,* the human family. People ask me sometimes, "Are you writing autobiographically, from what you know?" That's what you're supposed to do, but I am not writing so much out of what I know, as out of what I need to find out. People also ask, "Who do you see as your audience?" Like every writer, I imagine readers going on generation after generation into the future, but the people in the front row of my audience are friends with whom I've discussed issues and questions, or things that we're troubled with or that we're trying to come to terms with. That's where the books start, in a conversation with a friend, or with something that happens in the community, which is your larger family. These things start to puzzle you. There's nothing more boring than writing something when you already know how it's going to turn out, because then you're just the secretary.

Both novels are divided into sections. Has that been a useful structural device for you?

How to notate the novel? I think of it even at the level of sentences and paragraphs. Maybe because I began as a poet, I like to have my prose in movements, in stanzas. I can tell when a writer truly has a sense of paragraphing. Louise Erdrich does, and Amy Tan in *Joy Luck Club* has a wonderful sense of how to close a section, how to end a paragraph. I can just hear it. Sometimes I'll catch myself trying to rhyme the end of a paragraph or section—not a big thunder-clap rhyme, but a soft slant-rhyme for that slight punctuation. Going back to your earlier question about how my poetry has affected my fiction, I would say that one of my needs is to take the novel and divide it into smaller pieces, so that I can look at it all the way around.

In the entry about you in Contemporary Authors, *you quote Czeslow Milosz: "Language is the only homeland." You say that when your family landed in the United States, you "landed in the English language." Can you talk about that?*

I hate traveling in countries where I don't speak the language. I feel like a tourist there. When my husband and I were in Turkey, we took a car and drove into the interior. We finally developed this elementary, crude way of communicating. But I was frustrated the whole time. I said to my husband, "Next time, let's go to England, let's go to Spain. I don't want to go somewhere where I can't talk to the people." I think what Milosz meant was that the ability to create a place and feel like you belong in the human family happens through language. Coming to the United States, I was suddenly thrust into a new country, and everything I knew was left behind. Not being understood was like being in the tower of Babel, and I realized that language was going to be how I connected with these babblers! And so language became the bond I trusted; no longer did I want to sink my soul in a piece of land, a national culture, because I had seen how quickly that could go. Language was a portable homeland, so I became interested in words in a really intentional way, as I hadn't been with my native language, because I learned it as a baby. That's what I tell my students, too: "You have to do the same thing with your own language, you have to go back and relearn it, although you think you already know it. You don't know it from the inside. You have to go back and learn your own native language again as a writer. You have to ask yourself, 'Why am I using this little word instead of that little word?'"

You obviously identify with other women writers and ethnic writers. Do you also feel a special identification with those writing in a second language?

I feel a strong connection with other Latinos and Latinas. I think I identify with them culturally, especially with those who had English as a second language and so feel the divisions I do. When I left the Dominican Republic, I had what you might call classroom English. I had been to a little American school, but when I came to the United States I couldn't tell where one word ended and another one began. My ear didn't pick it up. Unlike in my class, people didn't say, "Hel-lo . . . My . . . name . . . is . . . Ju-li-a." A famous writer came to my college and said one could never write in a language one had not said "Mama" in. Hearing that comment caused me some radical self-doubt. As a defense, I acquired a list of writers who hadn't begun in English. In my own head I began to think, "Conrad." I guess I identify with anyone who comes from a place in the society where the dominant language isn't the mainstream language, like black English, where you speak another lingo or language and have to make all kinds of linguistic negotiations and adjustments. As Latino writers, my friends and I know that certain publications will reject a story if there are too many Spanish words. We know that we're always carrying the shadow-language with us. I have a student from Bosnia in my class now. His writing is awkward and riddled with errors, but some of his sentences and paragraphs are wonderful, because he hears English with a different rhythm than we do.

Don't you think that, as a Latina, you also have a distinctive sound?

I can detect it when I hear Sandra Cisneros or Ana Castillo read. I can hear that lilt in their voices, and I hear it in the way they put together sentences. But it's hard to hear it in my own voice, until someone points it out.

In the Contemporary Authors *entry you say that you "lost the island" but discovered a better world, a world of the imagination, and that "the boys in the school yard with ugly looks on their faces were not allowed into this world." To me that implies writing is an escape, but your actual fiction seems full of pain, and Yolanda says, "Violation lies at the center of my art." What about that?*

Those boys are the little sultans, and your job isn't done until you have transformed them. You have to be like Scheherazade, who makes the sultan penitent about his cruelty. You can't just write to a coterie of people who agree with you. But when I was little, words were a kind of defense, a wall those cruel boys couldn't violate.

The García Girls *ends with the episode of Yolanda and the kitten, when she is warned that to take the kitten from its mother "would be a violation of its natural right to live." Yolanda and her sisters are like the kitten in that they are taken away to the United States. The girls, then, are violators and are themselves violated. Is that a convincing reading?*

Absolutely. The world in which the García family are among the elite is a world of privilege and violation. And of course the girls are living in a society which treated maids very badly. The feeling there's something awry with the world is what sets you to write. The other night at this concert a friend of mine was in, I heard this line: "I surrender to the mystery." I want to be burned, so I don't want an epitaph, but if I did I would want that to be it. But there's a way that, as a writer, you don't completely surrender to the mystery. You want to understand and hold the mystery in your mind and do honor to it with the way you present it. As a writer, you feel there is something awry, and you feel the need to say something about it. I always tell my students that a story is always about trouble. Something's not right. Some tension is there that you need to work over and understand. What usually sends me to write is there's some windshield that needs to be cleaner. What sent me to the Mirabal story is that it needed to be told and told even across language.

The García Girls *begins with a family tree, tracing the family back to the conquistadores. Is that intended to extend the notion of violation to the whole family history? Does it serve a political purpose the same way inserting the characters' names into a list of Trujillo's victims does in* Butterflies?

There is a pretentiousness in any family tree that sets out to prove royal or divine lineage. My García family tree spoofed that kind of pretentiousness by exposing it. I never directly associated that device with the list of names in *Butterflies,* but it does seem to reflect the same sensibility. That list of names in *Butterflies* was a guiding idea as I wrote the novel. I told the publisher from the beginning I wanted those names to be there, because while the novel is primarily the story of three people, there were many, many more people involved.

Is Magdalena's devastating story about the de la Torre family in Butterflies *an indirect commentary on the family in the first novel?*

Those elite families where I came from once owned and controlled everything. The García girls grew up in a time when society was divided mostly into rich and poor. The Dominican Republic was a social and political world very different from the United States. When you come to America, especially America in the sixties, and you become politicized, you see your earlier life so differently, and it no longer has charm for you. That entitlement feels to you like a violation, like a curse. Part of the problem is the pact you make not to tell the story, to remain silent, to behave yourself. Otherwise you're violating their sense of your loyalty to them. The message is not to criticize and not to see things that you do now see. It's a matter of perspective. Maybe my political perspective would have developed even if I never left. There were political women in the Dominican Republic who might have stayed comfortably in their niche but saw things that bothered them and that changed them. But it's hard to change your vision if all around you people see things the same old way.

My sisters and I have talked about the fact that the people who actually raised us were the maids. The maids were the people who loved us, the people who held us, the people we saw all go sleep together six in a single room, where only two of us slept together in much bigger and airier rooms. And they told us their stories. They complained about how unfair things were, about how they had to work hard and late to prepare this party or that. So if you paid attention, that seed of awareness was there, and if you came to the United States, it got watered. The sixties culture of the U.S.A. was cooking with civil rights, women's rights, and anti-war protests. All of us, my mother included, were changed by coming here.

Doesn't Mami in The García Girls *say, "Better [to be] an independent nobody than a high-class houseslave"?*

People ask me, "In *The García Girls,* are you saying it's good to lose your accent?" They think I'm writing a novel with a message. I say, "If I had a message, I'd have written that message." It's more complicated than a message. Some things were lost, but some things were gained. I could never be the woman I am today in my original culture.

In the first section of The García Girls *when Yolanda goes back to the Dominican Republic, she says to herself she's not sure whether she will be returning to the United States. But by the end of that chapter she seems to realize she can't stay in the Dominican Republic.*

Not only that, she's operating by an American code—she is not attuned.

These two kind *campesinos* really are going to help her with the car, and she is thinking, "Inner city, these men are going to rape me or kill me." She's so un-at-home now that she can't even read the signals. She thinks she's tricking them, but she is operating now in English even when she speaks Spanish.

The other day Mami was telling me that Papi, who is probably the most Old World in our family, said, "If we had not come to this country, my girls would not have had all the struggles. They would not have gotten into so many wrong things because they didn't know better." We started with nothing, and none of us had fancy lives. My parents knew from my mother's background to send us to certain schools, but we were always the ones on scholarship. Mami tells Papi, "If we hadn't come, they wouldn't be the women they are today." I think a lot was gained, but it was such a turbulent time to come to America. My women friends and I are the generation that cut the cord. We didn't know what the hell we were doing. So many of my friends have been divorced, and remarried, and divorced, because we just didn't know how to do it. We felt loyalty to our mothers and wanted to honor their way of life, and yet new things were happening, there were new economic pressures. We didn't want to be traditional women, but we didn't know how to put it all together, so we made a bunch of mistakes. We didn't feel right being one extreme or the other, but we didn't know the combinations. And then throw on top of that, the cultural differences. Even American women were confused as to where they were going and not getting it right. As a Latina, there was a feeling you were messing up not only in this culture but in that culture. It was complicated, but I wouldn't give it up. Actually even in the Dominican Republic things are changing socially and economically now.

In The García Girls *you capture very well the sense of the gilded cage, especially with that aunt who says, "Look at me, I'm a queen. My husband has to go to work every day. I can sleep until noon, if I want. I'm going to protest for my rights?"*

To be a valued possession of a man, to be cosseted and taken care of! It's in my poems: "pretty heroines rattling the bars after their happy endings." They lived happily ever after, yeah, right! We don't hear how afterwards maybe they want to get out. I wouldn't want to give up my independence. But because of the way I was raised, when I was being wired inside my head, I didn't know how to do certain things. So I am still afraid to ask, "How much are you going to pay me?" Thank God, I have an agent now who can do that.

Do you think women in general believe it's not polite to inquire about money?
Yeah, or to say what we want in an assertive way. To say, "I don't want to teach

that." It's more like, "I'd rather not teach it, but if you need somebody…" It's all couched in a polite style.

Don't both novels emphasize struggle as a value, as part of engagement in life?

That is the way I live my life. My friends and I were just talking about that. We have lived and struggled to put it all together, and finally all my friends and I are sort of settled down, one way or another. But I don't want to have figured everything out and just play out my good luck. How do I serve now that I've got a certain kind of security? What do I do with it? Do I keep making it bigger? What now? Those are the questions I ask myself. I'm thinking about quitting teaching, not just to have additional time to write but also to devote myself to more political work. To spend some of the year in the Dominican Republic and to find a way of paying back. My husband's first love is agriculture, and he sees so many wrong ways of farming in the Dominican Republic. He has all kinds of ideas about what should be grown and how the crops should be rotated.

Is your husband a farmer?

No, he's an eye doctor. I met him here in Middlebury. I have an eye problem common to people in the tropics, and I went to see him about it. He said, "This problem is unusual for somebody living in Vermont." I said, "I'm not from Vermont. I'm from the Dominican Republic." He said, "I just got back from there." He does volunteer surgery in different countries. It turned out he had been working in the Dominican Republic at a charity clinic run by one of my cousins. So both of us feel like doing something in the Dominican Republic. People say to us, "Oh, you're going to go down to buy some land, some beach property." We don't want beach property. We don't want to be in the tourist community. We want to be in the mountains, in a small village. If it were simply a question of beautiful land, we wouldn't have to leave Vermont. We want to be part of a community, working and doing something there. The question is how to put together a life that makes meaning. I think we are here to do our work, and what we have to do is multifaceted.

You obviously reject the old romantic image of the male writer only interested in his art and willing to sacrifice everyone around him, including his wife.

Oh, definitely. But as with any craft, whether it's teaching or writing, the work does become consuming. It takes time. Sometimes when I ask my students to revise, they say, "God, this is like the third draft," and I say, "Third draft! You haven't even started." For my next class I'm bringing in a letter I got from an editor about a story I wrote. It goes on for five pages—change this, take that out, this sentence doesn't work. I want them to see that it happens to me, too. It's part of the process. But going back to the romantic image of the artist, I do think solitude has to be part of the life of a writer, and one reason is self-protection. Writers are like psychic sponges. That's what one of my therapist friends says. We take things in, so we need to pull back and sort it out. That's true at least for me. I can get overwhelmed, and for me pulling back and writing about experience is the way to sort it out. That doesn't happen much when I am in the Dominican Republic. I almost never write there: there is never any time.

Why is that?

There's always some project we're involved in. The last time I was in the Dominican Republic I went to see Aniana, a woman who was a revolutionary in the Mirabals' time. She was a guerrilla then, and she is still up in the mountains politicizing the *campesinos*. She's an amazing woman in her late sixties. I'm very concerned now, because her life is being threatened by supporters of a multinational mining company that wants to come in and do mining and pollute the five most important rivers that provide water for a large area of the country. She's got the *campesinos* organized against it; it could be another Chiapas. They've threatened to burn her house down. I wrote an essay about her, and articles to publicize what she's doing.

But to get back to why it's so difficult to write when I'm there . . . Last time I was visiting Aniana, and there is no electricity in the mountains where she lives, and my life was totally involved with the *campesino* group. Sometimes at night I would get inside the car, turn on the lights, and write. I just felt so overwhelmed that if I got into bed, without first sorting things out, my mind could not relax. All I knew to do was to put things down on paper, to get hold of them, I guess. Aniana lives in this little house that is the center of the *campesino* movement. There is a man named Patricio who has taken on the job of being the caretaker there. He would stay up with me, poor man, although he was almost dropping off. I would say, "Patricio, go to bed." I was feeling the need to write. And he would say, "I have to keep you company." I would tell him, "This is something I have to do alone." But he didn't feel right about that; it didn't have to do with gender. He couldn't believe that someone could be comfortable in isolation. The few times I took a book somewhere, people would come and talk to me. Reading was a sign you were unoccupied.

I tell my husband that if we do go to live down there, I will have to find a way to combine the writing and the active parts of my life. Otherwise I may go crazy. Or maybe it will just be wonderful. Maybe I'll turn into this woman of action. That has always been my private other—the life of total action. I mean, I'm in love with Aniana. This woman has been *en la lucha* for forty years. She even left her children behind with her mother to join the guerrillas.

So she is like a contemporary Mirabal sister?

Absolutely.

Is this private other, the life of total action, what drew you to write about the Mirabals? Did you identify with one of the sisters in particular?

Perhaps Minerva, the one known as the ringleader. People say that Minerva was a heroine, and the other two were martyrs, but I don't buy that. I think there are different ways to be a heroine, and courage comes out of many different sources. Hers came out of ideology. Patria's came out of her religion. Wherever it comes from, there isn't just one form. And the youngest, what started her was the romance of it. María Teresa moves from the romance of finding her husband in the underground to having to come to terms with the grim reality of a torture prison. She learns that *la lucha* is real, it's scary, it's not a love story that we can say ended happily. Sometimes I feel my life up here in Vermont, working with language, is too removed and too precious and unreal. My life while I'm in the Dominican Republic provides a balance. But mostly I consider myself blessed. I feel when I'm writing that I've found the work I'm meant to do. The birds sing, the trees grow, the rain rains, and the sun shines, and writing is what that set of genes and chemistry that is Julia Alvarez *does*.

Is the gringa Dominicana *in* Butterflies *a somewhat mocking self-portrait?*

Maybe. When I was in the mountains I got all those *campesinos* to do aerobics, and I tried to get Aniana to eat right and do exercises. That was my American sensibility kicking in. What interests me most is the border between cultures, those combinations that are strange and wonderful and painful and conflicting. For example, you're wearing your *asabache* on your bra and at the same time you're taking your SAT. Whose God do you serve? But I like those combinations, when things are topsy-turvy and you're forced to look at them in a different way. When I travel in the Dominican Republic, and I go into a *comedor* with my husband, that's already weird for a woman to be doing.

Is your new novel, ¡Yo!, *a continuation of the García family story?*

Some pre-publication reviews have seen it that way, but it's not really. You do find out about the other sisters and the family, but it is focused on Yolanda, and it's also very much a novel about writing and about how everybody is a storyteller. It suggests that the idea of the artist as an elite who has exclusive rights to the story is wrong. There are many versions. And part of the novel is what price the people in an artist's life have to pay. We're always hearing about the anguish and the pain of the artist but not about the people who have to put up with the artist—people who have loved her or tried to love her, and others who did not like her very much. Or people who have trusted her and then found parts of their lives in her fiction.

How has it been for you? Do your sisters feel that they or their stories have been taken over by you?

It has not been easy. What is interesting to me is that I've always written this autobiographical way, and it was never a secret. Who did I send all my stories to? My sisters. One of my sisters has this big cloth pocketbook with all my stories rolled up in it, and she takes one out when she is on the toilet, or used to. But suddenly, when they're published, there is this outcry: "You misrepresented me, people are going to think I'm anorexic." And I would say, "It's fiction," but it was enough like my own life that they were afraid of exposure. My feeling is that if the writer is not mean-spirited and makes an attempt to change or mask the facts, then the problem is one of vanity and control and the complaints are really about something other than a violation of privacy. I chose to write about the Mirabal sisters; that story has nothing to do with me directly, but who I am and my background are part of why I chose them. I, too, come from an all-girl family, and I'm sure my sisters would tell you they found themselves there, in something Minerva did or something Patria said, even if I didn't think about them when I was writing the novel.

By now, all my sisters have come to terms with what I write, and I think finally are very proud of me. My mother, on the other hand, didn't think I should write a book with a bedroom scene between a man and a woman. My mother keeps saying to me, "Why can't you write a book the way other people write books, nice books?" But then she thinks Eleanor Roosevelt's grandson was disrespectful when he described his grandmother, in his memoir, as a plain woman. I agree with Dorothy Allison, who said to tell the story all the way through is an act of love. I also agree with her that fiction is much kinder and more compassionate than facts, because the writer isn't out to expose but rather to make meaning. You have to love your characters to write about them, which doesn't mean you have to like them or agree with them or want them to do the things they do. But you have to love them. Otherwise, the characters will be flat. Now with my new book about to appear, some nights I wake up in dread. I don't think I'll have any trouble with my sisters. Maybe Mami. My father has been golden. He's always been very supportive. And I was most worried about him with the first book.

In The García Girls *you have first-person sections and third-person sections, but by the end of the novel it seems that Yolanda is telling the story, whether it is first-person or third-person, and that she dominates the book, even though she is only one of the four sisters.*

It reminds me in that way of *Love Medicine*, where Albertine is the framing personality even though the novel goes far afield. Or *Monkeys* by Susan Minot, where there's the sensibility of the one who is the writer, which is a kind of string that goes through the novel. Even though you hear different points of view within the family, she is the one listening. With *The García Girls* I wrote using whatever point of view seemed right for that character at the time, for telling that story. It's the same in the new book.

What is the chronology of this recent novel?

It starts out in the present, with the sisters really pissed off at Yolanda about this book she's written. They plot how they're going to get a chance to tell the story. Then we go to the beginning of Yo's life. The mother opens the book, and the father closes the book. In between we hear about her life from childhood to present day.

Is this new novel also being published by Algonquin Books?

Oh, yes, I love my editor there, Shannon Ravenel. She's an old-time editor who does line editing and is truly interested in your growth as a writer. It might be funny to some people, here I am a Latina with this Southern woman for an editor, but we have so much in common. I think there must be something about the South, and family, and that kind of storytelling culture that is akin to Latin culture.

So you're happy with your agent and your editor?

They're two more *sisters*. Shannon and I were discussing something about the novel, and she finally said, "It's up to you—this is your book." I said, "But, Shannon, it's *our* book." She really listens in a way that I trust. I wrote an essay, which the editor of this prestigious publication was ready to take. It would have been good to have it appear, especially with the new novel coming out. I showed it to Shannon and she said, "I just don't think it's very good, Julia. I wouldn't put it out there." I knew what she was saying, there was a glibness in the voice and she caught on to that. Sometimes I am so full of self-doubt, she has to say this is *good*, or not. I trust her sensibility.

What are your current plans? Are you already thinking about your next book?

These essays I've been working on might lead to a book, but frankly I'm not sure where they may be going. As I mentioned, I'm considering giving up my position at Middlebury. Because of my immigrant mentality, I'm not sure I'll be able to do that—give up my hard-earned tenure. But it's more than that. It would also mean giving up my students, my way of being in touch with the next generation, since I don't have any children of my own. It would also be giving up my place in a *community* in this country. And since it's Middlebury, my alma mater, it would mean saying good-bye to a part of my life that has been very enriching. I just don't know.

Andre Dubus

"Passion Is Better"

We spoke with Andre Dubus at his home in Haverhill, Massachusetts, forty miles north of Boston, near the New Hampshire border. Haverhill (pronounced "Hayvril" by natives) was known as "Shoe City" in better economic times, but now the red-brick factories that line the Merrimack River as it runs through town are mostly deserted. For Dubus's characters who reside there, life in Haverhill is often a discouraging prospect. "Our city," says one, "is no place for those drawn to suicide."

There is little depressing, however, about the rolling, forested countryside surrounding the town. Dubus lives in the country, though still within the city limits, just down the road from a llama ranch. A transplanted Cajun, he has called this part of New England home for more than twenty years.

Dubus has been a Marine Corps captain, a college teacher, a Guggenheim Fellow, and a member of the Iowa Writers Workshop. He is a devoted follower of the Boston Red Sox, and he is a Catholic who attends daily mass regularly.

In 1986, he was struck by a car and critically injured while trying to help a stranded motorist on Route 93 between Boston and Haverhill. He lost a leg as a result of the accident. Below he talks about how his injury has affected his writing.

Although he has turned more to nonfiction lately, short stories continue to be his love. "We short-story writers," he once observed, "are spared some of the major temptations: we don't make money for ourselves or anybody else, so the people who make money from writers leave us alone. . . . There is no one to sell out to, there is no one to hurry a manuscript for; our only debt is to ourselves, and to those stories that speak to us from wherever they live until we write them."

Dubus has published six books of short fiction, much of it collected in *Selected Stories* (1988). He is also the author of two novels, *The Lieutenant* (1965) and *Voices from the Moon* (1984), and a collection of essays, *Broken Vessels* (1991). His latest book of stories is *Dancing in the Dark* (1996).

He has received numerous grants and prizes, including, in 1988, a MacArthur Fellowship, or so-called genius grant. In 1991, he won the PEN/Malamud Award for Short Fiction.

You don't have much use for the image of the writer as the lone, suffering genius. What is your attitude toward the work you do?

It's a vocation. When it was hard for me to do anything after the accident, I kept trying to write, and the reason I gave myself—and I think it was real— was that God gave me this gift and I have to do it even though I don't always want to. It's like a bird can sing. It sings no matter how homely it may sound. That sense of vocation, by the way, is something my characters often lack. Peter Jackman ["The Winter Father" and other stories] started out to be an actor, but he abandoned it for the comparative security of working as a disc jockey. He lacked the courage necessary to pursue his vocation. It bothers me when people sell out.

Was there ever a danger you would do that?

I worried about it when I was younger. I knew I'd have to get a job to support the writing. But I've always tried to keep my desk clean, so I never felt like I had to pay a bill with the writing. It's hard enough to write without that financial pressure. I could never make a living as a writer, I only make a living because I write. People have given me jobs and grants because of my writing.

When I was in my late twenties, I was a Marine captain out in Washington state, and I've never had as good an income as that, until the MacArthur grant. But my first wife and I decided I would resign from the Corps anyway. I remember we were sitting in the kitchen sharing a bottle of Budweiser. I was subscribing then to the *Saturday Review of Literature,* and I was looking at the pages in the back, thinking maybe I could work for Sears and Roebuck in Australia or something. My wife said, call Iowa. I had a friend from the Marine Corps who taught there. So we called him, he spoke to R. V. Cassill, and they decided to let me in. We went in January and they gave us $180 a month until September when I started a $240-a-month assistantship. We were scared about leaving the security of the Marine Corps, but not terrified.

How was it at Iowa?

It wasn't bad. Everybody was broke. Things were tough, but our kids never even knew we were poor. We got food from the state, my wife made some plain meals, we all sold blood. It wasn't a big thing. But then you look back and realize a lot of people couldn't make that leap. Hell, you might die of an aneurism tomorrow. So you should do what you want. Especially white, educated people, for Christ's sake. It's not like we were born on the wrong side of the pigmentation border. I think it's just awful to want to be something, a lawyer, say, and settle for less. Or to want to be a mother and settle for less, if it's fear that's keeping you back. I mean, you're going to be afraid anyway, you can't avoid it. I'm scared all the time. But, boy, it ain't dull.

How has the accident affected your writing?

It took it away for a long time. Fiction has been very hard. You never know what's going to happen. I had a whole notebook of ideas, and I used to say I had enough ideas for the rest of my life, because I write slowly. The notebook is still there, but the notes seem written by someone else. They don't have any meaning for me. Only in the last year or so have I been getting new ideas for stories.

I really don't understand the effects of my injury enough to understand why the gift of writing left for so long. Although I was trying to write, nothing was happening. I talked to a psychologist about it. He said it had to do with severe shock. Now I'm just beginning to comprehend how deeply affected I was by the accident. I was a little nuts for a couple years. Then last year I managed to write a story and got back some of the processes I used to use. It's taken a great deal of patience. I've had to learn everything over. That doesn't make complete sense to me, because I didn't have a head injury. But then I did get hit by a fast-moving vehicle and had to have twelve operations. Also, the things I used to take for granted, like eating, were a challenge for a long time. Just in the last few weeks I've felt on top of getting through a day. Fatigue has been a great problem. This morning I got up at 8:00 o'clock and went to 9:00 o'clock mass, and I came home, made breakfast, and I wrote. I used not to be able to do that. By the time I got home from mass or ate breakfast, I'd have to lie down again. This morning I started a novella. I think I did. I pray, I pray.

Do you want to talk about it?

No, no way. I'll tell you why. Hemingway was right. If you talk about it, you ruin it. That's true for life as well as for writing. That's why, when men mature, you don't hear them talk about their girl friends anymore. It's an instinct. If you talk about it, it's gone. Once in college I had an idea for a story, a good story. I told it to my girl friend one night, the whole plot. She cried, it was so sad. We smooched. And I never wrote the story. I told that to a friend of mine recently, and he said, "It's a good thing you didn't get laid, Andre, because you never would have published a book."

You said once that to write well you have to "keep things tactile." What did you mean?

I have to become the character I'm writing about, feel who that person is. My difficulty in doing that lately may explain why I've written mainly essays since the accident. It's been frustrating, like being a designated hitter. It's good to have essays to fall back on, but stories are what I want to make, though I've never yet made the kind I wanted to. I have to get tactile. I have to work through a character's senses. I have to know what she feels like drinking a glass of cool lemonade, what it tastes like. How she feels when she's nervous. What she feels about food, whether it's something she looks forward to all day or it's just something to consume for nutrition.

I read what Oliver Sacks said about Robert DeNiro after the movie *Awakenings*. He said DeNiro doesn't know something until he can feel it in his flesh. I was working on a novella called *Adultery* many years ago and I came to a time in the story when the main character was very sad. I tried to figure out exactly how she felt. I closed my eyes and I remembered something—I don't know what—something that happened to me that hurt me in the way she was hurt. I could actually feel where the pain was then—right under the heart. And I could use that to write the story.

It sounds a little like method acting.

I used to say so myself. But I've heard method actors criticized for getting too much into themselves, for becoming too self-absorbed. If so, that's not what I'm talking about in writing. Writing is getting in touch with somebody else's feelings. In the same way, a child learns empathy from touching a hot stove. Later he sees another child touch the stove and he says, "Oh, I know what that feels like." Writing uses the senses in an imaginative way to connect with other people. It's not primarily a matter of getting in touch with your own subconscious. Finally, I think writing, in a strange way, connects not with the subconscious but with some mystery that's floating above us, like pollen or snow, something a lot more eternal than one person's subconscious.

You once said, "I always find fiction taking turns that I have not foreseen, and do not understand, but I feel to be inevitable and right. When that doesn't happen the story dies. . . . All my stories have changed in the writing." What has been the most surprising or unexpected change, either in a particular story or in your work generally?

Endings always surprise me. I never trust anyone who says they know where they are going with a story. I tell my students outlines are useless. An outline has nothing to do with writing. You just have to open yourself to things as they happen and hope some truth comes of it. You can't get the truth if you have an architectural plan. You have to say, "I don't know anything, I want to know what these characters will do in this situation." So the surprise for me is whatever I learn.

If you're not opening yourself to the subconscious in those situations, what are you opening yourself to?

Life, I hope. And if my own subconscious gets involved that's fine, but it's not my aim. I'm not really interested in finding out what I think about something. I don't believe that's a good reason to write. I'm more interested in finding out what my characters think, what they might do, what they might become. Thomas Williams, who died last fall, said writers write books because they have questions and they never get the answers they want. It's true that my characters sometimes do things I don't want them to, give me answers I don't approve of. I want to say, "Stop! Don't do that!"

I don't mean to get rid of the subconscious, I don't mean that at all. But what I try to get into is my soul. I believe that my soul connects with all of life. Swedenborg held that everything in the visible world is represented in the individual soul, every force and every breath of nature has a counterpart in the body. It's all one. I believe that.

You were once quoted as saying you believe in "absolute honesty . . . in not being afraid of what your characters might discover for you." Which of your characters discovered something for you that you might have been afraid to look at?

I wanted to avoid writing "Rose," the story of a woman who is the silent partner of a husband who beats up the children. I didn't want to write about it. Finally I had to. My wife said later I was messed up the whole time. But as I heard Rose speak, telling her story, the real truth for me was that she was redeemed, she just didn't know it. She had been made to feel powerless by forces that were too much for her—hard work, hard living, no future. But finally she did the right thing, she defied her husband, she saved her children.

The handling of point of view in that story is very unusual in your work. The first-person narrator is self-conscious and dramatized, tells us his age, that he lost a child in a car accident, et cetera. And the reader is overtly drawn into the story with sentences like "Don't you remember?" and "Imagine." Could you talk about these choices?

I think I developed the self-conscious narrative voice because the idea of harming children is so horrible to me that I could not write about it more directly, from the point of view, say, of the person doing it or even of the person who was letting it happen. So finally I decided to use somebody who wasn't there, who'd heard the story from Rose years later and could filter it. I really got the idea from Conrad, and for my narrator's name I tried to think of an acronym for Marlow. I never did get a name for him though. He wouldn't tell me his name, but I could hear him speaking very clearly.

You've written two novels, and you once said of the first [The Lieutenant] it should have been tightened up. You don't think of yourself as a novelist, do you?

I really don't understand how novelists' minds work. Nadine Gordimer says, in that great introduction to her selected stories, that a novel is something you stake out a piece at a time while a short story you can see whole. I'll bet that doesn't mean she can see the endings though. I don't know. I'd

love it if what I used to tell my students about Chekhov were said of me—
but I don't think it's true. I'd tell them Chekhov never wrote a novel because
he didn't have to, it's all there in his stories.

*You've praised Chekhov for the compassion he shows his characters, suggest-
ing this is the primary source of his greatness. How do you view your own relationship to your characters?*

It changes. Sometimes I'm a concerned father, sometimes I'm a repulsed
bystander. I remember writing *The Pretty Girl* [a novella] and coming to the
last scene, with man, woman, and gun all in the same room. Sitting there,
mulling over the possibilities, I was really hoping Polly and Ray could get
together. I listened to Ray talk and I thought he was making some sense, and
I didn't want Polly to shoot him, but she did, and that made me very sad. I
think that's why I wrote a final section from the viewpoint of Ray's grieving
brother, because I had to give expression to that sadness. As a writer or as a
reader, what pulls me back, makes me want to keep going in a story, is caring about the people. And that's true from Elmore Leonard to Nadine
Gordimer. Elmore Leonard's pull for me is his people. He's really not big on
plot. He's a character man.

*Your characters are often very passionate people, almost Russian in the depth
and extremity of their feelings. Why is that?*

I don't know. I do know that, while I was writing *Adultery*, I was reading
Love and Will [Rollo May], which makes the point that it's our awareness of
our mortality that causes our passions to be so strong. And I was working
with that theory in writing *Adultery*. I was also very lonely at the time. I think
loneliness is connected with that sense of mortality.

*You quoted, in another interview, a character from Jean Anouilh's The Re-
hearsal: "Practical. Every time someone says that word I know they're getting
ready to do something bad." Is that what you believe?*

Oh, yeah, it's so-called practicality that leads to war. Passion is better.

You begin The Pretty Girl *with a passage from The Apocalypse: "But because
thou art lukewarm, and neither cold nor hot, I am about to vomit thee out of
my mouth."*

Yes, Polly's sin is not that she's pretty but that she's lazy. That's why she
doesn't know what's wrong with her life. What's wrong with her life is that
there's nothing she loves and wants. She's passive. But don't get me wrong, I
love Polly, or I couldn't have spent so much time on her. I like Ray, too, in
that story. I love them all. I thought there was one thing Ray knew that she
didn't. He knew how to live, he knew the way he felt. He knew how to go out
into the world. Polly needs what a liberal arts education can give. She needs

some historical and spiritual connection to the world. She's got to stop being just a pretty girl.

How did The Pretty Girl *evolve?*

I wanted to write something suspenseful, a chase story. I actually spent some time trying to decide the gender of the person to be chased. At first, it was going to be a man, but then I thought, who would care if a man was being threatened by another man? The reader would say, "So, he should get a gun, take karate, lift weights. He's a grown man. Let him shut up and take care of business." For this reason, I think people who picket movies that supposedly exploit women don't understand what's really going on. It's simply more interesting, more frightening if the person in the harrowing situation is biologically weaker, if it's a woman. There are probably shabbier reasons, too, for what goes on in those movies, but at the same time we shouldn't overlook the obvious.

I told a woman friend, who is a mother, that being in a wheel chair has made me very frightened for my children, because I don't feel able to protect them physically any longer. I was always used to taking care of my kids. But now if some guy with pornographic and murderous intentions came along and grabbed my little girl there would be nothing I could do but watch. And this friend of mine said, "Yes, mothers feel that way a lot." Anyway the character of Polly grew, in part, out of my attempt to capture a feeling of vulnerability which is more obviously a part of women's experience than men's.

In that story, the sections that are from Ray's perspective are in the first person, while the Polly sections are in third person, with the effect that the reader isn't permitted to get quite as close to her. Why did you do that?

Except for very short stories I've never felt comfortable handling a woman's voice. Ray's voice was easier. He's a strange guy who does some terrible things, including raping his wife, but I felt I could understand why he did it. His anger is not about the past but the present. He can't stand the idea that he's separated from his wife and she's happy without him. Knowing she's happy without him is what really gets to him.

Your fiction often dwells on the differences between men and women. Joe, the priest in Adultery, *claims there's even a moral difference. Men tend to commit practical sins, he says, women instinctual ones. Partly as a result, he thinks, women feel less burdened by their transgressions.*

That makes sense to me. But women now are getting a lot more like men. They're dying sooner, too. Women didn't used to get strokes and heart attacks and lung cancer in the numbers they do now. I think it started when they began commuting and telling lies all day. That so-called practical male world out there is mostly lies. It bothers me to see women joining that world, which I've resisted joining all my life. I think I live more like a woman than a lot of women do. I'm not blaming them either. I think they got sold a bill of goods. A friend of mine, a writer, Marian Novak, said what really should have happened with the women's movement was that, instead of all the women carrying briefcases, the men should have learned to do domestic things. And boy, I agree with that. That's where the truth is. You feed a child, that's a sacrament. You sell a piece of real estate, I'm not sure what that is. It's a transaction.

You once said about the lack of understanding between men and women, "One of the first reasons is all the stuff a boy goes through to feel like a man, and what a girl goes through to feel like a woman. Everything that goes into this process only increases the isolation between them. I think that's why we're all essentially lonely." Do you think this situation has been changing, with the sexual revolution and the women's movement?

I guess I'm getting old and cranky, because I think things are changing for the worse. I think boys, in particular, have lost their rites of passage. We should have universal conscription at eighteen. Those who don't want to serve in the military should work with Habitat for Humanity or the Peace Corps, anything that would help teach them that they belong to a community of human beings. When I was young—whether you were an athlete or a lawyer or a bully or an English major—you had to become a man to get a girl. You either got out of high school and got a job or you went to college. Mark Costello said to a class of mine once at Bradford College that in the fifties every college man wanted three things: a diploma, a commission in the armed forces, and a marriage—preferably all in the same week. My friends who are now in their thirties and forties never went through that, and they really are different in the world. I think my generation understood that when a man loves a woman he changes his life for that woman. I think there are a lot of boy-men out there, dull boy-men with expensive haircuts. Mannequins!

You're a Catholic. Flannery O'Connor and Walker Percy addressed the difficulties facing a writer whose audience does not share his religious beliefs. Percy, for one, believed "the old words of grace" had lost their credibility. You, on the other hand, often write in explicitly religious terms about faith and the sacraments.

I got tired of concealing my Catholicism as a writer. Finally, I thought, to hell with it, I'm going to write about Catholics for a while. I figured, for one thing, if I had the sacraments to draw on as subject matter it would make the writing that much richer. The Catholic religion intensely interests me, and I like writing about characters who sometimes talk to God. As Flannery O'Connor said, it adds a dimension. When I write about people who don't have God, I feel as if there's something missing. Chekhov wrote that if you don't believe in something greater than yourself, all thoughts, all feelings, everything becomes just symptoms. Chekhov was not a man of faith, but he sensed something out there bigger than himself, whatever it was. If you don't have that, then anything, Chekhov said—a head cold, the screech of an owl—will throw you into a dither. This is, in fact, the history of modern literature, modern life: people desperately applying first aid to their symptoms.

You seem to like situations in which your characters are forced to make moral choices. Do ideas for stories sometimes come to you in the form of ethical dilemmas?

Yeah, I've been interested in moral choices for as long as I can remember. I'm sure that's because of the Catholic schools. I recall in the fifth grade—I think I was ten—I went to see *13 Rue Madeleine* with James Cagney. I asked the Brother at the school the next day about the cyanide Jimmy means to take if they catch him. See, he was operating behind enemy lines, and he knew when D-Day was going to be, so he had the cyanide to swallow so he wouldn't give away any secrets under torture. At ten, I thought that was just a fascinating moral quandary. So I asked the Brother, "Would it be wrong, would it be a mortal sin, to kill yourself in those circumstances?" He said, "Yes." I said, "Why is that any different from pushing a child away from a train when you know the train is going to hit *you*?" He said, "Because it is." So, in college, I asked my ethics teacher. He said, "If all human beings who were tortured broke under the strain, then you'd have to take the cyanide to save the lives of other human beings. But throughout human history we have examples of people who were tortured and didn't break. So that's why it would be wrong to take the cyanide—you can't play God in matters of life and death. You have to do what you know to be the right thing and trust in Him."

Your own characters, of course, do not always decide moral issues on such theologically correct grounds. For example, Adultery *ends with Edith's resolve to divorce Hank. We're encouraged, moreover, to see this as a positive thing. Do you feel uneasy about that as a Catholic?*

No, I think she does a great thing in ending that marriage. Along the way she's learned to change her patterns, she decides she's not going to be treated badly by a cheating husband anymore. So the fact is, that was a happy ending.

In "A Father's Story," do you think Luke does the right thing in covering up for his daughter who has killed a young man in a hit-and-run?

The moral right thing? No. He behaves as a father protecting his daughter. That's nature. If it had been a son rather than a daughter, Luke would have acted differently. A father with his daughter, that's an especially charged relationship.

He doesn't require that the daughter take responsibility for the terrible thing she's done. He seems to take her sin upon himself.

Yes, and his life changes as a result. He doesn't feel as close to God or to the priest who is his friend, or anybody, because ethically he knows he did the wrong thing. But when push came to shove he threw out ethics and went with his feelings, with the overpowering urge to protect his daughter.

That's his mistake?

I think he should have called the police, put his daughter in the car, and gone back with her to the scene of the accident.

Aren't you contradicting what you said earlier about passion being better than reason?

Personally, I like passion, but it causes me to make a lot of mistakes. The best thing is probably to develop instincts you can trust. But that requires a lot of moral harmony inside. I'll tell you how I got the idea for that story. A woman from Haverhill was killed driving down 495 when a car swerved in front of her and she hit a tractor trailer trying to avoid it. The driver of the car that caused the accident just kept going. The family of the dead woman hired a private investigator to find him. That made me wonder: what is that driver's moral responsibility if the victim is already dead? I got my answer by writing the story. I think there's a moral responsibility to give the bereaved family someone to blame, someone to hate. I think Luke knows that, but he sees his daughter crying there in his kitchen and he just has to help her get out of this mess. It isn't the right thing.

In reviewing your novella Voices from the Moon, *Updike said that "one of the [story's] theological implications is that in seeking relief from solitude we sin, and fall inevitably into pain. . . . So it is with a distinct sense of loss that the reader sees [Richie], at the end, turn toward a human comforter." Do you agree with this reading?*

That's not the way I read it, although it's true that our inability to live in isolation causes us all sorts of trouble. Before, Richie had always been solitary and at peace with it. Now his life is about to get a lot more complicated, for better or worse. I feel good about him at the end. I don't know whether he'll follow through with his intention to become a priest or not. I do know he's about to kiss that girl.

Whether or not you agree with Updike's interpretation of the ending, isn't it true that he describes an important tension in the lives of your characters? They seek love from other people, but in doing so the moral laws they try to live by are inevitably compromised. Isn't this Richie's situation? Isn't it also Harry's predicament in "If They Knew Yvonne"? Harry accepts his sister's view that the church isn't very smart about sex. Yet he still wants a priest's absolution for his sexual transgressions.

Yes, and he may never resolve that conflict. He's learned one thing by the end of the story though: he's learned moral responsibility. And when I say "moral" I'm talking not about obedience to law but the ability to love. Harry knows finally that lovemaking is not a matter of putting meat in meat, it's a sacramental act, with two human beings involved.

There's that quotation you use from John's gospel: "I do not pray that You take them from the world but that You keep them from evil." What does that mean to you?

It reminds me of Richie's view of things in *Voices from the Moon*. ["He saw the world as a tangle of men and women and boys and girls, thick and wildly growing as [these] woods; some embraced and some struggled, while all of them reached upward for air and rain and sun. He must somehow move through it, untouched by it, but in it too, toward God."] It means to take part in the world: to love, to make love and be loving. But it also means to do what's right—what's truly right for your daughter, say, instead of what feels right at the time, which is how Luke decides things in "A Father's Story." To have that sort of integrity requires a combination of judgment and experience and feeling. It requires a sense of historical direction. The trouble with a lot of people is that they seem to live as if the world began when they were born. Most of my students at Bradford knew frighteningly little about life, about history. The things they would say sometimes! It was like listening to somebody from another planet. Where were you for the past twenty years? I'd wonder. Where were your parents, your teachers, your community? Didn't anybody tell you anything? This is the main reason I want to live a long time, to keep telling my two young daughters everything I know, even as I realize I don't know anything.

Lori says to Hank at the end of Finding a Girl in America, *"We're not going to have American children." What's an American child?*

Secular, materialistic. It's not a very spiritual country we live in; it's a scary place to raise children. We're getting more and more greedy, and I deeply believe that if the country is going to be based on greed and selfishness, it doesn't really deserve to survive. The skeptical response to that is, "Well, you writers are always disgruntled and largely unpatriotic anyway. America's not so bad." But I look at the front page of the *Boston Globe*—eighty thousand hungry children in Massachusetts. Hungry! Anybody who looks away from that is a fool. What did Chekhov say in "Gooseberries"? Every happy man should have a hungry man banging on his door every night. I agree. Any man who is happy is a fool. True, ours may be the best country anyone has ever come up with. Still there are eighty thousand children hungry in Massachusetts. Twenty million in the country as a whole.

I think the main problem with the United States is that we lost God and we lost religion and we didn't replace God and religion with anything of value. I was just reading this column in the *National Catholic Reporter* by Demetria Martinez. Her main point is that ideologies arise when people have no firm faith to hold onto. Life is its own meaning, she says, it doesn't need an "-ism" to explain it. "When religion leaves the land," she writes, "it leaves ecstatic dancing and prophetic chant and life becomes increasingly a matter of verbal exhortation and moralistic rhetoric, in which people are told what to hear and believe."

If life doesn't need an "-ism" to explain it, does that include Catholicism?

Sure. True religion, whatever name it goes by, is believing that God is in everyone and treating everyone accordingly. Or there's Edith's idea in *Adultery:* she decides we've got to start treating each other like we're dying. That's the same idea as in that wonderful movie and novel, *Bang the Drum Slowly.* As sentimental as it may look in a movie, it's true. If you start treating everybody like they're dying, you start treating them better. I get better treatment now in a wheel chair. When I was just a biped, I didn't get nearly as many doors held for me, nearly as many offers of help. People do have compassion, but it doesn't get awakened often. What we've lost is the training— because it does take training—to love even the unlovable among us, not just the obviously and acceptably disabled, like somebody in a wheel chair, but the harder cases, too. Dorothy Day said one of her biggest troubles was in trying to love the rich. Or how about the powerful? How do you love them?

It sounds like for you the purpose of religious training is the better treatment of other people, developing this loving feeling for others.

I didn't say "feeling" though, did I? I'm not sure feelings are all that reliable. Compassion, that's the thing. I'm not sure compassion is a feeling. It's a direction, a condition, an action. You can't hope for a feeling of love for all people. That sounds like you're stoned or something. And the fact is, a lot of jerks show up looking for help at the shelters. Pains in the neck. Dealing with such people can be very trying. I read where Dorothy Day was about to unload on one of them one night down in the Bronx. A co-worker said, "Hold your temper, Dorothy." And Dorothy said, "I hold more temper in ten minutes than you've held in your life." I find that very human. So you can't love everybody, but you can make the right choices to help them in spite of that.

"I'm fascinated by the mystics," you once said, "those who transcend all that drowns me. The mystics remain in harmony with the earth and their fellow human beings and, yet, are above it all as they enjoy union with God." Do any of your characters approach this mystical state? Most of them, even the most religious, seem very much a part of the world.

Yes, I think that's true. It's very difficult to get in touch with that spiritual dimension—but it's there. It's said the Virgin Mary told those children she's been appearing to in Yugoslavia that when you pray for someone an angel sits on that person's shoulder. Isn't that beautiful? I have no trouble believing that, quite literally. I've had some strange experiences since the loss of my leg. Sometimes I feel as if it's come back. I feel like it's there. A doctor might say it's phantom sensations, a matter of the nerves getting disrupted or something. But the truth is, in some mystical way, the leg has returned to me at times. Once when it happened I asked my wife to touch the bedsheet where the leg would have been. She did, and it was warm. I'll tell you something else, my stump has "empathy." When I hear about somebody else's pain, the stump will start to hurt. William James said, where the spiritual world is concerned, we human beings are at about the same level of awareness as domestic pets. We think we have a sense of what's going on, but there's this whole other thing happening all the time just beyond our comprehension. Sometimes we catch glimpses of it, that's all.

Jayne Anne Phillips
The Mystery of Language

Jayne Anne Phillips began her writing career as a poet and published two books of stories, *Sweethearts* (1976) and *Counting* (1978), with small presses before her first commercial success, *Black Tickets,* which burst on the scene in 1979, when she was only twenty-seven years old. *Black Tickets* was praised for its richly sensuous language and unsentimental but deeply emotional stories. Critics applauded both the edgy, hallucinatory portraits of desperate, often violent characters and the generally longer, more realistic stories about ordinary, middle-class families.

Five years later, *Machine Dreams,* her first novel, told the story of the Hampson family—Mitch, Jean, their daughter, Danner, and their son, Billy—concentrating on the years between World War II and the Vietnam War. Once again, Phillips's powerful prose received critical acclaim. Reviewers and critics praised her ability to tell a gripping story, to evoke different time periods with visceral exactness, to provide political and social analysis, and to create vivid characters, each possessing memories and individual dreams. As one critic observed, "That *Machine Dreams* would be among the year's best written novels was easy to predict."

Fast Lanes (1987), her second major collection of short stories, further explored the themes of discontinuity and historical and personal isolation that are often at the heart of her earlier work. Several critics compared *Fast Lanes* to the work of the Beat generation, and one critic called Phillips "a feminized Kerouac."

In 1994, a decade after *Machine Dreams,* Phillips's much-anticipated second novel, *Shelter,* appeared. Set in 1963 in a West Virginia camp for girls, *Shelter* tells the story of four girls—Lenny, Alma, Delia, and Cap—and their relationships with Buddy, the son of the camp cook, Buddy's ex-convict stepfather, Carmody, and Parson, a holy man who lives nearby. Each chapter is an interior monologue of one of four characters—Lenny, Alma, Parson, or Buddy. The origins and effects of evil, the loss of childhood innocence, and the awakening of sexuality are among the central themes of this complex

Jerry Bauer

psychological and religious novel. Unlike *Machine Dreams,* which spanned several decades and closely mirrored political and historical developments in American culture, *Shelter* is internal, spiritual, and mythic. Its thematic and linguistic richness suggests Phillips continues to be one of our most interesting and unpredictable writers.

In the following interview, conducted in a restaurant near her home in Newton, Massachusetts, she talks about how and why she writes, the roots of her material, and the role of memory and mystery in her work.

How and when did you begin to write?

I started writing as a child, and then I stopped for quite a while. I started again in high school, doing just poetry. I thought of myself as a poet for a number of years, through college, and I was writing poems and publishing poems in various little magazines. Then I began writing prose fictions that were, I suppose, modeled after Rimbaud and Baudelaire. They were not event-oriented, yet they told a kind of story. They were extremely compressed. They were written like poems in the sense that the lines were stressed in a particular way, and my total attention was given to the language. Little by little, I began to break away from the restrictions of poetic form, and the first story I wrote that I consider a more conventional story was "El Paso," which is a series of monologues.

It sounds like you began publishing almost right away.

Just in college publications and small press magazines. One of my first publications was in *Truck* magazine, run by David Wilke. Then my first book, *Sweethearts,* was published by Wilke's Truck Press. That was a good association from the beginning, because he did very beautiful books. He would only do five hundred copies, and he paid in copies. It was a good way to break into publishing.

Did you think of writing in connection with publication from very early on?

Not really. I suppose I wanted to publish, but I didn't think of myself as publishing in magazines my parents might see or in magazines that people read. Writing was a secret thing for me and that was one reason I felt such freedom. I felt I could write about anything. I was insulated because the literary world was totally separate from the world of my family and my hometown and anyone who might have any judgment about it.

Have you maintained that sense of secrecy and separation?

That was important during the formative years of my relationship to writing. Now it's different and more complicated because I think your feelings about your primal family are very different from the feelings you have about your children. I felt I had a right to use whatever I experienced in my original family because our identities and boundaries were so permeable. I feel much more protective about my children; whatever I write that has seeds in the experience of raising them is going to be transformed a great deal more than what I have written about my own early years.

Did you get any encouragement to write during your childhood?

What encouragement I remember came from my mother. She was a reading teacher, though she failed to instill a love of words in all her children. She got one out of three of us involved in reading.

You're the only one?

The only one. I remember I was in a book club. I lived on a rural road and I got these books in the mail when I was seven or eight, and I became a voracious reader early on. I wasn't reading things that were particularly good, but I read anything I could get my hands on. I used to read my father's paperbacks, which were hidden high on a shelf in the bathroom. They were mostly books with scantily dressed women on the front covers—thrillers. However, I do remember reading *Rabbit, Run* during that period.

How old were you then?

I couldn't have been more than ten.

You read all of Rabbit, Run?

I wasn't able to read all of it, and I wasn't able to read it consecutively because I would have to read secretively, a few pages at a time in the bathroom.

You once said, "I'm interested in what home now consists of. Because we move around so much, families are forced to be immediate; they must stand on their relationships rather than on stereotypes or assumptions or a common history." Do you still look at home that way? Has having your own home and family changed your perception of home?

When I think about home I still think about times past and a sense of origins. I'm aware that what I'm living now are my children's origins; to me, this feels like real life as opposed to home.

In "Fast Lanes" Thurman asks the narrator, "Why do you go home?" Why do your characters, especially the young women, feel compelled to go home?

It has to do with settling issues. In many cases these are issues that have been inherited, not made by the characters. I think that is everyone's situation, vis-à-vis parental stories and myths. Family is partly a burden but also a treasure, because it is incredibly rich; the heart of it is a kind of mystery. Going home is a little like self-motivated analysis. It is a long process and unconsciously motivated in a lot of ways.

From comments you've made elsewhere, you obviously have a strong sense of belonging to a generation, the one that came of age in the sixties and seventies. Does a writer only really have a sense of his or her own generation's experiences?

Not necessarily. I get a sense of generational experience mainly through teaching now, which is not the same as living it. Also I view it differently, from the perspective of a parent and a teacher. A generation's identity has to do with political events, economic situations, information people are getting. People are getting far less information now than they did in the sixties.

Less information? Why?

When the draft finally ended and the volunteer army came in, people breathed a sigh of relief and went about their business. The government, particularly during the Reagan and Bush years, had this unquestioned military force at its disposal. Some of us may have bemoaned what was happening, but people didn't really feel it in their daily lives. I don't hope the draft is reinstituted, but I think a national service might make people pay more attention and live in a less isolated environment.

Apparently you did some wandering in the mid-seventies. How did you live? How did you support yourself?

I did all kinds of things. I worked in schools, in restaurants, sold bathrooms door-to-door.

How do you look at that period of your life now? Do you go back to it for material?

It does still influence my writing, not because of what I was doing then but because of all the voices I became familiar with. Once you start raising children, you're tuned into those children primarily. It is as though you are observing internal states, the basic mystery of the human heart, rather than different ways of speaking.

In "Blue Moon," Danner [a recurring character] says, "I didn't want to be the one who would remember everything." But she feels compelled to remember anyway. Is this partially how you define yourself as a writer, as the one who remembers?

In most families—and this has been borne out to some extent by family therapists—people take different roles, and there is usually one child who is the emotional barometer. Writers often turn out to have been those children. I don't know what distinguishes writers from those who don't become writers; maybe writers are power- or control-oriented and they have to have some way of taking control of what they have absorbed. When they are children, they begin to absorb and classify information in selective ways; at some point they are driven to make something of it, whether it is in the medium of words, music, art, cooking—whatever.

In your work there seems to be a constant tension within the characters of your generation between those who are "floating" and those who serve as the anchors of the family. Is the tension inevitable and irresolvable?

I used to think that going home was a rite of passage that people did at a certain age. As I have gotten older, it now seems to be something that people do continually, all their lives. If their parents are alive, it is all that much easier to do. It's like Eliot's quote about returning to the place you left and knowing that place for the first time. You make discoveries repeatedly if you enlarge as you go along.

Some of your characters stay at home in West Virginia, others move on. As the narrator in "Fast Lanes" puts it, some "stayed in one place and sank with whatever they had. But us—look at us . . . floating." The narrator in that story says she doesn't know how to sink. Would it be a good thing if she did? Or is sinking like drowning in quicksand?

That's the fear, you know. Leaving is a kind of metaphor for growing up. People don't grow up if they don't leave. And depending upon how much you've taken on within a family, leaving can be extremely painful. The extended period that many Americans go through, of going home and leaving and going home and leaving again, has to do, somehow, with the way we work at family.

What do you mean by "the way we work at family"?

The way we Americans work at family as opposed to the Europeans or the Japanese, where the whole idea of ancestors and lineage is formalized.

Leaving is not such an issue for them?

Leaving doesn't really happen. It's very American that you *must* leave and you must question everything that went before. It is related to the "Westward Ho" impulse. Family is difficult now because families are more isolated than they have ever been, and there is a diminishing sense of community, even in small towns. People are mobile and tend not to have extended families. The pressure on the tiny family unit is intense; there is always the option of moving on or breaking up, and people tend to do that more because they don't have extended family or community around. If you need help, you have to pay for it. If you can't pay, you don't have any help.

More than many writers you have shown an interest in what one critic called the "urban underbelly." We notice you recently wrote an introduction to Maggie: A Girl of the Streets. *May we assume the interest continues?*

It's classist to call it the urban underbelly. Who is making that judgment? I've always been interested in the people who are outside the myth, because they are the ones for whom the myth exists. My interest in children is similar in a way, because children are the ultimate outsiders. When you're looking at something as an outsider you are seeing it with a "beginner's mind," to use a Zen term. It redefines everything. People in extreme situations are like canaries in cages; you know, the old idea of testing the air by taking a canary into a mine and seeing if it keels over. Also, I don't view outsiders as urban particularly, because people struggle everywhere, and I guess I'm interested in looking at that.

Some of the outsiders in your fiction have poetic voices when they tell their stories, as in "How Mickey Made It," "Lechery," or "Black Tickets." These are among your most dense and lyrical stories. Is there something about their voices that is inherently poetic?

Their experience is less conventional. Material always dictates form in my work. If I'm writing something that is about relationships and family, I tend to write in a more conventional way because what I'm trying to do is establish a firm ground on which these characters can be seen. If I'm working with voice, usually an individual or internal voice, it's different. Internal voice is not bound by an event or a past. It's more dreamlike. The unconscious is closer to the surface. You are cut loose from all the conventions. Danner's section in *Machine Dreams,* for instance, is really clear in tone and not particularly poetic because it's not so much internal monologue as history. When I'm trying to work with language in monologue, I'm trying to unhinge everything, and I'm looking to the language to tell me where to go with it.

Gladys in Machine Dreams *talks about desperate people and says you have to be desperate to become pregnant. Danner's mother makes fun of her for saying that, and they laugh about it. It struck me that most of your characters could be described as desperate in one sense or another, not just people like the ones in "Black Tickets" and "Gemcrack," but the middle-class family members, too. Certainly Mitch is desperate, and Danner, too.*

Aren't you desperate? I'm desperate. I always think of it as a life force. From the time I was young, I never saw the point in contentment. It's a sort of cow-like state. I think desperation is just the nature of being alive. If you resolve one thing it really means that you're ready to take on something else. We certainly live in a state of chaos, entropy, where everything is in a process of transformation. It's a beautiful kind of desperation that makes us pregnant. Regardless of conditions most people do want desperately. That goes to the heart of what identity is, why we're here.

One critic said your stories tend to fall into two categories: the family stories and the stories about the outsiders, the more poetic stories. Do you look at it that way?

Not really. I think that was true in my first book [*Black Tickets*] but in *Machine Dreams* there was a change. Certain parts are more lyrical and other parts concentrate on moving the book along. I've been concentrating on writing novels for quite a long time. I haven't really written stories for ages. For me, it has all come together in novel writing.

Machine Dreams is divided into sections. Was that the plan from the beginning?

No. I work from language. In that sense I still work as a poet. That is why I write so slowly and with so little revision. I start with the language, just the sound of the sentence and move from there, because I'm working in an organic or subconscious way. To plan it from the outside would only get in the way of that.

So even when you're writing a novel, you don't envision the plot?

No. In the beginning of *Machine Dreams* I had about a hundred pages of another book, which I actually found recently. It was a book more like the story "Fast Lanes," in which there was this character similar to me at that time . . . blah . . . blah. Then, at some point, I began writing the first section of *Machine Dreams*, which is in the mother's voice. It is a different tone, and it was clear to me that I had found the beginning of the book. I put the other piece away, and from that point it was a much bigger undertaking and more interesting and dangerous for me to write. In the first two sections of *Machine Dreams* I was trying to look at the beginnings of this family, at the life stories of both parents. It went from there into being about the place, the community, that point in time, how those people experienced America at that time. I didn't draw any political lines but what I was trying to get across was that politics really goes on in people's lives, and the tragedy is that people often don't notice that the sky is falling until someone they love is in immediate peril. That was the way the book came together. Because I knew I wanted to cover a lot of time, I decided to use lapses of time to move the book and that made for the various sections. As for plot, it was almost self-evident where the book would go because of what happened during that period historically.

Did you do a lot of research, especially for the earlier sections?

It was memory research, embroidery of snippets and details. There were stories about the place where I grew up that I worked into the characters' lives. The sense of that little town was simply what I absorbed growing up in one place and feeling a lot of fidelity to it, even though I had left. The way a writer works with memory is almost religious. It has to do with a kind of redemption or an attempt to save something or to save a period of time or people in a particular period of their lives, to keep it from being lost. What you're trying to save is not reality but an illumined version of reality.

Bobbie Ann Mason said something similar. Part of her motivation, she said, was to save a time, a place, a certain people, all of which were passing—in her case, a way of life that existed in small Kentucky towns.

The impulse is especially strong in writers who come from disenfranchised, outsider areas; and small towns everywhere are outside the mainstream. A writer grows up absorbing a particular place, everything from diction, to sounds of accents, to what's important to those people and how it's reflected in what they do now. The writer is almost forced to leave. Of course, some don't. Eudora Welty didn't leave. But a lot of people have to, particularly women. What is it possible for a woman to do in those kinds of places? If you need to experience more than is allotted you, then you have to leave. Still, there may exist the redemptive urge in the writer, the desire to make that place known, to make it understood. I understand what Bobbie Ann Mason was talking about. I think it's a feeling a lot of writers have experienced.

One critic called Machine Dreams *"a political epic" and another said "the subject is history and the passing of time." Do you see it in those terms or more in terms of family?*

What I was trying to do in the book, what I try to do generally, is to write associatively, to convey information in a sensual way, to get at the way things smelled and tasted. I want to show the real experience, of absorbing something as a child or watching a relationship as a child. I want the writing to encourage that experience in the reader.

What is the relationship between Machine Dreams *and stories like "Bess" and "Blue Moon," which have some of the same characters? Were these originally part of the novel?*

"Bess" was. It was part of one of the long monologues at the beginning. I took it out later on because I realized the novel was meant to be about that little family, and Bess, though related, was something of a peripheral character. Moreover, the "Bess" story makes a case for Bess being Mitch's mother. To put that in the book would have completely skewed it.

Are you still coming back to those characters?

No, but the novel I'm finishing now does take place in 1963, the summer of '63, within a period of a few days. It takes place in a fictional town in that area. The town of Bellington [the setting of *Machine Dreams*] is mentioned as being nearby.

Does it have a working title?

I never say the title until the book is finished. I wanted to do something different. It's about several children who are isolated from their families. What I wanted to do, technically, was to set the book within a matter of a few days but somehow, through internal monologue, establish each of the characters' situations. So, in fact, the novel contains a host of characters almost telegraphed.

Back to Machine Dreams *for a minute. Although Danner and Billy are very close, the most profound connection seems to be between Jean and Danner. Do you think that reflects your feeling about mother/daughter relationships? That it's the main familial link? And is one of the things that links them the desire to pass on family history through telling stories?*

Yes, I think women pass down a real assignment, particularly to daughters. At least that was true in the South. But I also wanted to imply in the novel a generational shift. When Mitch goes to war he confides only in his male friends. But when Billy goes to war, it is his sister he talks to, not his parents. It's not something that would have happened a generation or so before. I think Jean has also passed down to Danner the responsibility to protect Billy, because she is unable to understand anymore how to do that. That responsibility for siblings is something taken on by the women in that culture.

Just in that culture?

I suppose it is more general: women nurturing and protecting. Men tend to deal with situations as they come up and women tend to anticipate them and then get accused of being hysterical and making a hard time for everybody.

One critic has said about Machine Dreams *that men's inability to "transform their losses into narrative fictions leads to their becoming weak or disappearing." The article argues that, in your novel, men tend to put their faith in machines because, unlike memories and dreams, "machines yield their secrets without risk to the self." Do you find that a resonant reading of the novel?*

That's an interesting take on it. Reading is almost like dreaming. A novel is a gestalt in which we project our sense of reality on the totem of the book and the characters of the book, which is fine. But whenever somebody tells me so-and-so said this about that, I always listen partly with an interest in what that person is playing out. The business about machines yielding secrets without risk to self is certainly true. What I wandered into in *Machine Dreams* was a source of myth. We're really dealing with myth every day in our life, even though we are not living in a time when people necessarily believe in mythic creatures. Every technological invention you can think of is a kind of manifestation of old magic: the idea of voices traveling through space, and the idea of flight, leaving the confines of the earth. You could view television as kind of a crystal ball. But there's a danger. Technological society takes control away from the individual.

I think the *Machine Dreams* idea developed in the section where Mitch is burying the Japanese soldiers on the beach. He has a recurrent dream about that experience. It becomes a touchstone for him because his whole identity is based on building, taking material and building things, driving machines, controlling machines. In that instance, he is using the machines to bury these anonymous men. It's an inversion of what he thought he was. That's often what happens in war. Billy has this idea of flight from the time he is a child; that's very male and mythic. It ends by being played out in the frame of war. It's such a waste. In this sense the novel is a warning, a way of saying that ordinary people are important. Governmental policy may take years to filter down to us. Once it does, it's usually too late to stop the machinery.

In "Fast Lanes" Danner says, "Nothing mechanical is easy." Are machines inevitably our betrayers? Do we expect too much from them?

No. Machines are just machines. In *Machine Dreams* the transistor radio is like an ear on the culture of that period of time, the song lyrics and the secrets.

Secrets are a motif in what you have been talking about today and in the novel. Mitch identifies with the leper in terms of secrets, and earlier you talked about the beginning of writing for you as being secretive.

I think we might substitute the word mystery for secret. The reason Mitch is interested in the leper or feels for the leper is that the leper reminds him of things he can't deny. There is so much about him that he doesn't know. His entire past is a mystery. It is a secret they are keeping from him in a way. In a larger sense, it is mystery that fascinates me. The reason we have art of any kind is to get at that over-arching mystery. Everyone experiences mystery in personal terms, but it's a replicated pattern. Getting at what we don't know is the reason for being alive.

In your career you moved from poetry to compressed short stories to short stories to novels. What is your sense of that change? Is an increased interest in storytelling behind it?

I may at some point write stories again but in the past few years I have felt a need for the space and time that you take with a novel. It's a different kind of relationship. It's just where my interest lies right now.

Could you talk about the difference in the way an image works in a novel as opposed to the way it works in a short story?

Probably the reason I'm attracted to the novel is the kind of patterning you can do or that almost emerges. I think if you stay focused on the material, in the way that I hope to, there is a kind of pattern that emerges in the writing that is sometimes a surprise to the writer. I think that's the real reason to stay with something over the long haul. It is something that is almost unconsciously worked out over the period of time that you live in the material and work with the material.

A number of writers have talked about how the length of the novel doesn't allow the writer to obsess over each sentence, to concentrate on each word. Has that been your experience?

I would write a lot more books if I didn't obsess over every word, but in fact I do.

You've mentioned that you write line by line. Do you mean that, unlike writers who do a quick draft and then go back and reword, you have to get one line right before you write the next line?

Yeah. I don't intend to do that necessarily, it's just the way I write. After I finish a book I may revise it and take out this or move this or that around, but I don't tend to race through it, get the story down, then do another version. I know people who write that way and it works for them. That's not the way I do it. Maybe it's the poet in me. I write slowly and I tend to have the line already formed in my head before I start. It's hard to say whether I hear it or write it, but I stay in the book by rereading what I've written and staying in the sound and the voice of the book. I never have approached a book as a deck of cards that I can shuffle and move around. I feel, rather, as if I were looking for something that already exists, trying to stay with it and find it and feel out the shape of it.

You've spoken of writing as "a metaphysical process." What do you mean by that?

It goes back to what we were saying before about secrets and mystery, why people write. It also has to do with what I think of as the religious passion of trying to be an artist of any kind. The art functions as a form of meditation in which thoughts arise and you watch them. You are moving with them, but you are not in them. That is the way memory and experience work for the writer. It all moves together, but the writer isn't bound by any one thing. Genesis speaks of the forces moving on the earth. Different colors of darkness meld together, and things emerge from that darkness. That's the way I see writing.

Talking about writers serving their material, you've said, "It's like being led by a whisper." Can you describe the nature of the whisper?

It's like a whisper that you can't quite make out. Something like the auditory hallucination people have of hearing their name spoken suddenly across the street. It is not as though they are really hearing someone shouting at them, but they have a sense of an internalized whisper. That's the way I experience writing. As I said before, there's a sense that the book is already there, whole, and I am trying to feel it out, to find out what it is and move into it and inhabit it. Find it in language.

Tobias Wolff

Citizens and Outlaws

"All my stories are in one way or another autobiographical," Wolff once declared. "Sometimes they're autobiographical in the actual events which they describe, sometimes more in their depiction of a particular character. In fact, you could say that all my characters are reflections of myself, in that I share their wish to count for something and their almost complete confusion as to how this is supposed to be done."

This autobiographical desire for prestige, which often figures in Wolff's stories, becomes central to his memoirs, *This Boy's Life* (1989) and *In Pharaoh's Army* (1993). At the time of our original interview with him (material from a follow-up interview has been included), *This Boy's Life* had just been published; it describes the author's troubled and sometimes harrowing childhood. The boy we come to know in this book wants to be admired, wants to be considered "a boy of dignity and consequence." What he becomes instead is a petty thief, a vandal, a forger, and, most of all, a liar—one particularly adept at counterfeiting conventional appearance and behavior to get what he wants.

Our interview took place in San Antonio, where Wolff had come to give a reading from the new book. In addition to talking with him about the memoir, we discussed the short-story collections *In the Garden of the North American Martyrs* (1981) and *Back in the World* (1985), as well as his novella, *The Barracks Thief* (1984), which won the 1985 PEN/Faulkner Award.

In a subsequent interview, conducted seven years later, we turned our attention to Wolff's Vietnam memoir, *In Pharaoh's Army*, and his most recent collection of stories, *The Night in Question* (1996). Wolff also elaborated, at this time, on a variety of topics touched on in our original conversation, including his conception of himself as a writer, the relation of truth to lies in his fiction, and the importance of moral choice for his characters.

Formerly a professor of creative writing at Syracuse University, Wolff now teaches at Stanford University. After serving with the army from 1964 to 1968, he attended Oxford University, where he received B.A. and M.A. degrees. He

Marion Ettlinger

also holds an M.A. from Stanford. Besides teaching and writing, Wolff is the editor of two short-story collections: *Matters of Life and Death* (1983), an anthology of contemporary American fiction, and *A Doctor's Visit* (1988), a selection of Chekhov stories.

What was your motive in writing This Boy's Life?

I started out jotting things down about my childhood, because I felt them slipping away, and I wanted to have some sort of record. Then I saw patterns emerging. Then I began to hear a voice telling it. Also, I recognized that my childhood made a good story. For years I had seen people perk up when I told them some of the things that happened when I was a kid.

Why did you begin the memoir where you did? You weren't born at ten. Why begin at that point?

That was the moment at which my mother and I had coincidental hopes. I was old enough then to share her desire to be fantastically rich, to be on top of the situation. I had enough of a grasp on reality to know that we were not on top of the situation and that life could be better than it was. And so the trip out West that begins the memoir was no longer a matter of her hauling her kid around. It was a joint venture. We both wanted that. We begin this book in transit, in hope, and we end it in transit, in hope. These hopes are going to be disappointed at the end as they were at the beginning, but the fact that hope persisted is what I wanted to leave at the end of the story.

You insist, throughout the memoir, on keeping a clear distinction between the boy and the adult narrator. It's as if you don't see them as different stages of the same person but as completely different people.

I don't bring the adult in very often.

He's there, you feel him.

Yes, you feel him there.

And while you don't want to make a bridge between the boy and the adult, the reader naturally finds himself wondering, How did the confused teenager we're left with at the end, this compulsive liar, become the adult fiction writer? You don't give us much help with that. Why not?

Why didn't I make a bridge? Gives too much solace to the reader. The boy doesn't know there's going to be any bridge. The boy lives this life ignorant of what is going to happen to him later, as we all do. The child is alone. The child, as I say in the book, moves out of reach of the man. To the extent that I start giving reasons for how this boy gets transformed into this incredibly wonderful adult who's now telling his story, the minute that bridge exists, and that explanation exists, the boy is no longer alone. He is simply in the process of becoming someone else. I think that would compromise the integrity of his experience, to come in with a comforting adult voice all the time. I don't like that tone in childhood memoirs, generally, letting the kid off the hook with this very adult ironical humor, when things really are quite serious. One of the things I took to heart when I was preparing myself to write the book was Graham Greene's *A Sort of Life*, in which he says that memoirs frequently go bad because writers fail to give due gravity to the things that were grave and serious matters when they were young. I wanted to keep a

rigid distinction between the child's perceptions and the adult's. It is a calculated risk, because it can seem to be an artificial distinction. After all, there
was a bridge of some kind. Was it being coy to withhold it? I would rather
run the risk of being coy than of crowding the kid out. You have to make those
decisions when you write anything, and you always risk one thing to get
another. You have to decide what you want most. I most wanted the reader
to have a sense of this kid very much on his own. My mother was certainly a
loving person and would give whatever support she could, but she couldn't
always give substantial support because her circumstances didn't allow it. So
this boy found himself on his own. Oh, once in a while, I felt I had to account
for the effect of some of these things later on, the way they echo into adult
life. But I didn't want to do it very often.

*Yes, there are selective leaps into the future. The first one is Vietnam. Was there
any calculation about which leaps to make, or in what order?*

Yes, I wanted the reader to be aware very early on in the book that this
boyhood is a progression to a place. That the boyhood obsession with weapons has a terminus somewhere, that it ends in war. There's a logical progression in the kind of life that boys are encouraged to lead and dream of in this
country. There's a lot of violence in the book—a lot of male violence. That
kind of thing all goes somewhere.

*You say in the memoir, "I wanted distinction, and the respectable forms of it
seemed to be eluding me. If I couldn't have it as a citizen I would have it as an
outlaw." The citizen/outlaw distinction is important throughout the book. Do
you think being a writer is a way of accommodating both the citizen and the
outlaw?*

Yes, I do. Exactly. Most writers I know consider themselves outlaws and
yet lead middle-class lives. There aren't too many Hart Cranes left. And so
the impulse to break the rules is in our work. The desire to subvert and to
probe and to question and to dig the foundations out from under everybody
and to represent fraudulent selves to the world, all that is contained and le-
gitimized in imaginative acts. What is destructive and also self-destructive
is transformed. You don't give it up. You just find a way of using it.

*For all the humor in the memoir, and the implied optimism—because we
know the boy did grow up to be a writer, to have success—there's a sense of fu-
tility, a sense that no one can really help another person avoid his or her most
self-destructive urges. There's a line in the book: "The human heart is a dark
forest."*

I stole that line. It's from Chekhov. It's in a letter of his. Actually, he says,
"The human heart is a slumbering forest." I didn't even know I'd stolen it.

But when I was reading his letters I found that line. This was after the book came out, and I thought, well, I must have read this before. But you're right. There is a certain sense of helplessness in the memoir at the way in which people's destinies and natures are going to work themselves out regardless. At the same time, the people I'm writing about do not make themselves available to lessons, to learning much, to being helped much. I have seen people allow themselves to be helped. I didn't. I was not of that sort myself. I seemed to have to learn everything the hard way, to stumble up against every wall before I'd acknowledge that it was there.

One of the things I like about the memoir is that you don't do what childhood memoirs so often do—put most of the blame on the adults. There are some very sympathetically portrayed adults in your book—the nun, the priest, Mr. Howard, Mr. Bolger.

Most of the grown-ups I knew, except for Dwight [his stepfather], were very well meaning.

So we get the sense that, if the boy is not being reached, it's because he's not there to be reached.

Doesn't want to be reached. That's right. Secrecy is very important to children. It's one of the only powers they can wield over grown-ups. Your powers are negative when you're a child. Refusing to eat is another power kids have. So, of course, is falsehood. These are ways kids can get even. I never wanted readers to see this kid in the memoir as a victim of the evil adult world. This kid really gets his own back at adults. He's a tough nut. The adults are often his victims.

You talk about your relationship with your best friend, Arthur. You write, "One night he kissed me, or I kissed him, or we kissed each other." I thought, well, that's an interesting formulation. Is it unimportant which of these three possibilities is true?

No, it's not unimportant. I wanted not to attribute a quality to the experience it didn't have. I wanted to be very careful about that, because I'm not exactly sure how it happened, and it might have been spontaneous on both our parts. I also wanted the language to reflect that it wasn't a traumatic experience. In fact, a lot of men have told me, on reading that, about similar moments they had with friends—and they went on being friends. Still, it did affect my relationship with Arthur afterwards. I mean, we were both wary. We just didn't know what it meant or how to deal with it. In fact, what did it mean? I don't know what it means *now*. I wanted the language to reflect that, too, by carefully avoiding giving the initiative to either of us. I wanted to show how you are at the mercy of these impulses at that age. Because you're not sure who you are, you're not sure what governs you at any given moment. Things sometimes pass over you like a wind. There's a random quality to many of the experiences of youth.

At one point in the memoir, you talk about defining yourself in opposition to Dwight. In The Counterlife, *Philip Roth talks about how there is no self except in opposition to others.*

That's an interesting proposition. I think one of the best things that ever happened to me was that I had this complete creep around me all the time who had no virtues and all the faults. I was going to push against whatever man was around anyway, but what a wonderful thing that the man I had to push against was Dwight.

One reviewer suggested that, in the title of the memoir, you were playing off Philip Roth's My Life as a Man *or Edmund White's* A Boy's Own Life. *Were you? I thought you were alluding to the scouting magazine* Boy's Life.

Exactly. I meant to suggest an ironic discrepancy between the ideal boyhood portrayed in the magazine, and my own experience. I had originally planned to call the book *Boy's Life,* but then I came up with what I thought was the more interesting title.

You said in talking to students earlier today that you try to help beginning writers to find their own voice and the distinctive story they have to tell. Were you implying that each writer has one essential story to tell?

No, I was talking about the story they have to tell at that moment. However, I do think that every writer has a kind of "take" on the world that is different from others'. Or has that potential anyway. The problem is to separate it from the models, the influences, the conventions, the temptations of convention, to try and sieve it out from those things so the writer can begin to recognize what is distinctive in his way of seeing things.

Reading your work, I wonder if your "take" has to do with imagination and truth and lying.

Those questions do keep coming up in my stories. They aren't just philosophical questions to me. They're questions about the conduct of life. They've been very influential in my experience. Imagination was my curse and my blessing when I was young, and I still feel the heavy hand of it.

With our students earlier, you said, "Because I could imagine myself becoming someone else, I could be someone else."

That's right. How can you be what you can't imagine being?

The curse of it was that it made you very unhappy, frustrated?

Yes, frustrated. Because the world doesn't agree with you. The world doesn't share your imaginings of yourself, unless you can pull some kind of an enormous trick on the world and get it to agree, which it will do for only a little while, unless you have the goods to back up that bluff.

Your life and your writing seem to me so directly related to Gatsby. I find it just an overwhelming comparison. Do you see it?

Sure, absolutely. I didn't when I was young.

I mean the imagination, changing your name.

Self-invention. I think it's very American. We can do that here. Gatsby even invented himself into another class. You can't do that in other countries. Your very speech identifies you. Here you can do that kind of thing.

I wondered if, in writing the memoir, you were like Nick writing about Gatsby.

A little bit. A little bit. Yeah, that's a nice image. I like that. That's about the way I felt. Nick sees through Gatsby, but he has a real affection for him, too. Then he sees that there was something interesting in what he did. He liked him better than a lot of the people around him, the foul dust that floats in Gatsby's wake. Yeah, I like that.

As long as lying was brought up . . . Most of your characters—many of them anyway—do tell lies. I realize it's hard to generalize, because they lie for so many different reasons. But what's at the bottom of it? Why is lying so necessary to your characters?

The world is not enough, maybe? I'd have to go through every story in which a character tells a lie to try to puzzle that one out. But to lie is to say the thing that is not, so there's obviously an unhappiness with what is, a discontent. Some of the lies are just destructive lies and at least one of them is a competitive lie. Father Leo ["The Missing Person"] listens to his friend's story, and he feels like he ought to have a story like that to tell. And at the same time, he lies as a way of establishing a common ground with his friend.

James ["The Liar"] is an interesting case. His mother has always complained that he can't carry a tune. But on the bus at the end, he's telling these outrageous lies to the passengers, even making up his own language, and he says, "I sang [emphasis added] to them in what was surely an ancient and holy tongue."

He's found his voice. He's keeping these stranded people distracted and happy here at the end. He's found something good to do with this craziness of his.

Then there's the boy in the memoir. He's writing out the phoney letters of recommendation that will help him get into prep school, and suddenly he sees his true image in this character he's created on paper. As in "The Liar," falsehood helps him discover an inner voice or an inner self. How important is it that these lies are told to strangers?

Strangers are more gullible. Also, you're not so accountable to strangers.

You're not going to have to live with them. You're free to experiment, so to speak, with a stranger. They're *tabula rasa* as far as you're concerned. It gives you freedom. When I hitchhiked as a kid I used to lay these incredible stories on people, as a way of entertaining them—and myself. I didn't even know what I was going to say. I'd just spin it out. Wing it. I used to lie a lot, but not anymore. That's something I reserve for my fiction now.

You mention "winging it." It occurs to me, you've got all these good citizens in your stories, and a fair number of outlaws, too. But there's another kind of character, less common, who is neither the good citizen nor the conscious rule-breaker. This is the character who "wings it." Like James, like Mary ["In the Garden of the North American Martyrs"] when she turns off her hearing aid at the end.

Even the outlaws are respecting the rules by being outlaws, allowing themselves to be defined by the social order, if only by opposition. Those who are winging it are really letting go of that connection, of wanting to be defined in some way by the world, either by being inside or outside. So yes, winging it is literally a kind of lifting off, letting go, listening to the voice within and speaking with the magic of that voice rather than the committee around you.

Continuing with the phrase "winging it," I noticed, in rereading "In The Garden of the North American Martyrs," all the bird imagery, and I thought I'll ask him what the students always ask me—did he have all that in mind or not?

Yes. I sort of stumble on things as I'm writing the first draft or two, but by the time I've put a story through several revisions I know exactly where every comma has to be. The bird imagery may be a little bit too overt in this case. I don't know. Because I'm so aware of it, it really sticks out when I read it. There may be impulses in the work that I'm not conscious of, but that kind of stuff I'm very conscious of.

Do you see your books of stories simply as collections or do you think of each as unified in some way?

I think the stories are connected by subject matter and style. The collections seem to me to be different. I mean, they're obviously by the same person, but each of the collections has a somewhat different character, and that comes from the stories being connected. Next you're going to ask me what connects them, right? It's one of those things I can't unravel backwards.

How about the title of your second collection, Back in the World? *To take one story and to use it as the title of the collection—as you did with* In the Garden of the North American Martyrs—*is fairly traditional. But to take a phrase from one story [in this instance, "Soldier's Joy"] and to use it as the title of the collec-*

tion is unusual. By calling it Back in the World, *did you mean to make the Vietnam background more pervasive?*

It wasn't just Vietnam. "The world" is what people in religious orders—nuns and priests—call secular life. That's the way Jesus talks about it: The world's yoke is heavy, My yoke is light. So "back in the world" is an expression which has many connotations. I thought it was an expression that caught the spirit of a lot of the stories. I didn't want to use just one story's title this time. When you use the title of one story for the title of a collection, that story really has to carry a lot of weight, because in some way it has to support the claims of all the other stories. I wanted the title to float free. As a matter of fact, I had some pretty good stories that were in the first person that I didn't use in this collection because I wanted a unity of voice and perspective from one story to the next. I wanted you to read this like a novel, with the same kind of narrative presence in each story.

One of my favorite stories in the second collection is "The Missing Person." When I teach that story, there's always a big disagreement among the students about Father Leo and finally about what that story is saying. Some read it as a story about a man with a sincere, deep vocation who is serving a church that does not appreciate his gifts and so wastes them. Others say, no, Leo is a selfish romantic. They don't accept his vocation as genuine in the first place, and they see a positive turn at the end when he says "I'm here" to that neurotic secretary who seeks his protection.

That's the way I see it. I see him as a romantic. At the same time, the church is not a benign presence in this story. The story describes how the foundations are rotting, the basement's filled with scummy water, and they're paying crooks to keep it going. I am a Catholic, but that's the way I see the institutional church—I think it's become the cross the believers have to bear. But still, that doesn't give Father Leo an out, because I think his notion of his vocation has been a romantic one. And I think that he has discovered by the end that his vocation is where he is at any given moment and that he has to bring himself completely to that moment. When he says "I'm here," people tend to think of that as a very sad ending. But I always thought of it as a hopeful ending. However, I don't think there's only one right reading. I have to say, too, that I don't think writers own their stories. I don't have the last word on these stories. I think the intention that impels the story for the writer becomes irrelevant after the story is finished, because the story is then an object. It's like a vase or a painting, and it is liable to the interpretations that people bring to it. The writer is not necessarily the best interpreter of the story, because the writer is bound by intention, by what he meant to say. The fact of the matter is, as we all know, some of the most interesting things we say are those things we do not mean to say. And stories contain that matter. I'm often disappointed by the interviews I read with writers. When they start talking about their own work, it seems to me that I have a much richer reading of it than they have, than they seem to have had in mind when they wrote it. So I hesitate to give hard and fast interpretations of my own work. Also, I wrote that story seven or eight years ago, and I had a million things in mind when I wrote it, and I don't remember them all now. I hope they're there to be discovered in the story, but I don't really know. I do know that my sense of the story when I left it was, Leo's been offered another way of seeing his place in the world and of becoming reconciled to it. I don't necessarily mean that he's going to lead this transformed existence afterwards.

I'm sometimes reminded of Flannery O'Connor when I read your fiction. Even some of the story titles are reminiscent of O'Connor—"Worldly Goods," "The Rich Brother," "In the Garden of the North American Martyrs."

"The Poor Are Always with Us."

Yes, the very titles suggest a moral, even religious concern. Are you aware of an influence there?

I've learned from her stories. They concern moral choice. Choices between good and evil. I think of my own stories as leading up to such a point. The difference is, the choice O'Connor's characters are presented with—or have forced on them—is an irrevocable one, a choice between salvation and damnation. That doesn't happen in such an obvious way in my stories.

In O'Connor's fiction, grace breaks through, usually accompanied by violence. I don't find comparable moments in your stories.

I haven't seen too many of those moments myself, so I tend not to write about them. O'Connor's not really a realistic writer. She's a writer of fables. I'm not. I've written a couple, but that's not my mode. Her fiction is made to receive that kind of moment without any sense of dissonance. In my fiction, I think that kind of moment would ring false.

Would you consider "The Rich Brother" one of your fables?

That's as close to a fable as I've written. But even there, what compels the rich man to go back for his brother is different from what you'd find in O'Connor. He's going back all right. And I suppose you could say that's an intervention of grace, because he can suddenly imagine his wife standing there and asking him the question God asks Cain: "Where's your brother?" But it's also a natural psychological event in his life. She's going to ask him that question if he goes up to the door without his brother. And he's not going to be able to answer. He's got to go back for him. I guess my sense of what saves people has as much to do with the ordinary responsibilities of family, adulthood, and work as it does these violent eruptions from heaven, which one might look for in vain. I mean, that's the nature of grace. It doesn't come bidden, it comes unbidden. And so I have a different sense of what saves people than O'Connor's. It's grace, but mine takes different forms than hers. She has a somewhat cartoonish idea of fiction. For the deaf, one must shout; for the blind, one must draw large and startling figures. I like her work a lot, though I like it better when she manages to have some affection for her characters, as she does for Parker in "Parker's Back." That's a great story. But sometimes I think the polemicist betrays her humanity. She sets up her characters as weak arguments for which she has a stronger alternative.

*I was reading your introduction to the collection of contemporary short stories you edited [*Matters of Life and Death*]. There, you express your boredom with self-conscious experimental fiction.*

It was overstated, because who's really writing experimental fiction now? I don't see much of it anymore. I'm not hostile to experimental fiction, but there's a kind of self-indulgence that just doesn't interest me.

Even if people aren't writing it all that much, I think there still is, in the academy, a good deal of respect for it.

It's fun to teach, because it means something in a comfortable way, and there's a competitive impulse behind its composition that provokes a competitive impulse to disassemble it.

The Barracks Thief *is your most experimental piece, especially in the handling of tense and point of view. There are shifts from third person to first person and back again, and shifts in tense, too. Why did you choose to tell the story in that way?*

I don't remember. I tried it all different ways. I spent more time on *The Barracks Thief* than I've spent on any other story. I could, at one time, have given you detailed explanations of why I did the things I did. But, in the end, they were also intuitive choices.

Hubbard talks about how he was taught to picture people doing things, but he can't picture Lewis doing the theft. Philip can though; in fact, he does picture Lewis doing it.

Philip recognizes his connection to Lewis. When the sergeant says a barracks thief is like someone who turns on his own family, Philip feels accused. That's why he feels such complicity with Lewis. Even in the end, he says, Lewis's face floats up to mine like the face in a pool when you're going to drink—it's your own face.

And it's also the face of the Vietnamese he saw, and the face of his brother, too. I thought it was a nice moral balance between Hubbard and Philip. Hubbard can't picture the theft but Philip can. And yet Hubbard's comment to Philip— "You just think what everyone else thinks"—is wonderfully apt. One lacks a kind of imagination and the other lacks the ability to have an unconventional thought.

As for the thief himself, I wanted to give the sense of a person who has no attachment to the past, who has been tremendously hurt by the past but is cut off from his consciousness of it. He lives in the present, almost like an animal. It's his awakening from this animal state that the story is partly about. The reason I wrote that part of the novel in present tense and took the quotation marks off the dialogue was to give it a less detached quality somehow, to make it more vividly immediate and present. So I was shifting point of view and tense in the novel partly as a way of exploring the characters and their different perceptions of time.

The end of the novel is a meditation on time and what time does to us all. Philip had once believed that Lewis's life would be ruined by what happened. Now he realizes that people get over things, for better or worse. He considers how his father seems to have gotten over leaving the family; now he has a new family. I'm also reminded of what the narrator in "Next Door" says—it's terrible what we allow ourselves to get used to. Is time the enemy?

No, not at all. It brings problems, but it also brings the answers to them. Things pass. Time acts in different ways in my stories. I don't have a theory of time that you're going to be able to use as a grid to read my fiction. Some writers do. I hear writers talk about time in very systematic ways. I won't do that. It's something I treat in its own way in every story.

The characters in The Barracks Thief, *like many of your characters, are looking for acceptance. That's what Philip wants in the army. It's what appeals to him about that night at the ammo dump when he and his two soldier buddies stand up to the local authorities. At the same time, he and the others seem compelled to destroy that very trust they pretend to value more than anything else. Lewis steals, Philip rejects his brother, Philip's father abandons his family.*

Yes, it's a paradox of our condition that we crave intimacy, and when we have it try to destroy it.

In this same connection, how important is Philip's denial of Lewis in precipitating the thievery?

That's a crucial thing, because that's the night Lewis goes off alone, meets the prostitute, and ends up stealing to pay her. After the anti-war people have come to the camp to protest, there's a feeling among the soldiers of unity through opposition. For the first time, Philip feels like one of the boys. Then Lewis comes along and asks him to go to the movies and Philip says no.

Philip's with these other guys now, and Lewis isn't cool. Philip doesn't want to risk being uncool with him. It's an important moment in the novel.

Is that one of the original sins in the world according to Wolff—this denial of another?

That's right.

And that's why Hubbard's line to Philip—"You just think what everyone else thinks"—is such a devastating one. Hubbard instinctively recognizes Philip's need to be one of the group, and that very need is what causes him to betray Lewis.

Yes, I think so.

The soldiers in this novel are going to be sent to Vietnam, although we never see them over there. Vietnam is often in the background of your work, but you tend not to deal directly with it in your fiction. You once said you haven't figured out a way to tell the truth about it. What do you see as the particular difficulty?

Part of the problem is that the war novel in American literature is one of the most powerful inheritances we have. The writer of a first-rate novel about Vietnam is going to have to invent a novel that will escape the pull of convention, instead of writing a World War II novel and sticking it in Vietnam. The other problem, too, is that the nonfiction about Vietnam has been so good—Michael Herr's *Dispatches,* Philip Caputo's *A Rumor of War,* Ron Kovic's *Born on the Fourth of July*—that I think it's going to take an enormous amount of invention to arrive at something fresh, something that people don't already know, to tell the story in a way that is redolent of the place, that grows from the ground of that particular experience and not from some other.

Do you think Tim O'Brien did that in Going After Cacciato?

In parts of it he did. I'm particularly admiring of his story "The Things They Carried," which seems to me to be the best piece of fiction about Vietnam. I mean, it's such an unusual approach to telling a story, through the physical weight of the things these soldiers carry. You begin to take on that weight as you read the story. You begin to feel it, one item after another. He knows exactly what he's talking about, the weight of each piece, how it goes on. It's a great story. And that's the kind of thing, that's the fresh eye I'm talking about.

*How did you come to write your memoir of Vietnam [*In Pharaoh's Army*]?*

I never intended to do a second memoir, but shortly after finishing *This Boy's Life* I wrote a short story about the war ["Casualty"]—something else I thought I'd never do—and that made me realize I had a great deal more to say about Vietnam, something interesting that was much closer to my own experience than that short story had been. I started another story, this one very autobiographical; in fact, as I was writing it, I decided to make it entirely autobiographical. The next thing I knew I was writing another one, and another, and that's how *In Pharaoh's Army* evolved.

You've described the special challenges Vietnam poses to the writer. Does the memoir provide you with particular advantages in meeting those challenges?

It let me focus on the elements of my experience that were unique. That, in turn, helped me resist the powerful conventions of American war literature, and especially Vietnam literature. There is no "typical" Vietnam experience, and yet our ideas about what that experience constituted are so strong that even someone who was there can fall into the trap and neglect to give his own account.

What seems unique or unusual to you about your experience in Vietnam?

Several things. I was with Vietnamese troops, for the most part, rather than Americans. I did not experience grinding, day-in-and-day-out combat. My experience of war in the Mekong Delta was more random—hit-and-miss. I rarely saw the enemy. Now and then a few people would be killed; the count did rise steadily, but nothing like in the North. Also, everybody thinks "jungle" when they think of Vietnam, but there was almost no jungle where I was. It was flat, with rice paddies marked off by tree lines. The Vietnamese division I was assigned to as an advisor was headquartered in My Tho; it was a beautiful old French town, with wide, tree-lined boulevards and houses with red tile roofs and flowerpots on the windowsills.

Reviewers have commented on how much like short stories the chapters of your memoirs are, each with its own beginning, middle, and end. Can you describe the difference between writing a memoir and a piece of fiction? That is, besides the obvious difference—one happened, the other didn't—how does it feel different, or does it?

It does feel different. With a memoir, I know where I'm going, because I'm following a trail of events that actually happened. When I'm writing a story, there's always the anxiety of invention; I'm trying to figure out what's coming next, what the story is really about. As for the similarity between the memoir chapters and stories, it's not something I'm aware of as I'm writing. I don't consciously impose a short-story structure on the episodes of my life; that's simply the form in which they come to me. My memory organizes things into narrative. As long as I can recall, I've told stories about the past. That's how I make sense of life, the way a painter organizes through images. I know that life doesn't happen in chapters or stories, so the order I impose is, in a sense, artificial. I don't apologize for that, though I know some writers feel differently. Mary McCarthy, in her *Memoirs of a Catholic Girlhood*, frequently stops between chapters to correct herself on details and consult other people. She'll come back and say, "I made a mistake. This event really happened the year before I said it did. And the handbag actually cost five dollars, not two." She seems very interested in getting things exactly right. Reading her, I thought that approach was interesting for a while, and then it wasn't interesting anymore. That sort of scrupulous concern for the smallest details seems unnecessary. Anyone who's ever sat around a table with friends or family disputing versions of the past knows that people's memories work differently. I expect an intelligent reader to understand that.

You mentioned feeling the anxiety of invention when you're writing fiction. Are there also anxieties involved in writing a memoir?

You feel them, but they're of a different order. You worry, for example, about how your writing will affect others, because you're describing real people. You may disguise them—change their names, their occupations— but they will recognize themselves, since you're still preserving the most important part of them on the page, which is their character. So you worry about being fair, and about being honest, too. The other anxiety, of course, which attends the writing of any memoir, is the natural terror of self-exposure. You think, my God, is it really necessary to tell people I did this? And it isn't always. You don't need to tell every little rotten thing you thought or said or did. What you have to do is discern patterns in your experience. Then when a certain incident illuminates a pattern, even if it's unflattering, you have an obligation to put it in. So the anxieties are there—including the anxiety of writing itself. You're never sure how it's going to go that day, and most writers aren't interested in—aren't reassured or consoled by—what they've already written. They're always interested in the project at hand, and that's the one that's giving them trouble.

At one point in the Vietnam memoir you're in a bar back in the States and you tell an anecdote about the war to some friends. It's the one about Captain Kale and the Chinook. You note how the story doesn't go over very well; you say the problem was, you couldn't find the right tone of voice in which to tell it.

That happened to me a lot when I got back. In Vietnam, when you talked about things with other soldiers, it was always in this harsh, joking way that concealed any feelings you might have had, if indeed you did have any. That sort of talk has its uses among soldiers, but it doesn't translate well into civilian conversation. It can be rather appalling. At the same time, you didn't want to strike a phoney note—put on a long face, oh, woe is me, what a slave of the system I was! My situation was complicated by the fact that many of

my civilian friends were against the war. I was against it, too, but in a different way, because I had been there and still had friends over there. So I was
reluctant to mouth the usual anti-war pieties; they would have helped me
blend in, would have made me appear principled and high-minded, but I
didn't like the way the words sounded coming from me, even though I believed some of them.

*Explaining your inability to tell the Captain Kale incident effectively, you say,
"As soon as you open your mouth you have problems, problems of recollection,
problems of tone, ethical problems. How can you judge the man you were now
that you've escaped his circumstances, his fears and desires, now that you hardly
remember who he was? And how can you honestly avoid judging him? But isn't
there, in the very act of confession, an obscene self-congratulation for the virtue
required to see your mistake and own up to it?" You might be commenting in
that passage on the problems of writing any memoir.*

Yes.

How did you try to avoid these pitfalls in the writing of your book?

Oh, I don't know. It came a little more easily with *This Boy's Life*. You can
depend on a certain amount of forgiveness from people when you're recounting the things you did as a child. The matters in the second memoir are
weightier, and the person I'm writing about is older and presumably more
responsible for his actions. Your instinct as a writer is to protect that person
who is closest to yourself, and it has to be resisted.

You're pretty hard on yourself in the book.

I still had a lot of growing up to do. The thing about the army is, you think
you're joining up to become a man, but what you end up doing is prolong-
ing your adolescence. The army takes care of all those things that force you
to grow up; it takes choice out of your hands in the most fundamental ways.
You're told what to do, and in exchange for that you get three squares a day.
You never have to cook a meal for yourself, you never have to choose what
to wear, you don't even have to buy your own clothes or take them to a laun-
dry. You never have to hustle an apartment or navigate public transporta-
tion or any of the things other people your age who are entering the adult
world have to do. All of this can have a corrosive effect on the character. It
did on mine. When you've got somebody else doing for you all the time,
you're apt to surrender authority pretty quickly in ways you shouldn't. In this
memoir I'm painting a picture of a person who is still an adolescent but is
too old to be an adolescent, who finds himself in a situation where his now
no-longer-charming youthful qualities are apt to do real damage. And that

wasn't true only of me. Frankly, that was pretty much the state of the American soldier abroad.

In selecting the stories for your most recent collection, The Night in Question, *did you notice any unifying threads?*

Many of the characters are somewhat self-deceived, as most of us are in one way or another. We are continually negotiating the position we occupy in the world, and there is always a tension between the person we represent to the world and the person that we, in our most honest moments, recognize that we are.

If I can put it this way, I can imagine the people in these stories passing each other on the street. Though the stories are all different, the people in them breathe the same moral and spiritual atmosphere. I don't force them to live in the same town; they don't all live in Dublin or Winesburg, Ohio. But they inhabit, for me, a common plane of existence. They are all working, by default or calculation, on a similar problem. They are caught in webs of friendship, family, community, and institutions; they also feel a need to stand apart from these things at times and please themselves. These are the competing claims all of us face, and it's the continual work of our consciousness and conscience to sort out these various claims and decide which deserve our loyalty, where our obligations lie, what is true and what is right.

I was interested to hear you mention the theme of self-deception. You seem to focus, in these more recent stories, on the lies people tell themselves rather than on the ones they tell others. The sister in the title story ["The Night in Question"], for example—isn't she self-deluded? She sees herself as a fighter on her brother's behalf, whereas really she's just a fighter, someone who needs to encounter resistance and battle against it.

That's a complicated question. Having had an abusive father, she has a hard time hearing her brother speak about God as the loving patriarch, the Father of us all. Something in her revolts against that because of her own experience with fatherhood. She, who took her brother's part in life and stood beside him, sees this new-found religion of his as a desertion and betrayal. As she sees it, he's going over to the very power that has victimized them both. I have a great deal of sympathy for the sister. I know her heart. At the same time, her brother is trying to move beyond her angry, combative instincts; he's opening up, albeit in a very immature way, to a broader, more forgiving view. Given the way this drama between them is unfolding, I don't see a simple right or wrong. And I don't see her as simply self-deluded. She's got a stake in this. She's got a history.

I want to ask you about one of my favorites in the collection, "Bullet in the Brain." An amazing thing about that story is the way it presents an apparently irredeemable soul—Anders, the utterly cynical book reviewer—and then, in the space of two or three pages—redeems him. Through his recollection of a childhood memory, in the instant after he's shot, Anders rediscovers his capacity for joy and innocent delight. How did you come to write that story?

A friend told me about someone he knew who had been in a bank robbery, someone like Anders, a very jaded and cynical man. And apparently the robbers used hackneyed language, of the sort Anders finds so laughable in my story. I was interested in the fact they would use such language, as if they'd learned it from TV or the movies. I also began to think what would have happened if I'd been present at that robbery, hearing the robbers talk that way. "One of you tellers hits the alarm, you're all dead meat. Got it?" That sort of thing. To tell you the truth, I share some of Anders's qualities. I tend to review things that are going on around me. It's a writer's habit, and a critic's habit. And it occurred to me that, in a situation like the one Anders is in, where he starts to snicker at these cliché-spouting robbers, this extreme critical perspective could actually become physically dangerous. So, in that story, it wasn't just me looking at this worm of a man; Anders is enough like me that I could write about him from the inside out.

Among other things, it's a very funny story. My students love it, though some of them thought it should have ended when Anders gets shot.

Up to that point the story was pretty easy to write. But really, it would be no more than an anecdote if I'd stopped there. The second part of the story came late to me—the whole thing about the memories that pass through Anders's brain before he dies, and those that don't. I was *given* that idea in some way; I guess we could call it inspiration. I wasn't in control of the process. The story is about the brain, literally and figuratively, and that second part gave the story something of the shape of the brain, with a left and a right hemisphere. You've got the straight, logical half of the story, and then you have the intuitive, unpredictable half. So that pleased me, it gave me a chance to do something in a different way.

Where did Anders's final memory come from, about the baseball game and the boy from Mississippi who says, "Shortstop's the best position they is"?

That's a memory of mine, and it's funny how it's haunted me over the years. It happened just as I described it in the story. I was at a pick-up game with my friends and this boy said this wonderful line. And when I went home, I kept saying it all day long—"They is, they is." It came up in the writing of the story. Let's see, I'm fifty-one, and I was probably nine or ten at the time. Forty years ago! It's strange the way writing calls things up.

Do you still get the same pleasure from short-story writing as you did?

I love writing stories if it's going well. I hate it if it's going badly, and then I hate everything. But no, I love short stories, especially when something comes to life or you can feel it starting to come to life. But you don't always know. Some of the stories I like best in *The Night in Question,* like "Flyboys" and "The Other Miller," came hard, and I almost didn't finish them. You're not always soaring above the canyons when you're writing. You're down in the mines most of the time, and you don't know what your work is amounting to until you get to the end of it.

You once said that writing is an essentially optimistic act, that it assumes people can be reached, that they can be touched, and even changed in some cases. Do you feel that you write out of one of those impulses? Do you want, for example, to change people?

To sit for a moment and realize that other human beings have reality is a change for most of us. Most of us operate on the unacknowledged assumption that we are the only real human beings in the world and the only ones who matter. Stories have the power, I think, to suddenly fill us with the knowledge of other lives and with the importance of those lives to the people who lead them. And, in that way, yes, I write to change people.

Index

Algren, Nelson, 67

Allison, Dorothy, 142

Alvarez, Julia: attraction to a life of action, 140, 141; effect of writing poetry on her fiction, 130; handling of point of view, 132, 133, 143; identification with Latino writers, 135; life in the Dominican Republic, 137–40; poetry as first love, 128–31; Scheherazade as favorite heroine, 130, 136; sisters and sisterhood, 133–34, 142; use of autobiographical material, 133

—works by: *How the García Girls Lost Their Accents* (1991), 132, 136–38, 143; *In the Time of the Butterflies* (1994), 130–31, 136–37, 141–42; *¡Yo!* (1997), 133, 141–43

Anouilh, Jean: *The Rehearsal*, 151

Aristotle, 17

Auden, W. H., 20, 69

Babel, Isaac, 7, 94

Barth, John, 31

Barthelme, Donald, 6; "The Indian Uprising," 14

Bass, Rick: decaying of America, 82; effect of Jim Harrison's *Legends of the Fall* on, 76; effect of Richard Ford's *Rock Springs* on, 76–77; handling of point of view, 80; happiness as a learned attitude, 81–82; love of nature, 82; Montana as state of rebirth, 81; parents as storytellers, 77; starting to write professionally, 75; use of autobiographical material, 81; use of geological metaphors, 73–74; vitality as a value, 83–84; working with wife Elizabeth, 77; writing essays, 74–75

—works by: "Choteau," 80, 84; *The Deer Pasture* (1985), 77; "Mexico," 80; *Oil Notes* (1989), 72, 83; "Redfish," 79–81; "The

Watch," 79–80, 84; *The Watch* (1989), 76, 79; "Wild Horses," 80; *Winter* (1991), 77, 82

Baudelaire, Charles, 161

Beattie, Ann, 7, 19, 48

Bergholz, Susan, 132

Bellow, Saul, 7

Berriault, Gina: attitude toward creative writing classes, 64; attitude toward writing about characters like herself, 69; beginning to write in childhood, 62; effect of childhood reading, 62; interviews for *Esquire*, 66; mother's blindness as metaphor, 63; reading as collaborative effort, 65; as short-story writer, 65; use of autobiographical material, 68–69; as woman writer, 67–68; writing screenplays, 65

—works by: *Conference of Victims* (1962), 60, 69–70; *The Descent* (1960), 60, 69; "God and the Article Writer," 66; *The Lights of Earth* (1984), 60, 68, 69; *The Mistress and Other Stories* (1965), 60; *The Son* (1966), 60, 70–71; *Women in Their Beds* (1966), 60

Bombal, Luisa, 94

Borges, Jorge Luis, 14, 56, 90, 94

Boyle, T. Coraghessan: attention to, as a personality, 47; attitude toward television, 56–57; comic writing, 43, 50–51; ideas as starting points, 46; inventing characters, 50–51; as ironist, 44–45; literature as entertainment, 46–47, 56; opposition to political correctness and censorship, 49; reading and writing as imaginative journeys, 57; relationship to magical realists, 54; resistance to happy endings, 51; self-confidence, 53–54; as stand-up comedian, 55; teaching, 47–48; treatment of women and minorities in works by, 53; writing

process, 57–58; use of autobiographical material, 58–59; use of determinism, 44; use of historical fact, 52
—works by: *Budding Prospects* (1984), 51; *East Is East* (1990), 43–44, 50; "Greasy Lake," 49; "If the River Was Whiskey," 45; "Ike and Nina," 45; "King Bee," 55; "The Miracle at Ballinspittle," 45; *The Road to Wellville* (1993), 50, 52–53; *The Tortilla Curtain* (1995), 49–50, 52; *Water Music* (1981), 44–45, 51; *World's End* (1987), 44, 51, 53
Brecht, Bertold, 69
Brown, Mary Ward, 94
Bunin, Ivan, 64

Caputo, Philip: *A Rumor of War,* 183
Carver, Raymond, 6, 7, 48, 64, 76
Cassill, R. V., 147
Castillo, Ana, 132, 135
Cheever, John, 7, 45–46
Chekhov, Anton, 7, 91, 151, 154, 156, 174
Cisneros, Sandra, 132, 135
Clemons, Walter, 18
Conrad, Joseph, 131, 135, 150
Coover, Robert, 6
Costello, Mark, 153
Crane, Hart, 174

Day, Dorothy, 157–58
DeLillo, Don, 5, 48
Dickens, Charles, 42, 47
Dickinson, Emily, 128
Didion, Joan, 10
Dobie, J. Frank, 75
Doctorow, E. L., 7
Dos Passos, John, 67
Dostoevsky, Fyodor, 105, 108, 123, 126; *The Brothers Karamazov,* 123
Douglas, Ellen, 19
Dubus, Andre: Catholicism, 153–54, 157; effect of accident, 147–48, 152, 158; endings of fiction, 149; ethical dilemmas in fiction, 154; handling of point of view, 150, 152; on becoming his characters, 148–49; sexual revolution and the women's movement, 153; writing as a vocation, 147
—works by: *Adultery and Other Choices* (1977), 148, 151, 152, 154, 157; "A Father's Story," 154–56; *Finding a Girl in America*

(1980), 156; "The Pretty Girl," 151–52; *Voices from the Moon* (1984), 155–56
Duchamp, Marcel, 19
Dybek, Stuart, 117

Elkin, Stanley, 10
Erdrich, Louise, 48, 132–34; *Love Medicine,* 133

Faulkner, William, 5, 6, 22; *Absalom, Absalom!* 22
Ford, Richard: attitude toward postmodernists, 5, 6; beginning a novel, 5; on being a Southerner, 5, 10–12; characterization, 12–13; characters, 3–4; characters' names, 15, 17; characters' relationships to fictive places, 16; concern with language, 2, 3, 5; dancing as metaphor for writing, 16; endings of stories, 13; humor, 10; importance of physical action in his novels, 17; influence on Rick Bass, 76; Mississippi as home, 20; moving, 19; on not being a "male writer," 8; rejection of racism, 11; relationship to mother, 9, 10, 20; response to critics, 17; similarity to protagonists, 8; teaching, 21; use of autobiographical material, 19; verisimilitude, 13–14; wife Kristina, 7, 10, 13, 20; writing for readers, 22; writing short stories vs. writing novels, 6
—works by: *Independence Day* (1995), 4, 5, 18, 20; "Jealous," 9; "Optimists," 15; *A Piece of My Heart* (1976), 9; *Rock Springs* (1987), 7, 9; *The Sportswriter* (1986), 11, 13, 15–17; "Sweethearts," 7; *The Ultimate Good Luck* (1981), 7, 18; *Wildlife* (1990), 9, 15, 17, 18, 20; "The Womanizer," 19
Forster, E. M., 3
Friedman, Bruce J., 10
Fuentes, Carlos, 94

Galeano, Eduardo, 67
Garcia, Cristina, 94
García Marquez, Gabriel, 54; *Chronicle of a Death Foretold,* 94
Gass, William, 6
Gilchrist, Ellen, 48
Gogol, Nikolai, 68
Gordimer, Nadine, 150–51
Gottlieb, Robert, 110

Greene, Graham, 47, 53; *A Sort of Life*, 173
Gunn, Thom, 87

Hall, Donald, 3, 7, 15
Hall, Oakley, 7
Halpern, Dan, 3, 7
Hannah, Barry, 10, 19
Harrison, Colin, 117
Harrison, Jim, 19, 78; *Legends of the Fall*, 76;
    A Woman Lit by Fireflies, 8
Hawthorne, Nathaniel, 55
Heller, Joseph, 15; *Something Happened*, 16
Hemingway, Ernest, 114, 148
Herr, Michael: *Dispatches*, 183
Hills, Rust, 13
Huddle, David, 132
Humphreys, Josephine, 19

Irving, Washington, 55

Jackson, Jon, 118
James, Henry, 13
James, William, 158
Johnson, Denis, 48
Jones, Edward P., 94
Jones, Thom: beginning a novel, 125–26; be-
    ginning stories, 115; breaking stories into
    scenes, 116; competitive impulse, 122; ef-
    fect of epilepsy, 123; effect of working as
    janitor, 117–19; experience as boxer, 119;
    importance of drugs for functioning, 126;
    influence of Schopenhauer, 114, 117, 120,
    123; pessimism, 114; similarity to character
    Ad Magic, 120; spiritual quests and reli-
    gious faith, 123; teaching, 127
—works by: "Australian Dream Time," 123;
    "Cold Snap," 126; *Cold Snap* (1995), 112,
    116–17, 126; "I Need a Man to Love Me,"
    122–23; "I Want to Live!" 117–20; "The
    Pugilist at Rest," 116–18, 121–22; *The Pugi-
    list at Rest* (1993), 112, 114; "Quicksand,"
    120; "Rocketfire Girl," 115; "Rocket Man,"
    118; "Way Down Deep in the Jungle," 125;
    "A White Horse," 120

Kafka, Franz, 94
Kovic, Ron: *Born on the Fourth of July*, 183

Leonard, Elmore, 94, 151
Levi, Primo, 64, 97–98

Loewinsohn, Ron: *Magnetic Fields*, 48
Lubbock, Percy, 3

Machado de Assis, Joaquim Maria, 94
Mason, Bobbie Ann: celebration in her
    work, 141; characters' language, 29; dif-
    ference between *Shiloh* and *Love Life*, 36;
    effect of moving on her work, 27–28;
    effect of social class on characters, 30;
    effect of writer's block, 30; family as
    source of characters, 27–28; importance
    of style, 42; Kentucky as inspiration,
    27, 40; naming and writing as motifs,
    38–39; popular culture, 26–27; religion,
    37; resistance as source of energy, 24–25;
    as a Southerner, 25, 27; use of tense,
    32–34; writing as reclaiming lost mate-
    rial, 25
—works by: "Detroit Skyline, 1949," 35–36;
    In Country (1985), 25, 27, 37–39; *Love Life*
    (1989), 32–33, 36; "Marita," 33–34; "Mem-
    phis," 26; "Midnight Magic," 36;
    "Shiloh," 38; *Shiloh* (1982), 32, 36; *Spence
    + Lila* (1988), 23, 28–29, 33, 39–41; "State
    Champions," 29
Maugham, Somerset, 127
McCarthy, Mary, 185
McDonald, George: *At the Back of the
    Northwind*, 62
McGuane, Tom, 19
McMichael, James, 3
Meredith, James, 11
Michaels, Leonard: acquiring mother's
    fears, 89; burning first novel, 93; effect of
    a pogrom on family, 89–90; Herman as a
    new voice, 98; Holocaust and art, 97; im-
    portance of voice, 88–89; Jews, 90; lyrical
    impulse, 86; narrator of *The Men's Club*,
    95–96; Phillip Liebowitz as recurring
    character, 90–93; the Phillip stories, 92;
    working from sound, 87; writing screen-
    play for *The Men's Club*, 97
—works by: "City Boy," 92; *Going Places*
    (1969), 93; "I Would Have Saved Them If
    I Could," 97; *The Men's Club* (1981), 95–
    97; "Murderers," 90–91; *Shuffle* (1989),
    87–90; "Sticks and Stones," 92
Miller, Henry, 114
Milne, A. A., 62
Milosz, Czeslow, 134–35

Minot, Susan, 143
Morrison, Toni: *Jazz,* 97

Nabokov, Vladimir, 25, 34, 35, 64
Nietzsche, Friedrich, 124
Novak, Marian, 153

Oates, Joyce Carol, 93, 111, 126
O'Brien, Tim: *Going After Cacciato,* 183; "The Things They Carried," 22
O'Connor, Flannery, 5, 43, 45, 153–54, 180–81; "A Good Man Is Hard to Find," 43; "Parker's Back," 181
O'Connor, Frank, 13

Paz, Octavio, 94
Percy, Walker, 10, 153
Phillips, Jayne Anne: early career, 161; outsiders' voices in her fiction, 165; secrets as motif, 169; working as poet, 166; working with memory, 166–67; writers as emotional barometers, 163; writing as metaphysical process, 170; writing process, 169–70
—works by: "Bess," 167; *Black Tickets* (1979), 165; "Blue Moon," 163, 167; "Fast Lanes," 162, 164, 166, 169; *Machine Dreams* (1984), 165–69; *Shelter* (1994), 167
Poe, Edgar Allan, 55
Pynchon, Thomas, 52

Raab, Larry, 3
Ravenel, Shannon, 132, 143
Rhys, Jean, 64
Rilke, Rainer Maria: "The Archaic Torso of Apollo," 131
Rimbaud, Arthur, 161
Robison, Mary, 7
Roth, Philip, 7, 10, 94, 176
Ryan, Michael, 3

Sacks, Oliver, 149
Salgado, Sebastião, 67
Salinger, J. D.: *The Catcher in the Rye,* 126
Santiago, Danny, 50
Sartre, Jean-Paul, 14, 70
Schopenhauer, Arthur, 114, 117, 120, 123, 124
Smith, Carol, 79
Steinbeck, John, 67; *Cannery Row,* 49; *Tortilla Flat,* 49
Stone, Robert, 19, 58

Tan, Amy: *The Joy Luck Club,* 134
Taylor, Peter: *The Collected Stories of Peter Taylor,* 7
Tilghman, Christopher: connections between place and history, 103; family, 108; family in stories, 109; first two unpublished books, 108; need for compassionate empathy, 104; range of characters, 102, 103; starting with visual image, 100–101; storytelling, 110; teaching, 104; writing as grappling with holy mysteries, 104–6
—works by: "A Gracious Rain," 106; "Hole in the Day," 101; "In a Father's Place," 102, 107; "Mary in the Mountains," 107–9; *Mason's Retreat* (1996), 99, 111; "On the Rivershore," 101–2
Tolstoy, Leo, 53, 105
Trollope, Anthony, 108
Turner, Alice, 117, 120
Twain, Mark: *Life on the Mississippi,* 10

Unamuno, Miguel de: *Tragic Sense of Life,* 64
Updike, John, 155–56

Vonnegut, Kurt, 56

Welty, Eudora, 5, 6, 10, 11, 167
White, Edmund: *A Boy's Own Life,* 176
Wilke, David, 161
Williams, C. K., 3
Williams, Joy, 7, 19
Williams, Thomas, 150
Wolff, Tobias: anxiety of invention, 184–85; on books about Vietnam, 183–84; character vs. narrator in *This Boy's Life,* 173; citizen/outlaw distinction in *This Boy's Life,* 174; comparing his stories to Flannery O'Connor's, 180–81; experimental fiction, 181; on imagination and lying, 176–78; motive in writing *This Boy's Life,* 172–73; self-deception as theme, 187; unified nature of story collections, 178, 187; writers' limited interpretations of own work, 179–80; writing memoirs vs. novels, 184–86; writing to change people, 189
—works by: *Back in the World* (1985), 171, 178–79; *The Barracks Thief* (1984), 171, 181–83; "Bullet in the Brain," 188–89; "Casualty," 183; "Flyboys," 189; *In Pharaoh's Army* (1993), 171, 183–87; "In the Garden

of the North American Martyrs," 180; *In the Garden of the North American Martyrs* (1981), 171, 178; "The Liar," 177; "The Missing Person," 177, 179–80; "The Night in Question," 187; *The Night in Question* (1996), 171, 187; "The Other Miller," 189; "The Poor Are Always with Us," 180;

"The Rich Brother," 180–81; *This Boy's Life* (1989), 171–75, 186; "Worldly Goods," 180

Yates, Richard, 7

Zangwill, Israel, 62

BONNIE LYONS is a poet and professor of English at the University of Texas at San Antonio. Among her publications are *Henry Roth: The Man and His Work* and articles on contemporary fiction and American Jewish literature.

BILL OLIVER is a short-story writer who teaches at Washington and Lee University and the Virginia Military Institute. His fiction has appeared in *Virginia Quarterly Review, Carolina Quarterly, Florida Review, Indiana Review,* and *Kansas Quarterly,* among others. He is also the author of a collection of stories, *Women & Children First* (Mid-List Press).